AN INTRODUCTION TO THE PHILOSOPHY OF NĀGĀRJUNA

An Introduction to the Philosophy of Nāgārjuna

MUSASHI TACHIKAWA

Translated by
Rolf W. Giebel

MOTILAL BANARSIDASS PUBLISHERS
PRIVATE LIMITED • DELHI

First Edition: Delhi, 1997

ISBN: 81-208-1466-5

MOTILAL BANARSIDASS

41 U.A. Bungalow Road, Jawahar Nagar, Delhi 110 007
8, Mahalaxmi Chamber, Warden Road, Mumbai 400 026
120 Royapettah High Road, Mylapore, Chennai 600 004
Sanas Plaza, Subhash Nagar, Pune 411 002
16 St. Mark's Road, Bangalore 560 001
8 Camac Street, Calcutta 700 017
Ashok Rajpath, Patna 800 004
Chowk, Varanasi 221 001

PRINTED IN INDIA

BY JAINENDRA PRAKASH JAIN AT SHRI JAINENDRA PRESS,
A-45 NARAINA, PHASE I, NEW DELHI 110 028
AND PUBLISHED BY NARENDRA PRAKASH JAIN FOR
MOTILAL BANARSIDASS PUBLISHERS PRIVATE LIMITED,
BUNGALOW ROAD, DELHI 110 007

PREFACE

The starting point of our study of the *Madhyamakakārikā* (referred to hereafter as the *Middle Stanzas*) was the doubts that we had come to entertain in regard to statements to the effect that Nāgārjuna's philosophy of emptiness as exemplified by the *Middle Stanzas* represents a "logic transcending logic" and that therefore Nāgārjuna set a positive value in his arguments on logical contradiction and paradox. Even though it may be true that the philosophy of emptiness does embody certain elements of something that transcends logic, it was inconceivable that the complex and persistent arguments of the *Middle Stanzas* should have been formulated with a disregard for such laws as those of the excluded middle and contradiction, both basic to logic, and it also seemed improbable that the passion of the Indian Nāgārjuna to follow his arguments through to the very end should not be supported by sound logical operations. But even so, how would it be possible to retrace Nāgārjuna's attempt to grasp by means of logic something that would appear to clearly transcend logic? A hint in reply to our continued questioning was provided by the perspective proposed by religious scholars and consisting of the two poles of the "sacred" and the "profane." This perspective is usually employed in order to clarify the nature of group religious acts, but the process leading from the profane to the sacred is the same in the case of individual religious acts too, and we wondered whether this perspective might not also be applicable when considering the philosophy of emptiness in Mahāyāna Buddhism, possessed as this latter is of features characteristic of individual religious acts. In particular, the two vectors existing between the sacred and the profane and pointing in opposite directions proved to be most suggestive in their implications.

If, after having taken into our field of vision the two poles of the sacred and the profane and the two vectors between them, we then consider the *Middle Stanzas*, the logic of this work gradually becomes clear. When Nāgārjuna repeatedly emphasizes that "things do not arise," he means that "things do not arise" with own-being or as substantive entities, and the negation of the profane *possessed of own-being* is thus emphasized. The momentum of the process in the course of which such negation is performed (corresponding to religious praxis) becomes the vector pointing from the profane to the sacred. When, on the other hand, Nāgārjuna says that "things arise by dependent co-arising," he means that "things *without own-being* arise" by the principle of dependent co-arising or truth, and it is to be surmised that the vector in this case points from the sacred to the profane and that its momentum is bestowed by truth or the sacred on that which has come in contact with truth.

The "time" involved in the first vector is relatively slow in its movement, and in this process as delineated in the *Middle Stanzas* logical consistency is thoroughly pursued in all facets of Nāgārjuna's arguments. But the moment when the profane touches the sacred and that same moment in which there occurs the sacralization of the profane, corresponding to the second vector, is the moment of religious awakening and does indeed "transcend logic." Although Nāgārjuna does describe what takes place there "by provisional designation," in contrast to the cumulative logic of the first vector, he is rather spare in words in regard to this second vector.

The misunderstanding that the logic of the *Middle Stanzas* is from the first supralogical, the attitude which by interpreting what might be termed "immanentistic realism" in its overly popularized form would rest in the profane without having passed through the stage of negation, and the existence of a tendency to emphasize the union of opposites by again simplistically superimposing the sacred and the profane—these could probably have been all avoided by correctly discerning the nature of the above two vectors. The dynamic significance attached by Nāgārjuna to the central concepts of emptiness and dependent co-arising also becomes clearer if we take into consideration these two vectors. The realization that one source of the various misunderstandings of the logic of the *Middle Stanzas* probably lies in a confusion of the two types of negation employed in the

Middle Stanzas, namely, non-affirming or absolute negation and affirming or implicative negation—corresponding in the case of the *Middle Stanzas* to the negation of a proposition and the negation of a term respectively—also resulted from our reading of this work on the assumption that it had been composed with a view to observing logical consistency.

In the ancient India where Nāgārjuna lived "things" (*bhāva*) were probably far less sophisticated and of a far more natural form than they are today, and they would have existed in a state closer to man, sometimes even inspiring him with awe. It is difficult to comprehend the powerful will to completely extinguish all existing things at least once without taking into account the premise that this may indeed be possible. For us who live in the present age, overwhelmed by things that are frightfully distant towards us and of such profusion, the philosophy of emptiness that would hold that "all things do not exist" is at the most nothing more than something to be given fleeting thought while we are being totally immersed in the profane. We live surrounded by circumstances such that it is impossible to do otherwise. With our strong proclivity towards the pragmatic, it is necessary to realize that there is a risk of our minimizing that aspect of rigorous negation in Nāgārjuna's thought and interpreting the *Middle Stanzas* with a bias towards their aspect of the sacralization of the profane. Both the great Indian genius for the negation of the profane, as evidenced for example in *yoga*, and the optimistic confidence in ultimate salvation common to all Indian religions must be accepted as a single unity, and Nāgārjuna's philosophy of emptiness is of course a case in point. The object of Nāgārjuna's inquiries, pursued with an intensity that is directly sensed by us readers living close to two thousand years later, was how to master the actuating moment that brings about the overlapping of the sacred and the profane. In this sense the *Middle Stanzas* represent a religious work expounding the path to liberation.

A variety of views in a variety of spheres and on a variety of planes are doubtless possible in regard to what the *Middle Stanzas* have to teach us who live in a situation so remote from that of ancient India. But in all cases one must start with as accurate as possible an understanding of Nāgārjuna's intent. We would like the reader to regard the present work as one attempt in this direction.

The present book has come into existence only through the help and kindness of a number of people. Here I would like to express my particular gratitude to Prof. F. Staal (Professor Emeritus, University of California, Berkeley), Prof. P. Griffith (University of Chicago), Prof. G. Paul (University of Karlsruhe), Prof. S. Bahulkar (Central Institute of Higher Tibetan Studies, Sarnath) and Dr. M. Kolhatkar (Deccan College, Poona), who all gave invaluable suggestions regarding this book.

The present volume is an English translation of a revised version of my Japanese book entitled *Kū no kōzō* (The Structure of Emptiness; Daisan Bunmeisha, 1986). I would like to thank Mr. Rolf W. Giebel for having taken great pains to translate it.

Musashi Tachikawa
Professor,
National Museum
of Ethnology,
Osaka, Japan

TABLE OF CONTENTS

CHAPTER ONE

THE HISTORICAL POSITION OF NĀGĀRJUNA'S THOUGHT

Mahāyāna Buddhism arose between the first century B. C. and first century A. D. from a vast reform movement that stood opposed to the earlier conservative forms of Buddhism such as Abhidharma Buddhism. In contrast to the "scholastic" Abhidharma Buddhism, which was primarily the domain of renunciant monks, Mahāyāna Buddhism was born with a broader form of salvation that also gave consideration to the spiritual salvation of lay believers as its goal. It was in such a context that the early Mahāyāna scriptures such as the *Aṣṭasāhasrikā Prajñāpāramitā* and *Saddharmapuṇḍarīka-sūtra* appeared. While adhering to the original standpoint of Early Buddhism that all things are impermanent, Mahāyāna Buddhism propounded by means of its own original methodology the non-reality of the world in contrast to the methods of Abhidharma Buddhism which had sought to define the world as existent and possessing a specific structure. Nāgārjuna (A. D. 150-250 or 100-200), the first person to give a logical exposition of the early Prajñāpāramitā scriptures, provided early Mahāyāna Buddhism with a clear theoretical model and laid the foundations of Mahāyāna Buddhism. The presentation of his ideas was somewhat singular in its style, and this is no doubt a major reason for the great diversity of interpretations to which Nāgārjuna's thought has given rise. Although syllogisms such as appear in the system of the later logician Dignāga (6th cent.) do not yet appear in Nāgārjuna's arguments, he was consistently *logical* in his assertion of the non-reality of the world. His theories represent one of the most noteworthy achievements in the history of Indian logic.

While describing on the one hand concrete, although fictional, examples of the activities of hosts of bodhisattvas, the early Mahāyāna scriptures such as the Prajñāpāramitā corpus also sought to upset the very foundations of the world view of those whom they were criticizing. The Mahāyānists' methods of arguments were quite startling, for they began saying things that ran directly counter to everyday logic. One of their favourite such expressions was "form is emptiness" (*rūpaṃ śūnyatā*). "Form" signifies anything with colour or shape, but here it further refers to the world of delusion or the profane world, while "emptiness" refers to enlightenment or the sacred. The existence of any third possibility other than delusion or enlightenment is not recognized, and the sum of these two constitutes everything. Thus ostensibly the statement "form is emptiness" would appear to be saying that "A is B," but in actual fact it is saying that "form is non-form," namely, "A is non-A." The *Vajracchedikā Prajñāpāramitā* which belongs to the corpus of Prajñāpāramitā literature, contains the statement that "the perfect wisdom (*prajñā*) taught by the Tathāgata (i. e., Buddha) is not perfect wisdom." Although qualified by the words "taught by the Tathāgata"—and this qualification is in fact the key to an understanding of the distinctive nature of such statements—this expression may be considered to belong to the mode of expression "A is non-A." Expressions of this kind appear not only in the Prajñāpāramitā literature but also in other Mahāyāna scriptures. Particularly in later Tantric texts this paradoxical expression serves as a veritable magic wand that solves all problems at a single stroke.

A situation corresponding to "A is non-A" cannot occur in the everyday world, and the Mahāyānists were fully aware of the fact that neither everyday thinking nor formal logic permits it. The Mahāyānists themselves recognized that form and emptiness are contradictories and that the sum of the two represents everything. Yet the very fact that the statement "A is non-A" is impossible in everyday linguistic activity was all the more reason for them to use such expressions. This represented an articulation *in our everyday language* of the idea that the world of absolute truth or enlightenment rejects language. The fact that *truth rejects language* must also be expressed by means of language. Man is permitted only one type of language, and there is no language other than our everyday language for describing absolute truth itself.

"Delusion and enlightenment" represent, as do also for example "man and God" and "the profane and the sacred," the two poles that always exist in religion. These two poles stand opposed to one another and correspond to A and non-A. But at the same time interaction between the two poles is also possible, and a *sine qua non* of any religion is that the two poles at times become completely identical, namely, that the "sacralization" of the profane be possible. The manner in which this interaction or identification takes place is a question concerning all religions, and the *Vajracchedikā Prajñāpāramitā* could be described as an example of an attempt to link the two poles in the most direct manner possible.

This identity of opposites came to constitute the basic spirit of Mahāyāna Buddhism. It was because this spirit was expressed in a form such as "A is non-A," which made logicians feel the need to demonstrate its truth, that later Buddhist thinkers were to take the content of such expressions up for consideration in a field that might be termed the study of "logic," and it became the task of Mahāyānist thinkers to prove that "A is non-A."

Nāgārjuna, who is considered to have provided Māhāyana Buddhism with its theoretical model, does not in fact employ the expression "form is emptiness." Although he makes free use of the logic of the identity of opposites as a basis for his assertion of the non-reality of the world, he would appear to be almost purposely avoiding this more or less central thesis of "form is emptiness." This stance of Nāgārjuna's, who as spiritual successor to the Prajñāpāramitā scriptures sought to elucidate their spirit, is a point which we must bear in mind when studying the *Middle Stanzas*, and it is in itself a subject deserving further inquiry.

As a work summarizing the basic tenets of Nāgārjuna's thought, the *Middle Stanzas* are looked upon as his *magnum opus*. This work consists of approximately 450 verses and is divided into 27 chapters. Each chapter deals with a topic apparently unrelated to the immediately preceding and succeeding chapters, and as a whole it gives the impression that it is not an ordered inquiry into a single theme. But a careful examination reveals that the *Middle Stanzas* maintain a consistent attitude from first to last in regard to both their subject matter and their method of presentation.

Although the fact that the *Middle Stanzas* provided scriptures such as the Prajñāpāramitā corpus with a theoretical model has come to be generally recognized by researchers, to date there has been no detailed study of the structure of this model. There has been considerable discussion of questions relating to the thought of the *Middle Stanzas*, such as its standpoint as a religious work, and many views worthy of our attention have been put forth. Insofar that the *Middle Stanzas* represent first and foremost a religious work, it is obvious that such questions are of prime importance in this treatise. But in order to be able to discuss these questions precisely and in direct relation to Nāgārjuna, it is necessary when elucidating the theoretical structure of the *Middle Stanzas* to understand correctly what Nāgārjuna is saying. This is necessary not simply because "manner of presentation and content are one," but because in this work Nāgārjuna is from first to last making an issue of language, dealing with language, and discoursing with language as his means. In the case of the *Middle Stanzas* the form of presentation reflects the very structure of the content of the ideas embodied therein.

It has been said that "Nāgārjuna bestowed logic upon the 'world of emptiness' to which the Prajñāpāramitā scriptures had attempted to point by means of allegories and irritating repetitions."[1] The aim of the present work is to comprehend this logic in as precise a form as possible and to thereby gain a correct understanding of the thought of the *Middle Stanzas*.

At the same time, we would also like to consider the ideas of the *Middle Stanzas* in the broader context of philosopical and religious thought in general and to apprise ourselves of their religious characteristics. This is a task that is necessary not only in order to gain a general overall view of the *Middle Stanzas*, but also in order to throw their content into clear relief from a broad standpoint. To this end it will be necessary to integrate our various perspectives into a number of axes of thought.

---

1. Kajiyama Yūichi and Uryūzu Ryūshin, *Ryūju ronshū* (Treatises by Nāgārjuna), *Daijō butten* (Mahāyāna Scriptures), Vol. 14 (Tōkyō: Chūō Kōronsha, 1974), p. 419. (Here and below Japanese names are given in the Japanese order, with the family name preceding the given name, except in the case of Western-language publications where the author's name appears in the Western order.)

CHAPTER TWO

THE RELIGIOUS POSITION OF THE *MIDDLE STANZAS* (*MŪLAMADHYAMAKAKĀRIKĀ*)

1

All religions incorporate the two poles of the "sacred" and the "profane" as one axis of their structure. These two poles do not signify two mutually unrelated fixed points; rather, there exists a dynamic relation between the two. It is this dynamic relation or interaction between the two poles that is in fact the essence of all religions. The question of what kind of interaction between the two poles each religion posits represents perhaps the most important perspective in any consideration of religion.

An example in which these two poles stand furthest apart from one another may be seen in the relationship between God and mankind in the Old Testament. In this case, God is the creator of heaven and earth while Adam, meaning literally "man," is his creation. The leader of none of the twelve tribes of Israel can claim God as the forefather of his own tribe. Even when God speaks to Moses, he does not show himself, and their interaction is limited to the act of speaking. In the New Testament God is born as the son of man. But unlike in the case of Indian religions, there is no union of man and God through meditation. In Christianity the sacred remains the sacred to the very end, and consequently the Gnostic school, which asserted that it was possible to comprehend the sacred through knowledge, was rejected as a heretic sect. The sacred manifests itself unilaterally within the profane as a sacrifice through its own self-denial. This is incarnation by grace.

In the Indian religions it is generally emphasized that the two poles are in essence identical. The *Chāndogya Upaniṣad* expresses the relation between these two poles with the words "that art thou" (*tat tvam asi*). This dictum points to the essential identity obtaining between the pole of the cosmic self (*brahman*)—referred to as "that" —and that of the individual self (*ātman*)—referred to as "thou." However, the interpretation of this essential identity did not remain uniform throughout the history of Brahmanic thought. A variety of views were born concerning the question of how to understand this concept, and in accordance with these differences of opinion a number of schools arose within Hindu philosophy. In the case of the typical poles of Buddhism, such as delusion and enlightenment, man and Buddha, and conventional truth and ultimate truth, the identity of the two poles is also emphasized. Although Buddhism initially made its appearance in reaction to the Brahmanic thought that was dominant at the time, in regard to this point it belongs to the same category as Brahmanism, differing from Christianity, which belongs to another category of religions. Just as in the case of Brahmanism, there were established a variety of schools within Buddhism too. It is possible to divide Buddhism into two major currents according to how, assuming the essential identity of the two poles, the relation between them is interpreted. One is that which would posit a great many stages between the two poles and asserts the need for rigorous spiritual training in order to reach the desired pole, while the other maintains that since the two poles are essentially identical, it is possible to attain the desired pole by means of a special method and without going through a long process of religious cultivation. This latter way of thinking appears prominently in some types of later Tantric Buddhism.

During the last century or so the concept of the "sacred" has come to be moulded by a great many researchers into a concept extremely useful for the study of religion. The scholar who deserves the greatest credit for having made of the "sacred" a valid scholarly concept is probably R.Otto. According to him, the sacred is that which not only gives rise to a creature-feeling in which one senses one's lack of worth, but also possesses elements of "awe-inspiring mystery" (*mysterium tremendum*), "fascinating mystery" (*mysterium fascinans*), and "majesty" (*majestas*). Commenting on Otto's achievements in studies on the history of religion, M. Eliade writes,"Most probably, Otto tacitly claimed for himself a similar role, that of mediator between *revelatio generalis* and *revelatio specialis*, between Indo-Aryan and Semitic religious thought, between Eastern and Western types of mysticism."[1] Although Otto's conception of the sacred as defined in his main work *Das Heilige* (1917; *The Idea of the Holy*, 1923) was modelled upon the God of the Old Testament, it is potentially applicable as a scholarly concept also to the study of other religions such as Hinduism and Buddhism.

Today, however, when we employ the two concepts "sacred" and "profane" together, we use the former in a far broader sense than did Otto. It was Eliade who, under the influence of Otto, used these two concepts as a pair and succeeded in interpreting religion in the context of the interrelationship between the referents of these two concepts. In the "Introduction" to his *Das Heilige und das Profane* (1957; *The Sacred and the Profane*, 1959), he points out that Otto's *Das Heilige* overemphasizes the irrational aspects of the sacred, and he declares that "we adopt a different perspective."[2]

Having proposed that the first possible definition of the *sacred* is that it is the *opposite of the profane*, Eliade declares that the sacred manifests itself. According to Eliade, it is this manifestation of the sacred (hierophany) that constitutes the factor common to all religions from the most primitive to the most highly developed. It is, in other words, the essence of religion. This hierophany always takes place in the profane. Thus, for Eliade, religion represents the manifestation of the sacred within the profane.

Likewise R. Caillois also considers that a distinction between the sacred and the profane lies at the basis of religion. He begins his work *L'Homme et le sacré* (1939; *Man and the Sacred*, 1959) with a statement to the effect that every religious conception of the universe implies a distinction between the sacred and the profane, and that it is important to take note of the fact that all unconditionally valid definitions relating to religion subsume this opposition between these two poles. According to Caillois, the experience of the sacred occurs as the sum total of the various relationships obtaining between man

---

1. M. Eliade (tr. Willard R. Trask), *The Quest: History and Meaning in Religion* (Chicago: The University of Chicago Press, 1969), p. 23.
2. M. Eliade (tr. Willard R. Trask), *The Sacred and the Profane: The Nature of Religion* (New York: Harcourt Brace Jovanovich, 1959), p. 10.

and the sacred. In other words, the sacred is related as a common property to certain objects (instruments of the cult, etc.), certain beings (kings, priests), certain places (temples, palaces), and certain times (festive days, etc.).

According to Eliade, any object, including the sun, stars, mountains, rivers, trees, animals and parts of the human body, may become a "locus" of hierophany; stones and trees assume the power of the sacred not because they themselves have this sacred power, but as a result of the actions of man. The actions here referred to by Eliade are mainly ritual acts involving the manipulation of symbols. E. Durkheim, who also considered the distinction between the sacred and the profane not to be based on the nature of the object itself, holds that societal factors lie at the base of the sacred. For him, ritual both strengthens the sense of solidarity among members of a society and also has as its goal the rebirth of the whole of society.

M. Mauss, who belonged to the Durkheim school, also emphasized the social character of the sacred. He maintained that religious phenomena were in fact social phenomena and that social phenomena could in turn be understood in the same manner as linguistic phenomena. For the members of a particular society, language already exists as a datum of experience from the day of their birth into that society. When someone learns a language within a particular society, or even when he or she uses it after having mastered it, language represents the act of an individual who represents a "*signifiant*" (significant) acting upon the "*signifié*" (significatum) or meaning-content functioning as an already given unity. Likewise, religious acts may also be understood as separate pieces of information passing through an integrated circuit containing information on various conventions relating to the sacred and the profane that have historically evolved in the particular group to which the individual belongs.[3]

2

Both Eliade's ideas on the interrelationship existing between the sacred and the profane and the social and historical understanding of these same concepts as presented by Durkheim and Mauss are particu-

3. C. Levi-Strauss, "Introduction à l'oeuvre de Marcel Mauss," in Marcel Mauss, *Sociologie et anthropologie* (Paris: Presses Universitaires de France, 1950).

larly useful for our purpose. It is, however, possible to further extend the sphere of that referred to by the sacred and the profane.

The sacred and the profane are scholarly concepts that have been proposed to facilitate our understanding of religion. Therefore, it does not necessarily follow that the language that has nurtured the form of religion happening to represent the object of one's investigations possesses terms translatable as the "sacred" or the "profane," nor will the existence of a perduring entity definable as the sacred be always recognized in that particular form of religion. The "sacred" refers to an absolute power which we cannot see, to an "incarnation" of that power in visible form, or even to shrines and ritual implements in which a deity is believed to indwell. In other words, it signifies not only the power of the sacred but also any object that has been vested with this power, such as the image of a deity, a shrine, a mountain or water. The "profane," on the other hand, is anything that has not been vested with this sacred power. For example, human beings as distinct from gods, as well as natural and artificial objects with which we come in contact on a daily basis, are designated as profane in relation to the sacred.

The sacred and the profane represent the two poles of a single unity, and they may be compared to the two poles between which electricity flows. Just as the plus and minus poles do not function independently of one another, so do the sacred and the profane, the two poles of the single unity comprising religious phenomena, invariably function as a pair. Even in the most simple religious phenomenon there exists the "direct current" of human action in the form of the movement of energy between these two poles which represent important constituent elements of that phenomenon.

The important point is that the agent in a particular religious act must to some degree be aware of the difference between these two poles in religion. When, through the code of "meaning-content" that has already evolved historically in the social group to which the agent belongs, a difference or disparity is understood by the agent to exist between the two religious poles, there flows an "electric current" between the two poles and a religious phenomenon occurs.

Needless to say, the strength of the current and the difference between the two religious poles, namely, the "voltage," vary according to the form assumed by a particular religious act. When the current between the two poles ceases to flow, that is to say, when the difference between the two poles no longer holds any meaning for the agent nor for those who are participating in the act as onlookers or petitioners, then there is no religious phenomenon even if the act should still continue.

It is of course rare for all the participants in a particular religious act—for example, a festival procession—to be aware of the difference between the sacred and the profane, and generally there is a difference in the degree of awareness of the individual participants. In the case of such religious acts as those that have evolved and been preserved over a long period of time, as long as one observes the conventions of that group—for example, marching in procession along a specified route wearing special attire—this festival procession will function as a religious act of that group even if one is not personally conscious of the difference between the two religious poles. The difference between the sacred and the profane must, however, be understood by at least some of those who organize such an act on a regular or irregular basis.

The sacred and the profane are meaningless in the absence of human action. It is only through the acts of people who have become aware of the difference between the sacred and the profane that the dynamic relation between these two religious poles becomes possible. The study of religious phenomena is the study of the interaction of the sacred and the profane, and in the final analysis it is nothing other than the study of the acts of people involved in the interaction of these two poles. Religion may be described as a form of goal-oriented action performed with an awareness of the difference between the sacred and the profane.

Although almost all human action is goal-oriented, religious acts are particularly so. This is because they consciously incorporate the difference between the sacred and the profane as a constituent element of the act and seek to achieve a particular goal. Different religious acts accord with their respective goals and conform to the secular world in their respective forms.

3

Scholars of religion have from their various standpoints attempted to classify the great variety of religions into a number of types. Today the most common classification is that which would divide religions into (1) the religions of primitive peoples, (2) folk religions, and (3) the religions of advanced cultures (or world religions). Examples of (1) include the totemism of the Australian Aborigines analyzed by Durkheim and the cult of *mana* (a supernatural and ubiquitous power) discovered by R. H. Codrington in Melanesia. Religions such as Judaism, Hinduism and Shintō, on the other hand, belong to (2). As in (1), these religions have no specific founder, and the various elements of their respective forms may be said to have developed naturally. Religions of this type are usually confined to a particular ethnic group and do not spread to areas not inhabited by that group. As is well-known, Christianity, Buddhism and Islam belong to (3). Religions of this type often evolve with a certain folk religion as their basis. For example, Christianity developed out of Judaism, while Buddhism inherited a great many elements from Brahmanism. Unlike (2), however, religions of type (3) generally have a historical founder, such as Jesus, Śākyamuni and Muhammad, and as the designation "world religion" suggests, they spread among different ethnic groups.

It should be noted that in actual practice religions of type (3) are often found in a form combined with a religion of type (2). For example, Buddhist Tantrism absorbed indigenous elements of India and other regions to which Buddhism had spread—elements that are both prominent and important in folk religions—without losing its distinctive features as a world religion. Reference is also often made to the amalgamation of Buddhism and Shintō in Japan.

The above threefold classification still retains its significance today. It would appear, however, that the time has come for us to reconsider the basis of this classification into three types. As may be inferred from the terms "primitive" and "advanced culture," the above classification presupposes a theory of evolution. This threefold classification is, namely, founded upon the assumption that, just as in the case of science and technology, religion too evolves and develops from the "primitive" to the "advanced."

It is of course true that, when considered historically, elements that were not present or were at least not particularly conspicuous in types (1) and (2) came to assume utmost importance in religions of type (3). For example, the spiritual salvation of the individual as exemplified by the enlightenment that Śākyamuni advocated or by the salvation taught by Jesus is virtually ignored in the case of religions of type (1), and even in the case of (2) it would not have played any important role in Brahmanism, centred as it is on rituals based on the Vedic scriptures, or in Shintō prior to Buddhist influence. But for religious thinkers of Hinduism in later times, such as Śaṅkara and Rāmānuja, and also in the case of Shintō after it had come to possess its own doctrinal system under the influence of Buddhism, the spiritual salvation of the individual did also become a central issue. In this sense, although the thought of Śaṅkara and Rāmānuja did not, unlike Buddhism, come to exert any great influence in lands far removed from the Indian subcontinent, it may still be said to have many elements in common with religions of type (3).

To interpret religious phenomena throughout the world in this manner within the framework of a process of evolution and development is probably to a certain degree historically correct and will no doubt retain its significance in the future too. Belief in a theory of evolution, however, tends to give rise to a value judgement that would regard the initial stages of development as "inferior" and the final stages as "superior." In point of fact, the threefold classification of religions into the religions of primitive peoples, folk religions and the religions of advanced cultures is linked to the idea that since the first group of religions is still undeveloped and backward and the third group represents the supreme form of religion, all people should be led to the third type. But have religions actually evolved and developed in this manner? If an adherent of a "world religion" should define the "religions of primitive peoples" as being inferior, then has he not rather discarded that which is most fundamental to religion?

Today the focus of interest in religious studies would appear to be on religions of types (1) and (2), and there is little interest being evinced in religions of type (3), especially not in questions concerning the spiritual salvation of the individual. Scholars specializing in Christian theology, on the other hand, virtually ignore the religions of types (1) and (2) and even less do they attempt to understand (1) and (3) by means of a single integrated theory. Researchers in the field of Indian and Buddhist studies are also split into those studying (1) and (2) and those studying (3), and it cannot be said that they are considering these three types in any coordinated fashion. The various forms of religions which have thus hitherto been looked upon as belonging to three totally different groups may, however, possess structures more similar to one another than has until now been realized. Although the concepts of the sacred and the profane as propounded by eminent scholars of religion such as Eliade, Durkheim and Mauss have for the most part been employed in connection with religions of types (1) and (2), we believe that their dynamic understanding of these two poles may be valid also in regard to religions belonging to type (3).

If, placing the thought of Nāgārjuna, who provided a theoretical model for Mahāyāna Buddhism, in the context of the sacred and the profane within the structure of religion as a whole, we then seek to clarify its religious characteristics, it will be found, as is explained below, that the dynamic understanding of the above-mentioned scholars in regard to these two poles is extremely helpful. No one would take exception to defining Nāgārjuna's religious thought as belonging to (3) insofar that it has its roots in the teachings of Śākyamuni and aims primarily at individual salvation. But the interactions of Nāgārjuna's thought with the various forms of religion that it encountered in later times are of particular interest when considered from the vantage point of the above three types of religion. After Nāgārjuna's death Mahāyāna Buddhism was, in the course of its "development," to come in contact with many indigenous cultures, as well as experiencing conflict and interpenetration with Hinduism and other religions. Thus, although endowed with the characteristics of a religion of type (3), Mahāyāna Buddhism was, historically speaking, closely linked to religions of types (1) and (2). In this process of interpenetration, Mahāyāna Buddhism was to create many rituals. In religions of types (1) and (2) almost all religious acts take the form of ritual, whereas in type (3) ritual acts tend to be avoided since they are considered to be either an obstacle to or unnecessary for the attainment of the ultimate goal. For example, in the Shin sect of Japanese Pure Land Buddhism and in Ch'an (Zen) Buddhism, or at least in their early stages, little importance was attached to ritual in the form of external acts, even though today some ritual elements may have come to be incorporated. The same thing may be said in the case of Protestantism too. But in the various Tantric sects ritual occupies an important position, and in other religions of type (3) too acts such as chanting a magical formula will, when considered objectively, be found to represent rituals in a broad sense with a specific purpose just as in religions of types (1) and (2).

All religions, whether they belong to type (1), (2) or (3), may be considered to aim at either the manifestation, attainment or rejection of the sacred through the negation or transformation of the profane. Buddhism utilized the ancient practice of *yoga* as a means for attaining ultimate knowledge. The "four meditations" described in early Buddhist scriptures are clearly a form of *yoga* that was incorporated into Buddhism, while the Vijñānavāda school was also known as the Yogācāra or "Yoga Practice" school because *yoga* constituted its main method of practice. As is repeated over and again by Eliade in his work *Le Yoga* (1954; *Yoga*, 1958), *yoga* represents a means for making possible the manifestation of the sacred through the negation of the profane.

When considered in this light, it may be said that the aim of Nāgārjuna's *Middle Stanzas* is to make possible the experience leading to the sacred under its aspect of "emptiness" (*śūnyatā*) by putting an end to the profane world in the form of linguistic proliferation (*prapañca*), held to be the root of karma and mental defilements. Nāgārjuna's view that "*nirvāṇa* is no different from transmigration (*saṃsāra*)" adds a special qualification to the manner in which the profane is brought to cessation.

4

The interaction between the two poles in religion is marked by two vectors pointing in different directions. One vector points from the profane to the sacred, while the other points from the sacred to the profane. Religious praxis such as points in the direction of the former may be seen, for example, in the instance of a "profane" human being approaching or seeking to attain the "sacred." The opposite direction is to be seen in a situation where the sacred manifests itself in the profane or in the power that the profane receives from the sacred. These two vectors differ not only in direction but also in quality. The first vector arises through the will and action of the practitioner, while the second vector is born of the energy possessed by the sacred itself. Since the sacred and the profane are not fixed points, the two vectors do not describe a straight line but come to assume a more complex aspect.

The two religious poles as they appear in the *Middle Stanzas* are "linguistic proliferation" (*prapañca*), representing the sum total of human language and its referents, and emptiness, in which this has been extinguished. (Alternatively, they may be said to correspond to *saṃsāra* and *nirvāṇa* or the conventional and ultimate truths.) Thus the first vector corresponds to the act of attempting to extinguish linguistic proliferation, while the first aspect of the second vector (the manifestation of the sacred in the profane) is to be found in the meaning of emptiness (*śūnyatā-artha*) and its functioning (*prayojana*), and the second aspect (the power that the profane receives from the sacred) is to be seen in the state of being an entity the essence of which is emptiness but which has been provisionally named by means of language (*upādāya prajñaptiḥ*). Nāgārjuna discusses in detail the negation of the profane, but he says almost nothing about the sacred itself. When he says, "We declare dependent co-arising to be emptiness" (*Middle Stanzas*, XXIV.18), the two poles in religion are extremely close to one another, for that which has arisen in dependence upon conditions (the profane) is here termed the sacred. But at the same time, asserting as he does that all linguistic proliferation must be extinguished in order to attain emptiness (*ibid*., XVIII.5), Nāgārjuna does not forget to touch on the rupture existing between the two poles. Insofar as he insists upon the absolute extinction of linguistic proliferation, Nāgārjuna may be said to be emphasizing the first vector and relying on the inherent power of the profane to proceed by its own efforts. But, unlike Abhidharma Buddhism, he does not ultimately recognize any distance separating the sacred and the profane. The first vector as described in the *Middle Stanzas*, representing the long path of negation, calls to mind a parabola projected through the vast realm of the profane towards its point of contact with the realm of the sacred, while the implied second vector suggests countless straight lines that diffuse instantaneously throughout the entire realm of the profane. The two aspects of the second vector are, furthermore, closely related to one another in the *Middle Stanzas*, for the contact between the two poles (the first aspect) continues to repeatedly exert influence upon the subsequently sacralized world (the second aspect). In this manner, by availing ourselves of a perspective provided by the twin concepts of the sacred and the profane and by further considering the differences in the length and direction of the two vectors between these two poles, it is possible to elucidate the characteristics of

Nāgārjuna's thought which, although a form of exoteric Buddhism, was later to provide the theoretical basis for esoteric or Tantric Buddhism.

5

As was noted above, it is human action that makes possible the interaction between the two poles of the sacred and the profane. The actual forms assumed by the interaction between the two poles may be seen in ritual acts such as rites of offering and in religious praxis such as *yoga*, and the sphere of our observations is confined to those religious acts that take concrete forms, including the mental functions that arise in the consciousness of a *yoga* practitioner. Natural objects (flowers, stones, etc.) and artificial objects (effigies, etc.) often serve as religious symbols, and here again it is human action that makes them function in this fashion. As is pointed out by Eliade, it is action in the form of ritual that might, for example, give meaning to plants as symbols of life and cause this meaning to function within human existence.

There are two types of religious acts. The first is ritual acts performed by several people (group religious acts), and includes festivals and funeral rites. The second is praxis whereby the individual, acting on his own initiative deliberately and repeatedly, brings about a movement of energy between the two religious poles (individual religious acts); this latter includes meditation and chanting. The first of these two types of religious acts is to be found in all of the aforementioned three types of religions, but its importance is greater in the religions of primitive peoples and folk religions than in the third type of world religions. The second type of religious act is performed in both folk religions and world religions, and is especially prominent in the latter.

Although both of these two types of religious acts are concerned with the difference between the sacred and the profane, the content of the two poles differs according to the nature of the act. In the case of group religious acts, the sacred and the profane often appear in the form of external objects. Let us consider the example of *caitya* worship among the Newars in Kathmandu. In order to celebrate the birthday of the head of a household, a Buddhist monk is invited to perform a fire rite (*homa*) in front of the *caitya* or memorial for the dead, during which oil and grain are thrown into the fire. At the same time, offerings of flowers and lamps are made in front of the *caitya*. In this case the monk, *caitya*, fire, oil and so on are each transformed into the sacred and endowed with an electric charge, as it were, corresponding to the relative importance of their respective functions. In rituals such as the full-moon and new-moon sacrifices that have been practised since the times of ancient Brahmanism and in many other Hindu rituals too various objects appear as symbols of the sacred and the profane.

Judging from the works that are today considered to be genuinely attributable to him, Nāgārjuna did not attach any value to group religious acts, and in the *Middle Stanzas* he concerns himself solely with individual religious acts. But later, when the idea of emptiness became the theoretical basis of esoteric or Tantric Buddhism, Tantric Buddhism was to "internalize" group ritual acts and thereby seek to integrate them with individual religious acts. In later times the idea of emptiness would link up with Brahmanic religious rituals such as the *homa* rite and with *yoga*, Hindu myths and even shamanistic elements. According to the Tibetan tradition, the author of the *Middle Stanzas* is said to have also composed a great many Tantric treatises. The elucidation of what aspects in Nāgārjuna's thought contained elements facilitating this internalization of group ritual acts in later times will provide an interesting topic for future study, and even when considering the *Middle Stanzas*, concerned as they are with individual religious acts alone, it is important to bear in mind the probable latent existence of such elements.

6

For the sacred to manifest itself within the profane, the profane must "die" once. This is because it is only following the sacrifice of the profane that the sacred is able to manifest its power in the "*topos*" formerly occupied by the profane. When the Brahmins of yore threw butter and pieces of rice cake into a fire as offerings, these offerings symbolized the profane, and through being consumed by fire they were able to invoke the deities to the ritual site. So that the great goddess Devī could be born in India, the corpse of Śiva's wife Satī is said to have been cut up into pieces. In rites of offering (*pūjā*) there is always something that is presented to the sacred as something that must die (or be dismembered).

In addition to religious acts for the aggrandizement of worldly riches and benefits such as wealth, power and ability, religious acts aiming at emancipation from the cycle of birth and death or at the acquisition of metaphysical knowledge through the death of the profane by abnegating worldly riches and controlling to the utmost limits both one's physical and mental activities are found to be especially prevalent in India. In acts of this latter type, all human actions and activities are directed towards "cessation." In the former type of religious act, on the other hand, human activities are "promoted." Traditionally, these two types have been known as *nivṛtti* (cessation) and *pravṛtti* (activity) respectively. In this case, "cessation" does not necessarily refer to a state of tensionless repose or to the process leading towards such a state, for in order to bring profane human action—including not only desires but also the cognition of objects of desire—to a state of "death," it often becomes necessary to traverse a path far more demanding than that of the path of "activity." In other words, those acts aiming at the extinction of the profane may be said to be not themselves in a state of cessation but rather in a state of activity.

The *yoga* practitioner, motionless and silent, seeks to control his mind. The thoughts that arise one after another in his mind must be brought to cessation. *Yoga* is a method for making possible the manifestation of the sacred as a result of the absolute cessation of the profane. In the case of an individual religious act such as the practice of *yoga*, all one's actions are, as it were, immolated on the altar of one's own body and thus brought to death. Compared with butter and pieces of rice cake, the profane that dies here is of infinitely greater import. This is of course no mere death, but death in preparation for rebirth. The ultimate goal of *yoga* is, after having brought the activities of one's body and mind under control, to obtain the wisdom of enlightenment or to come in contact with the light of the cosmic self (*puruṣa*).

The term "*nivṛtti*" is used in the sense of "withdrawal from a certain thing (*x*)," and the "cessation" (*nivṛtti*) with which we are here concerned also embraces this meaning. In the case of the Sāṃkhya school it is withdrawal from the activity of the primordial matter constituting the world, but in Buddhism the situation is somewhat different. This is because Buddhists—we shall disregard the Tantrists for the time being—seek not so much to withdraw from karma and mental defilements but rather to extinguish them. It is not only the act of withdrawing oneself from a certain object *x* or its influence, but also the act of negating the very functioning or existence of *x* that has traditionally been termed "*nivṛtti.*"

The content of the profane that is to be negated through the act of *nivṛtti* is most diverse. By considering what sort of things are brought to cessation in what degree or by examining the content of what is negated and the degree of its negation, it is possible to understand the various schools of Indian philosophy as forming a single gradated sequence, with the objects of negation and degree of negation revealing the distinguishing features of the respective religious sects and philosophical schools.

In the case of Buddhism, human existence has been equated with suffering, and this suffering was held to result from craving. For suffering to be extinguished, its cause must be extinguished. The method towards this end was expounded by Śākyamuni in the form of a teaching that has been known as the "four noble truths of suffering, the origination of suffering, cessation, and the path." The truth of cessation (*nirodha-satya*) here signifies the cessation (*nivṛtti*) of the profane in the form of craving and so forth.

The extinction of the profane as it appears in the form of mental defilements and ignorance has been a fundamental characteristic of Buddhism throughout its history, and religious acts in pursuit of the realization of emptiness are oriented towards *nivṛtti* itself. In order to experience emptiness, it is necessary to negate as fictitious linguistic proliferation (*prapañca*) or the everyday world that is the source of karma and mental defilements. When Nāgārjuna states that "linguistic proliferation is extinguished in emptiness" (*ibid.*, XVIII.5), a great distance separates linguistic proliferation and emptiness insofar that a long process of negating linguistic proliferation lies ahead, and the acts of cessation performed in order to close this gap cannot be but thorough. The point in which this process differs from yogic practices is that it concerns primarily linguistic proliferation.

Although Abhidharma Buddhism (in particular, the Sarvāstivāda school) did not deny the major premise of Buddhism that "all things are impermanent," elements of realism were more marked in this school than in any other in the history of Buddhist thought. Indian schools of realism such as the Vaiśeṣikas held this world to be made up of indestructible constituent elements, and the Sarvāstivādins also considered the world to be composed of a number of elements (*dharma*)—in the *Abhidharmakośabhāṣya*, for example, they are given as numbering seventy-five. Hence, for this school, the profane negatee consisted primarily of the mental defilements and so forth pertaining to the individual. The standpoint of this school, in which the activity of the self (*ātman*) is negated but the elements (*dharma*) constituting the world are not negated, has thus traditionally been expressed as "the self is empty but the elements are existent."

It was the corpus of Prajñāpāramitā scriptures that was to repeatedly negate the profane world with the slogan of "form is empty," namely, "the physical and mental constituent elements of matter, perception, conception, volition and mental inertia, and consciousness are empty (*śūnya*) [or emptiness (*śūnyatā*)]." Nāgārjuna is thought to have been influenced by early Prajñāpāramitā scriptures such as the *Aṣṭasāhasrikā Prajñāpāramitā,* and in regard to their respective attitudes towards the negation of the profane there are many points in common between the two.

The content of the twenty-seven chapters of the *Middle Stanzas* represents nothing other than the nullification of linguistic proliferation. "Linguistic proliferation" (*prapañca*) here signifies (1) verbal expression, (2) concepts or ideas, (3) acts of expression, (4) referents of verbal expression, and (5) the very structure incorporating all the above elements, namely, the entire world, including the cognition thereof.[4] Therefore, according to the *Middle Stanzas,* the profane negatee comprises not only the mental functions of the individual but also the external world as well. The second and third centuries A. D. when Nāgārjuna (*ca.* 150-250) was active and when the majority of the early Mahāyāna scriptures such as the *Aṣṭasāhasrikā Prajñāpāramitā* and *Gaṇḍavyūha-sūtra* were already circulating was also a time when the orthodox Brahmanic schools were making efforts to formulate their respective systems of thought. Resting on the conviction that it

4. Cf. Tachikawa Musashi, "Gengo katsudō no shimetsu to kūshō—purapancha ni tsuite" (The Extinction of Linguistic Proliferation and Emptiness: On *prapañca*), *Bukkyōgaku,* Vol. 9-10 Special Issue (1980), p.146 ff.

was possible to gain cognizance of the very structure of the world, Brahmanic schools such as the Sāṃkhya, Nyāya and Vaiśeṣika attempted to describe the world from their respective standpoints and in accordance with their respective methods. According to the Vaiśeṣika school, the world is composed of six, or in later times seven, categories (substance, quality, movement, universality, particularity, inherence and non-existence) and may be likened to a multistoried structure. The constituent elements of this structure, as well as the connections between them, are extremely stable, and the categories themselves that compose the world are imperishable. The formative changes that occur in the world are nothing other than changes in the connections between these categories. In a system such as this of the Vaiśeṣikas the existence of the world is by no means something profane that must be negated, and the target of the negation of the profane in this school is sought in something other than the existence of the world. Although a Buddhist school, the Sarvāstivādins held views similar to those of the Vaiśeṣika school in regard to their understanding of the structure of the world, and for them too the profane negatee was not the world itself. It was Nāgārjuna who, taking note of these philosophical trends in Brahmanism and similar tendencies within Buddhism, was to level severe criticism at such views. Among the various currents of thought in India, all evincing a strong interest in describing the structure of the world, Nāgārjuna's attitude, an attitude retraceable to none other than Śākyamuni, was singular, for he maintained that it was wrong to try to describe the structure of the world insofar that any world possessing a describable structure was not real. This attitude of Nāgārjuna's was the most radical even in the traditions of *nivṛtti*.

Although the greater part of the arguments contained in the twenty-seven chapters of the *Middle Stanzas* represents a critique of the Sarvāstivādins seeking to uphold a solid world structure, Nāgārjuna's arguments were also applicable to realists such as the Nyāya and Vaiśeṣika schools. In the course of the controversy that was to continue between Mahāyānist and Hindu realists for nearly one thousand years after Nāgārjuna's death, adherents of the Mādhyamika school, the successors to Nāgārjuna, continued to adamantly deny the existence of the world. For them, any description of the world was from the first quite out of the question.

7

Linguistic proliferation that has been brought to cessation does not, however, remain forever in a state of "death." Instead it is reborn as a referent of verbal expression that, although non-existent as a real entity, has been provisionally named (*upādāya prajñaptiḥ*). But as was noted earlier, the author of the *Middle Stanzas* does not have much to say on the vector pointing from the sacred to the profane, alluded to in the statement that "emptiness is provisional designation" (*ibid.*, XXIV.18). It was this, when the once negated profane had been reborn as something positive through the power of the sacred and when this reborn profane was functioning as the sacralized profane, that represented the final goal of the *Middle Stanzas*. Nāgārjuna's goal was not emptiness itself in which linguistic proliferation had ceased; rather, he aspired to the redemption of all existence as it is through the actualization of linguistic proliferation that had been reborn by the power of emptiness and thereby sacralized.

Such a perspective is one that "arises," as it were, following a long process of total negation of the profane, and while embodying a vision of emptiness that transcends language, it is alive to everyday linguistic activity. Except for the statement that "emptiness is provisional designation," the *Middle Stanzas* remain silent on the quintessence of this state. The length of the first vector and the speed and complexity of the second vector, mentioned above, may be said to reflect the relentlessness of the negation of the profane and the stratification of that which is affirmed.

In this chapter we have attempted to shed light on various characteristics of the ideas elaborated in the *Middle Stanzas* by considering them within the context of a number of axes of thought. In the next chapter we wish to survey the discussion of spiritual cultivation in the *Middle Stanzas* by relating it to the process leading from the profane to the sacred and to that leading from the sacred to the profane. This will be our final preparation before setting out to probe in detail the nature of the logic of the *Middle Stanzas*.

CHAPTER THREE

THE CONVENTIONAL AND ULTIMATE TRUTHS IN NĀGĀRJUNA'S THOUGHT

While recognizing the basic identity or homogeneity of the two poles in religion, the different schools of Indian Buddhism conceived of the distance separating the two poles in a variety of ways. But the understanding that from delusion, the "cause" of enlightenment (the profane), one traverses a "path" of cultivation (medium) to reach the "fruit"of enlightenment (the sacred) was common to all Buddhists. Nor was Nāgārjuna's thought any exception to this general understanding. He called the state of the cause the "conventional" (*saṃvṛti*) and the state of the fruit or result the "ultimate truth" (*paramārtha*). For Nāgārjuna religious praxis meant to perceive that our everyday linguistic activity (*vyavahāra*), which serves as a medium for the profane, is unable to describe the ultimate truth as it actually is and to thereby realize that everything that exists is "empty" (*śūnya*).

Human action (karma) leads to further action, and this endless chain of action binds man to transmigration or the cycle of birth and death. Mental defilements such as desire, ignorance and anger, which plague and afflict the body and mind, also keep man shackled to delusion. Such is the everyday world of the profane. In the *Middle Stanzas* (XVIII.5a) Nāgārjuna states that "through the extinction of action and mental defilements there is liberation." And, according to Nāgārjuna, action and mental defilements arise from "discriminating thought" (*vikalpa*; XVIII.5b).

Furthermore, this discriminating thought is born of linguistic proliferation (*prapañca*; XVIII. 5c). The original meaning of "*prapañca*," here translated as "linguistic proliferation," is "expansion" or "diversity," but here it refers to verbal expression, the essence of which is expansion or diversity. Here "verbal expression" signifies both language and the act of causing language to function as language.

Expansion or diversity indicates the "division" into diverse elements that is unavoidable in verbal expression. Normally our thinking presupposes a dichotomy between affirmation and negation, active and passive, agent and action, one and many, and so on. In almost all cases, a statement that is made without assuming a dichotomy between the affirmative and the negative, or between *A* and non-*A*, is meaningless. A single judgement already presupposes at least two concepts. For example, the judgement "the chalk is white" requires the two terms 'chalk' and 'white' and presupposes the two concepts of 'chalk' and 'white'. In addition, the concept 'white' also presupposes the referent of the term 'not white'. In other words, it presupposes a dichotomy between *A* ('white') and non-*A* ('not white'). Then again, if one were not to recognize a dichotomy between the active and the passive, it would become impossible to discuss the relation between the seer and the seen, the knower and the known, and so on. The expression "a person walks" is based on a dichotomy between the agent and the action. A proposition, the basic unit of language, is not feasible without two or more elements.

This kind of dichotomy between the affirmative and the negative or the active and the passive corresponds to the expansion or diversity that constitutes the essence of *prapañca*. For Nāgārjuna, language as characterized by this expansion or diversity, as well as the phenomenal world that is based thereon, represented the profane that had to be negated.

We noted earlier that the *Middle Stanzas* represent Nāgārjuna's refutation of his opponents who maintained that "things really exist." His method of refutation was to negate the validity of the propositions that his opponents presented by bringing to light the contradictions into which these propositions, expressed by language inevitably characterized by "expansion," had to lapse on account of this "expansion."

While basing himself upon the logical consistency of language, Nāgārjuna demonstrated by his own original methods the reasons for the non-validity of propositions such as "the traverser traverses" and "a cause has an effect." Nāgārjuna, looking as he did upon the entire phenomenal world as the sum total of "linguistic proliferation" (*prapañca*), was a merciless critic of language, but at the same time in his arguments he was absolutely unrelenting in his pursuit of the logic of language.

Taking up for consideration various "interdependent relationships" in a phenomenal world that exists merely on account of interdependence or "dependent co-arising" (*pratītya-samutpāda*), Nāgārjuna demonstrated that these interdependent relationships are, properly speaking, logically impossible. His thesis, expressed in such startling terms as "things do not arise" (Chap. I) or "a traverser does not traverse" (Chap. II), asserted that there exists neither an agent, nor the object of an action, nor an action. By such methods Nāgārjuna completely denied the existence of all things as "own-beings."

The propositions dealt with in the different chapters of the *Middle Stanzas* are diverse in nature, but the majority of them lead to a conclusion that negates linguistic proliferation. As will be seen below, Nāgārjuna's arguments demonstrating the non-validity of his opponents' assertions are unrelenting, and his determination to exhaust the subject under discussion is overwhelming. This relentlessness of his represents the length of the path leading from the profane to the sacred, or the length of the first vector, in his conception of spiritual cultivation, and it also reflects the propensity in his thought towards radical cessation (*nivṛtti*).

At the conclusion of this long and gruelling process to completely extinguish linguistic proliferation there awaits the perspective of a vision of emptiness in which "nothing exists (or everything is empty)."

> Linguistic proliferation is extinguished in emptiness.
> (*prapañcas tu śūnyatāyāṃ nirudhyate//* XVIII. 5d)

The *Middle Stanzas* begin with the following verse of salutation, and it is what is here referred to as "auspicious dependent co-arising" (*pratītyasamutpādam...śivam*) that represented Nāgārjuna's goal of "ultimate truth."

> I offer salutation to the Enlightened One, the best of preachers, who taught dependent co-arising, which has no ceasing, no arising, no nullification, no eternalness, no unity, no plurality, no coming, and no going, is quiescent of linguistic proliferation, and is auspicious.

(*anirodham anutpādam anucchedam aśāśvatam/*
anekārtham anānārtham anāgamam anirgamam//
yaḥ pratītyasamutpādaṃ prapañcopaśamaṃ śivam/
deśayāmāsa saṃbuddhastaṃ vande vadatāṃ varam//)

It is in such terms that the ultimate truth attainable when linguistic proliferation, inherently doomed to a dichotomy between being and non-being, has ceased following a long process of negation is described at the start of the *Middle Stanzas*. In this verse, ultimate truth is termed "dependent co-arising" and is qualified by the modifier "auspicious." Although Nāgārjuna relentlessly denied the existence of all dependently co-arisen things, the ultimate truth to which he finally attained was also designated "dependent co-arising," and there is no doubting the fact that this dependent co-arising was something positive. That reached at the end of a process of rigorous analysis of language was not a "graveyard of thought" in which all modes of thought had simply been extirpated, but was a point where "dependent co-arising" or the "dependently co-arisen" was nothing other than the sacred.

But the *Middle Stanzas* have little to say on the "positive" structure of ultimate truth itself. Although they do contain two or three passages touching on ultimate truth, the content of these may be said to be encapsulated in the verse of salutation cited above. This means that ultimate truth does not exist apart from the conventional and with its own independent structure. In other words, the sacred, in some indiscernible manner, indwells in the profane.

Was the goal of the vision of emptiness a pinpoint summit upon which one could not even stand and rest? If it were a point where, on account of the extinction of everyday language, people could neither speak nor think, what meaning would the mode of being that this implied have for human life? Even if someone were to complete the complex practices of this vision of emptiness and reach ultimate truth, would it then not be incumbent upon him or her to simply dissolve into nothingness? Is there in fact any difference between the vision of emptiness and nihilism? In reply to such misgivings, Nāgārjuna answers as follows:

> The Dharma-teaching of the Buddhas is based on two truths:
> The conventional truth and the ultimate truth.

(*dve satye samupāśritya buddhānāṃ dharmadeśanā/ lokasaṃvṛtisatyaṃ ca satyaṃ ca paramārthataḥ//* XXIV. 8)

The "conventional truth" represents the verbalization of "ultimate truth." On the one hand language is totally rejected and ultimate truth is held to be ineffable, but on the other hand it is possible to give verbal expression to ultimate truth in the form of conventional truth. If touched by the power of ultimate truth, the modes of thinking that had until then been negated are reaffirmed. For example, following the statement "linguistic proliferation is extinguished in emptiness" quoted above, the *Middle Stanzas* continue as follows:

The Buddhas have both indicated that there is a self and taught no-self,
And they have also taught that there is no self nor no-self whatsoever.
(*atmety api prajñapitam anātmety api deśitam/ buddhair nātmā na cānātmā kaścid ity api deśitam//* XVIII. 6)

And in verse 8 of the same chapter it is stated that

Everything is either true, or not true, or both true and untrue,
Or neither true nor untrue: This is the teaching of the Buddhas.
(*sarvaṃ tathyaṃ na vā tathyaṃ tathyaṃ cātathyam eva ca/ naivātathyaṃ naiva tathyam etad buddhānuśāsanam//* XVIII. 8)

Here Nāgārjuna himself is giving expression to modes of thought such as "there is a self" and "everything is true" that had to be negated during the process of religious cultivation. What is the reason for this? The key to solving this question lies in the expressions "the Buddhas have...taught" and "this is the teaching of the Buddhas." Namely, the Buddha, who has already attained ultimate truth, is, in view of its practical utility in the secular world, here giving expression in the form of conventional truth to ultimate truth which, properly speaking, it is impossible to express by means of language. Conventional truth represents language as used when those who have been granted contact with ultimate truth after having undergone spiritual training in the vision of emptiness descend to save the world. Thus there exist two types of language, one linguistic proliferation in the form of "false verbal expression" and the other conventional truth in the form of the teaching of the Buddhas.

Therefore, those who have attained to ultimate truth do not

simply disappear into nothingness. The world of this conventional truth is one in which those who have reached ultimate truth work for the benefit of others or guide those who have not yet attained to ultimate truth.

The following two verses are of special interest in that they demonstrate the contrast between the negation of linguistic proliferation and the verbalization of ultimate truth.

Contingent upon (*apekṣya*) fuel there is no fire, and not contingent upon (*anapekṣya*) fuel there is no fire. (X.12ab)

In dependence upon (*pratītya*) an action there arises an agent,
And in dependence upon an agent there arises an action. (VIII.12abc)

The former of these two verses resolves into

Contingent upon *x* there is no *y*,
And not contingent upon *x* there is no *y*.

Here the word "contingent" is understood to be invariably complemented by "not contingent." In other words, it implies a dichotomy between *A* and non-*A*, and therefore both must be negated.

The second verse, on the other hand, takes an affirmative form, namely:

In dependence upon *x* there is *y*,
And in dependence upon *y* there is *x*.

This "in dependence" does not presuppose "not in dependence." Thus the words of this verse are not torn by a dichotomy between *A* and non-*A*. The word here used for "in dependence upon" (*pratītya*) is also found in "dependent co-arising" (*pratītya-samutpāda*), which represents ultimate truth. In this manner VIII.12 gives expression to ultimate truth in verbalized form.

Nāgārjuna conceived of the world of ultimate truth in terms of dependent co-arising. The idea of dependent co-arising had in fact been one of the mainstays of Buddhism ever since its beginnings. The doctrine of dependent co-arising as expounded in Early Buddhism, however, was one declaring that things begin to exist and cease to exist in dependence upon other things, and emphasis was placed primarily on the temporal aspect of causal relationships.

Among the various theories of dependent co-arising that were to evolve in later times, that most widely known is one positing a twelvefold chain of dependent co-arising. By identifying the first member "ignorance" as the basic cause whence the second member "formative forces" (*saṃskāra*) is born, to be followed by the third member "consciousness" and, at the end of the chain, the twelfth member "old age and death" as the final outcome, it seeks to explain the human condition in terms of a concatenation of causes and effects.

Nāgārjuna adapted this conception of dependent co-arising stemming from Early Buddhism in a still broader context. He sought to consider all existent things, which in the twelvefold chain of dependent co-arising had been understood in terms of temporal causality, in terms of a synchronous logical relationship.[1] According to him, movement and its locus, action and its agent, active and passive, being and non-being, etc., also all stand in an interdependent relationship to one another. The manner in which all existents in the phenomenal world are "interdependently related" is known as dependent co-arising, while a correct grasp of this mode of being of all existents represents dependent co-arising as ultimate truth (although this does not, of course, exhaust Nāgārjuna's ideas on dependent co-arising).

While referring to ultimate truth on the one hand as "dependent co-arising," Nāgārjuna also calls it "emptiness," as for example when he says, "linguistic proliferation is extinguished in emptiness" (XVIII. 5d).

"Emptiness" (*śūnyatā*), which constituted the central concept of the Prajñāpāramitā scriptures upon which Nāgārjuna's thought was to be based, means that existents have no eternal and unchanging essence (*svabhāva*: own-being). In the Prajñāpāramitā scriptures "emptiness" refers to the world of enlightenment, but it is also stated that this world of enlightenment is not separate from the world of delusion: "Form (the world of delusion) is emptiness, and emptiness is form." Here, "form is emptiness" may be considered to point to the path leading from delusion to enlightenment, while "emptiness is form" points to the path descending from enlightenment to delusion. The

1. For Nāgārjuna, the very fact that something could be expressed by language or by a proposition meant that it was dependently co-arisen.

Prajñāpāramitā scriptures do not, however, explain in detail the nature of these two paths which point in opposite directions.

In his consideration of the process of the "path," which had not been sufficiently elucidated in the Prajñāpāramitā scriptures, Nāgārjuna, while still basing himself upon the concept of emptiness, turned his attention to the different aspects of emptiness. There were some people who, mistaking Nāgārjuna's emptiness for mere nihilism, advanced the following opinion:

If all this is empty, then there is no arising and no decay,
And for you it follows that the Four Noble Truths do also not exist.

(*yadi śūnyam idaṃ sarvam udayo nāsti na vyayaḥ/*
caturṇām āryasatyānām abhāvas te prasajyate// XXIV. 1)

Nāgārjuna's reply was as follows:

You understand neither the purpose of emptiness,
Nor emptiness, nor the meaning of emptiness, and so you thus exert yourself in vain.

(*...śūnyatāyāṃ na tvaṃ vetsi prayojanam/*
śūnyatāṃ śūnyatārthaṃ ca tata evaṃ vihanyase // XXIV. 7)

The "purpose of emptiness" refers to the objective of extinguishing linguistic proliferation and the efforts leading towards this objective; "emptiness" corresponds to ultimate truth, namely, the state in which linguistic proliferation has been extinguished; and the "meaning of emptiness" signifies all existents relating to our everyday life in which emptiness is an actually established fact.

The opponent with his one-sided understanding of emptiness had completely overlooked the aspect of the "meaning of emptiness." Stated in terms of what we have said earlier, it represents the world of conventional truth in which ultimate truth has been verbally expressed. It is the world in which those who have attained to ultimate truth dwell from the very next moment and the world to which they lead those seeking to proceed from the secular world to ultimate truth.

The fact that a correct understanding of the manner in which existents are "interdependently related" corresponds to dependent co-arising as ultimate truth and that this ultimate truth is called emptiness is explicitly expressed by Nāgārjuna in the *Middle Stanzas* XXIV.

18ab, where he says,

Whatever is dependent co-arising, that we declare to be emptiness.

(*yaḥ pratītyasamutpādaḥ śūnyatāṃ tāṃ pracakṣmahe/*)

The same verse continues:

It is provisional designation and it is the middle way.

(*sā prajñaptir upādāya pratipat saiva madhyamā//*)

"Provisional designation" refers to the verbalized form assumed by ultimate truth, and it may be said to correspond to language in which the vector leading from the sacred to the profane is grounded. The term "middle way," on the other hand, also refers to ultimate truth, but in the *Middle Stanzas* it is used by Nāgārjuna only this once. It is in fact this word "middle" (*madhyamaka*) from which the title "*Middle Stanzas*" (*Madhyamakakārikā*) derives, but although it refers to something transcending any dichotomy into "being" and "non-being," "attribute" and "substance" or "cause" and "effect," and although it was later to give rise to the appellation "Mādhyamika" school for the successors to Nāgārjuna's thought, Nāgārjuna may have avoided excessive use of it because it is a positive term without any negative connotations. One may conjecture that after having explained ultimate truth by means of terms such as "dependent co-arising," a word of strongly negative implications in that it denies the autonomous substantiality of things, and "emptiness," which points explicitly to the non-substantiality of things while also giving succinct expression to the sacred, Nāgārjuna perhaps finally used just once this term "middle path"—the term most befitting the content of the *Middle Stanzas*—in order to reveal the real hidden depths of the truth. It is a term which, in no simplistic sense, "transcends language and transcends logic" and which is directly to the point in expressing Nāgārjuna's negation of the real existence of things. On no account, therefore, does this "middle" refer to something intermediary, nor does it signify a "mean" from which extremes have been rejected.

By establishing his own original methods of argument, Nāgārjuna pointed to a path negating the conventional and leading to ultimate truth (the first vector). But in addition to this, he also shed light on the course leading back to the conventional after the attainment of ultimate truth (the second vector). The latter is not practised in stages as is the first vector, but is realized instantaneously. Ultimate truth is not a goal where one can abide forever, but is like a flash of light, and after one has come in contact with it, the conventional becomes something that has been sanctioned; its continuing existence is, namely, acknowledged as conventional truth. At the same time, ultimate truth also comes to serve as a support for further advances towards this conventional truth.

Conventional truth (ultimate truth in verbalized form) is necessary in order to put into practice the vision of emptiness directed towards ultimate truth. Guided by the teaching of someone who has already attained enlightenment, one is able to advance along the path towards ultimate truth. When one negates an example of linguistic proliferation such as "A traverser traverses" by saying, "A traverser does not traverse," one has already been illumined in some form or another by the light of ultimate truth. The analysis and criticism of language undertaken by Nāgārjuna were in fact based on conventional truth. The basis of Nāgārjuna's negation by means of *reductio ad absurdum* of the linguistic proliferation of "the traversing of that which is being traversed" lay in the idea of dependent co-arising, according to which a point being traversed can exist only in conjunction with the act of traversing.

Thus, for Nāgārjuna, ultimate truth and the conventional are not two separate entities, but overlap in such a manner that it is difficult to differentiate one from the other. This derives from the thesis that "form is emptiness, and emptiness is form," central to the Prajñāpāramitā scriptures, and on the basis of this Nāgārjuna formulated an integrated dynamic theory of praxis. His weapons in doing so were a series of arguments based on formulae of negation, a broader interpretation of dependent co-arising, and also his heedfulness of that aspect of the "meaning of emptiness" inherent in emptiness.

Although they are only hinted at, the sacralization of the profane in the final stage of the path leading from the profane (the conventional) to the sacred (ultimate truth) and the overlapping of the sacred and the profane that then occurs are conceived of in the *Middle Stanzas* in extremely dynamic terms, but in later times there was to appear a tendency to substantialize and fixate them. This tendency is also to be seen in certain schools of Tantric Buddhism, and as has already been noted in the previous chapter, in this current of thought Nāgārjuna was regarded as the founder of Tantrism. After having come under the influence of Tantrism, the praxis of Mahāyāna Buddhism also came to assume aspects of group religious acts centred on ritual, even though it was grounded in visualization practices aiming at personal salvation.

But the overlapping of the sacred and the profane in the *Middle Stanzas* represented the centre of a state of tension or the starting point of a parabola, and although following the moment in which the profane has come in contact with the sacred there might be born a world in which the sacred indwells in the profane, this world must be always sustained by a recurrent momentary point of origin. This is because the second vector leading from the sacred to the profane would probably lose its power of movement if it lost contact with this point of origin. The function of this point of origin is fulfilled by the cessation of linguistic proliferation.

In regard to its conception of enlightenment as a total affirmation following upon rigorous negation and its optimistic belief in this ineffable state of enlightenment, Nāgārjuna's theory of praxis was consistent with the traditions of India's religions. At the same time the fact that, faithful to the thought of the Prajñāpāramitā scriptures, he attached great importance to emptiness and returned to the idea of "no-self" in Early Buddhism is also an aspect of Nāgārjuna's thought that cannot be overlooked. Furthermore, his originality as a Mahāyānist lay in the fact that he grasped the nature of spiritual progress subsequent to enlightenment and delineated a unique world of his own in which the conventional and ultimate truth overlap one another.

CHAPTER FOUR

STATEMENTS TO BE TREATED IN THE *MIDDLE STANZAS*: THE STRUCTURE OF THE PROFANE

The *Middle Stanzas* consist of twenty-seven chapters. The titles of the individual chapters are as follows:

I. An Examination of Conditions (*Pratyaya-parīkṣā*)

II. An Examination of the Traversed and the Non-traversed (*Gatāgata-parīkṣā*)

III. An Examination of the Organs of Sight, etc. (*Cakṣurādīndriya-parīkṣā*)

IV. An Examination of the Aggregates (*Skandha-parīkṣā*)

V. An Examination of the Elements (*Dhātu-parīkṣā*)

VI. An Examination of Passion and the Impassioned (*Rāgarakta-parīkṣā*)

VII. An Examination of the Conditioned (*Saṃskṛta-parīkṣā*)

VIII. An Examination of Action and Agent (*Karmakāraka-parīkṣā*)

IX. An Examination of the Prior Entity [Controlling All Physical and Mental Functions] (*Pūrva-parīkṣā*)

X. An Examination of Fire and Fuel (*Agnīndhana-parīkṣā*)

XI. An Examination of the Prior and Posterior Extremities [before Birth and after Death] (*Pūrvāparakoṭi-parīkṣā*)

XII. An Examination of Suffering (*Duḥkha-parīkṣā*)

XIII. An Examination of Formative Forces (*Saṃskāra-parīkṣā*)

XIV. An Examination of Association (*Saṃsarga-parīkṣā*)

XV. An Examination of Own-being (*Svabhāva-parīkṣā*)

XVI. An Examination of Bondage and Liberation (*Bandhanamokṣa-parīkṣā*)

XVII. An Examination of Action and Its Effect (*Karmaphala-parīkṣā*)
XVIII. An Examination of Self (*Ātma-parīkṣā*)
XIX. An Examination of Time (*Kāla-parīkṣā*)
XX. An Examination of Conjunction (*Sāmagrī-parīkṣā*)
XXI. An Examination of Occurrence and Dissolution (*Saṃbhavavibhava-parīkṣā*)
XXII. An Examination of the Tathāgata (*Tathāgata-parīkṣā*)
XXIII. An Examination of Erroneous Views (*Viparyāsa-parīkṣā*)
XXIV. An Examination of the [Four] Noble Truths (*Āryasatya-parīkṣā*)
XXV. An Examination of Nirvāṇa (*Nirvāṇa-parīkṣā*)
XXVI. An Examination of the Twelve Causal Factors (*Dvādaśāṅga-parīkṣā*)
XXVII. An Examination of [False] Views (*Dṛṣṭi-parīkṣā*)

The first stage in the arguments of the *Middle Stanzas* is to demonstrate that "things do not exist." As was mentioned earlier, in refuting the assertion of his opponents that "things do exist," Nāgārjuna employs arguments based on a type of ***reductio ad absurdum***, and the aim of the following chapters is to grasp in concrete terms the actual nature of this *reductio ad absurdum* and the structure of Nāgārjuna's negation when he maintains that "things do not exist." His methods of demonstration fall into a number of patterns, but in each case his method aims at covering the entire field under discussion and it represents an integrated system. In this system it is propositions describing two entities standing in a relationship of dependent co-arising to one another that represent the focus of discussion and serve as the pivot for all subsequent logical developments.

There is no doubting the fact that not only in the *Middle Stanzas* but also in Buddhism in general one aspect of dependent co-arising (*pratītyasamutpāda*) is that it represents a type of relationship or that it is a teaching or truth concerning relationships. For a relationship to be possible, at least two constituent "factors" are necessary. In his discussions in the *Middle Stanzas* Nāgārjuna often takes up for consideration a pair of factors or entities that are inseparably connected to one another and expresses the relationship obtaining between these two factors in the form of a single proposition. Of the

450-odd verses comprising the *Middle Stanzas* there are more than eighty verses composed of or containing such propositions, and in the arguments developed in these verses Nāgārjuna employs a line of argument consistent from first to last. The remaining verses of the *Middle Stanzas* are devoted primarily to supplementary explanations of these propositions.

As an example of such a verse containing a proposition describing two interdependently related factors or entities, let us consider VIII. 12, a verse to which we have already referred (p. 28).

Example 1

pratītya kārakaḥ karma taṃ pratītya ca kārakam /
karma pravartate... // (VIII.12abc)

(In dependence upon an action there arises an agent,
And in dependence upon an agent there arises an action.)

In this verse Nāgārjuna takes up for consideration two factors, namely, action (*karman*) and agent (*kāraka*), and describes the relationship obtaining between them. This operation represents the first step in Nāgārjuna's arguments in the *Middle Stanzas*. The assumption on which this operation is based is that these two factors or entities, namely, action and agent, are interdependently related. The main topic of Chapter VIII in the *Middle Stanzas* is the interdependence of action and agent or, in other words, the fact that they stand in a relationship of dependent co-arising to one another, and verse 12 quoted above as Example 1 concludes the arguments of this chapter.

In each chapter of the *Middle Stanza*s Nāgārjuna deals with the relationship between two or three (and sometimes four) factors. As an example dealing with a triadic relationship, we may consider XIX. 1.

Example 2

pratyutpanno 'nāgataś ca yady atītam apekṣya hi/
pratyutpanno 'nāgataś ca kāle 'tīte bhaviṣyataḥ//

(If the present and the future are contingent upon the past,
Then the present and the future will exist within past time.)

This verse mentions three factors, namely, the present

(*pratyutpanna*), the future (*anāgata*) and the past (*atīta*), and describes the relationship obtaining between them. This triad is, however, divided into two groups. The two factors comprising the first group are the present and the future, while the second group consists of a single factor, the past. Since the two factors comprising the first group are dealt with as a single factor in relation to the past, it may be assumed that in effect only two factors are being dealt with in this verse (and the same applies to verses 2-3 of the same chapter too).

In the *Middle Stanzas* there are to be found a variety of similarly inseparably connected pairs of factors or entities standing in a relationship of dependent co-arising to one another. If it were possible to extract all such pairs of factors appearing in the *Middle Stanzas*, it would become clear between what sort of entities Nāgārjuna considered an interdependent relationship to exist. The following table is an attempt to do so, and it lists the pairs of factors appearing in each chapter of the *Middle Stanzas*. In order to gain a clear understanding of the distinguishing features of the arguments developed in the *Middle Stanzas*, especially the arguments concerning dependent co-arising, we hereby hope first of all to clarify the context of these arguments.

*Verse numbers follow the Poussin edition (*PP*).

TABLE 1

Chapter	Verse	Two Factors	
I	1	Existent or thing (*bhāva*)	Arising (*utpāda*)[1] from self (*sva*), arising from another (*para*), arising from both (*dvi*), or arising without cause [i.e., neither from self nor from another] (*ahetu*)
I	4ab	Function (*kriyā*)[2]	That which has conditions (*pratyayavat*) or that which has non-conditions (*apratyayavat*)
I	4cd	Condition (*pratyaya*)	That which has functions (*kriyāvat*) or that which has non-functions (*akriyāvat*)

I	6	Condition (*pratyaya*)	Existing entity (*sadartha*) or non-existing entity (*asadartha*) ·
I	11	Effect (*phala*)	Condition (*pratyaya*)
I	14	Effect (*phala*)	That which is composed of conditions (*pratyayamaya*) or that which is composed of non-conditions (*apratyayamaya*)
II	1	Traversing (*gamana*)[3]	That which has been traversed (*gata*), that which has not been traversed (*agata*), or that which is being traversed (*gamyamāna*)
II	8	Traversing (*gamana*)[4]	Traverser (*gantṛ*), non-traverser (*agantṛ*), or third person other than a traverser and non-traverser ("*anyo gantur agantuś ca...tṛtīyaḥ*")
II	12	Beginning [of traversing] (*ārambhaṇa*)[5]	That which has been traversed, that which has not been traversed, or that which is being traversed
II	15	Standing still (*sthiti*)	Traverser, non-traverser, or third person other than a traverser and non-traverser
II	18	Traversing	Traverser
II	24, 25ab	Traversing	Really existent traverser ("*sadbhūto gantā*"), not really existent traverser ("*asadbhūto [gantā]*"), or really and not really existent traverser ("*sadasadbhūto [gantā]*")[6]
II	24, 25ab	Traversing	That which has been traversed, that which has not been traversed, or that which is being traversed (according to Piṅgala's interpretation)[7]

III	5	Seeing (*darśana*)[8]	Organ of sight (*darśana*)[9] or that which is not an organ of sight (*adarśana*)
III	6	Seeing	Seer (*draṣṭṛ*)
IV	1	Matter (*rūpa*)[10]	Cause of matter (*rūpakāraṇa*)
IV	4	Matter	Cause of matter
IV	6	Cause (*kāraṇa*)	Similar effect ("*sadṛśaṃ kāryam*")[11] or dissimilar effect ("*asadṛśaṃ kāryam*")
V	1	Space (*ākāśa*)[12]	Characteristic of space (*ākāśalakṣaṇa*)
V	3	Characteristic (*lakṣaṇa*)	That which has characteristics (*salakṣaṇa*) or that which is without characteristics (*alakṣaṇa*)
V	7ac	Space	Existent (*bhāva*) or non-existent (*abhāva*)
V	7bc	Space	That which is characterized (*lakṣya*) or that which characterizes, i.e., characteristic (*lakṣaṇa*)[13]
VI	2cd, 3ab	Passion (*rāga*)	One who is impassioned (*rakta*)[14]
VI	4	Passion	One who is impassioned
VI	10	Passion	One who is impassioned
VII	14	Arising (*utpāda*)	That which has arisen (*utpanna*), that which has not arisen (*anutpanna*), or that which is arising (*utpadyamāna*)
VII	20	Arising (*utpatti*)	That which exists (*sat*), that which does not exist (*asat*), or that which exists and does not exist (*sadasat*)[15]
VII	21	Arising (*utpatti*)	Existent that is being extin-

			guished (*nirudhyamānabhāva*) or existent that is not being extinguished (*anirudhyamānabhāva*)
VII	22	Standing still (*sthiti*)	Existent that has stood (*sthitabhāva*), existent that has not stood (*asthitabhāva*), or [existent] that is standing (*tiṣṭhamāna*)
VII	26	Extinction (*nirodha*)[16]	That which has been extinguished (*niruddha*), that which has not been extinguished (aniruddha), or that which is being extinguished (*nirudhyamāna*)
VII	27	Extinction	Existent that has stood (or abided) or existent that has not stood
VII	28	Extinction[17]	This state ("*sā avasthā*") or another state ("*anyā avasthā*")[18]
VII	30ab, 31ab	Extinction (*nirodha*)	Existing existent (*sadbhāva*) or non-existing existent (*asadbhāva*)[19]
VII	32	Extinction (*nirodha*)	Oneself (*svātman*) or another (*parātman*)
VIII	1	Performing really existent action ("*sadbhūtaṃ karma*") or performing not really existent action ("*asadbhūtaṃ karma*")[20]	Really existent agent ("*sadbhūtaḥ kārakaḥ*") or not really existent agent (*asadbhūtaḥ kārakaḥ*)[21]
VIII	7	Performing really and not really existing action ("*sadasat tat*")[22]	Really and not really existent agent ("*sadasadbhūtaḥ kārakaḥ*")[23]
VIII	8a	Performing not existing [action] (*asat*)[24]	Existing [agent] (*sat*)

VIII	8b	Performing existing [action] (*sat*)[25]	Not existing [agent] (*asat*)
VIII	9, 10, 11	Performing really existing action or performing really and not really existing action	Really existing agent, not really existing agent, or really and not really existing agent
VIII	12	Action	Agent
IX	5	Something ("*kiṃcit*")	Someone ("*kaścit*")
X	1	Fire (*agni*)	Fuel (*indhana*)
X	12	Fire	Fuel
XI	3, 4, 5	Birth (*jāti*)	Old age and death (*jarāmaraṇa*)
XII	1	Suffering (*duḥkha*)	That which is self-produced (*svakṛta*), that which is produced by another (*parakṛta*), that which is produced by both ("*dvābhyāṃ kṛtam*"), or that which is without cause (*ahetuka*)
XIII	5	Change (*anyathābhāva*)	One thing (*tat*) or another thing (*anya*)
XIV	7	Otherness (*anyatva*)	That which is other (*anya*) or that which is not other (*ananya*)
XVI	1	Transmigration (*saṃsāra*)[26]	That which is permanent (*nitya*) or that which is impermanent (*anitya*)
XVI	6	Bondage (*bandhana*)	One who has attachment (*sopādāna*) or one without attachment (*anupādāna*)
XVI	8	Liberation (*mukti*)[27]	One who is bound (*baddha*) or one who is not bound (*abaddha*)
XVII	28	Living being (*jantu*)	Agent (*kartṛ*)

XVII	29	Action (*karman*)	That which has arisen from conditions (*pratyayasamutpanna*) or that which has not arisen from conditions (*apratyayasamutthita*)
XVIII	1	Self (*ātman*)	[Five] aggregates (*skandha*)
XVIII	7	Dharma-nature (*dharmatā*)	That which is non-arisen (*anutpanna*) or that which is non-extinguished (*aniruddha*)
XVIII	8	Everything (*sarva*)	That which is true ("*tathyam*"), that which is not true ("*na tathyam*"), that which is both true and untrue ("*tathyaṃ cātathyaṃ ca*"), or that which is neither true nor untrue ("*naivātathyaṃ naiva tathyam*")
XIX	1, 3	Present (*pratyutpanna*) and future (*anāgata*)[28]	Past (*atīta*)
XIX	5	Time (*kāla*)	That which has stood (or abided) (*sthita*) or that which has not stood (*asthita*)
XX	11	Cause (*hetu*)	Effect (*phala*)
XX	12	Past effect (*atītaphala*)[29]	Past cause (*atītahetu*), future cause (*ajātahetu*), or present cause[30] (*jātahetu*)[31]
XX	13	Future effect	Future cause, past cause, or present cause
XX	14	Present effect	Present cause, future cause, or past cause
XX	17	Non-empty effect ("*aśūnyaṃ phalam*")	Arising (*utpāda*)[32] or extinction (*nirodha*)[33]
XX	18	Empty effect ("*śūnyaṃ phalam*")	Arising or extinction
XX	19	Effect (*phala*)	Cause (*hetu*)
XX	21	Effect with really existent	Cause

		own-being ("*svabhāva-sadbhūtaṃ phalam*") or effect with not really existent own-being ("*svabhāvāsadbhūtaṃ phalam*")	
XX	24	Effect	That which is produced by conjunction (*sāmagrīkṛta*) or that which is produced by non-conjunction (*asāmagrīkṛta*)
XXI	1	Occurrence (*sambhava*)	Dissolution (*vibhava*)
XXI	7ab	Occurrence	That which is destructible (*kṣaya*) or that which is not destructible (*akṣaya*)
XXI	7cd	Dissolution	That which is destructible or that which is not destruct ible
XXI	8	Occurrence and dissolution ("*sambhavo vibhavaś ca*")	Existent *(bhāva)*
XXI	9	Occurrence and Dissolution	That which is empty (*śūnya*) or that which is not empty (*aśūnya*)
XXI	10	Occurrence	Dissolution
XXI	12ab	Existent (*bhāva*)	Being born from an existent (*bhāva*) or being born from a non-existent (*abhāva*)[34]
XXI	12cd	Non-existent (*abhāva*)	Being born from an existent or being born from a non-ex istent[35]
XXI	13	Existent (*bhāva*)	Being born from self, being born from another, or being born from self and another
XXII	1	Tathāgata	[Five] aggregates (*skandha*)
XXIII	3	Self (*ātman*)	Existence (*astitva*) or non-existence (*nāstitva*)

XXIII	5	Defilement (*kleśa*)	One who is defiled (*kliṣṭa*)
XXIII	7, 9	Form, sound, taste, touch,smell and things ("*rūpaśabdarasasparśā gandhā dharmāś ca*")	Purity (*śubha*) or impurity (*aśubha*)
XXIII	10, 11	Purity	Impurity
XXIII	17, 18	Error (*viparyaya*)	One who has erred (*viparīta*), one who has not erred (*aviparīta*), or one who is erring (*viparyasyamāna*)
XXIII	20	Existent (*bhāva*)[36]	Being born from self, being born from another, or being born from self and another
XXIII	24ab, 25ab	Defilement	Those that already exist by their own-being ("*bhūtāḥ svabhāvena*") or those that do not already exist by their own-being ("*abhūtāḥ svabhāvena*")
XXV	10, 13, 16	Nirvāṇa	Existent (*bhāva*), non-existent (*abhāva*), existent and non-existent ("*abhāvo bhāvaś ca*"), or neither existent nor non-existent ("*naivābhāvo naiva bhāvaḥ*")
XXV	17	The Blessed One after death ("*param nirodhād bhagavān*")	Existing,[37] not existing, existing and not existing, or neither existing nor not existing
XXV	18	The living Blessed One	Existing,[38] not existing, existing and not existing, or neither existing nor not existing
XXV	19	Transmigration	Nirvāṇa
XXV	22	Everything (*sarvadharma*)	That which has a limit (*antavat*), that which is without a limit (*ananta*), that which both has a limit and is without a limit ("*anantam antavac ca*"), or that which neither has a limit nor is without a limit

			("*nānantaṃ nāntavac ca*")
XXV	23a	Everything [39]	That very thing ("*tad eva*") or something else (*anyat*)
XXV	23bcd	Everything[40]	Eternalness (*śāśvata*), non-eternalness (*aśāśvata*), eternalness and non-eternalness ("*aśāśvataṃ śāśvataṃ ca*"), or neither eternalness nor non-eternalness ("*nobhayam*")
XXVII	3, 9	Past age (*atītādhvan*)	The fact that I existed or the fact that I did not exist[41]
XXVII	8	Self	Attachment
XXVII	13	Past age	The fact that I existed, the fact that I did not exist, the fact that I both existed and did not exist, or the fact that I neither existed nor did not exist
XXVII	14	Future age	The fact that I shall exist or the fact that I shall not exist[42]

Notes to Table 1

1) In the Chinese translation by Kumārajīva "arising" is expressed by the verb "to be born" (*shêng*), while in the Sanskrit text it is expressed in the form noun+verb, i. e., "*utpannā vidyante*" ("are [things] that have arisen").

2) In the Chinese translation *kriyā* is understood in the sense of function as effect and translated accordingly (*kuo*: "fruit, effect"; Taishō Tripiṭaka, Vol. 30, p. 2c, l. 6).

3) "Traversing" (*gamana*) is expressed by the verb "is being traversed" (*gamyate*). The expression "that which is being traversed is being traversed" (*gamyamānaṃ gamyate*) in v. 1 later (v. 3a) reappears as "the traversing of that which is being traversed" (*gamyamānasya gamanam*). This rewording shows more clearly that the two factors in question are "traversing" (*gamana*) and "that which is being traversed" (*gamyamāna*).

4) As in II. 1, here too "traversing" (*gamana*) is expressed by a verb,

this time "traverses" (*gacchati*). The content of the proposition "a traverser traverses" (*gantā gacchati*) appearing in v. 8 is later (v. 10cd) rephrased "the traversing of (=by) a traverser" (*gantur gamanam*). This rewording shows more clearly that the two factors in question are "traversing" (*gamana*) and "traverser" (*gantṛ*).

5) The "beginning of traversing" (*PP*, p. 101, l. 1: *gamanārambha*) is here expressed by an infinitive followed by a verb, i.e., "*gantum ārabhyate*" ("begins traversing").

6) In the Chinese translation v. 25ab is translated, "Be traversing determinate [i.e., really existent] or non-determinate [i.e., not really existent], the three [types of traversing] are not applicable to a traverser" (*op. cit*., p. 5b, l. 27), and this is then interpreted to mean that regardless of whether traversing be determinate or non-determinate, a traverser traverses neither that which has not been traversed nor that which has been traversed nor that which is being traversed (*ibid*., p. 5c, l. 7). Poussin's Sanskrit text, on the other hand, gives v. 25ab as "*gamanaṃ sadasadbhūtaḥ triprakāraṃ na gacchati*," with the modifier "*sadasadbhūtaḥ*" (Sing. Nom. m.) qualifying "*gantā*" which appears in v. 24. But since *sadasadbhūta-* is interpreted in the Chinese translation as qualifying "traversing," there is a possibility that the Sanskrit text used by Piṅgala had "*sadasadbhūtam*," qualifying not "*gantā*" but "*gamanam*" (taken to mean "that which is traversed" in the Chinese translation).

7) According to Piṅgala's commentary, the three factors dealt with by Nāgārjuna in vv. 24-25ab are traverser, traversing and that which is traversed. The "traverser" is further divided into three types, i. e., "really existent," "not really existent" and "really and not really existent," while "that which is traversed" is divided into "that which has not been traversed" and "that which is being traversed." Therefore, it may be considered that the relation between traversing and a traverser and the relation between traversing and that which is traversed are linked in these two verses. In Candrakīrti's commentary (*PP*, p. 107, l. 11), on the other hand, "three" (*tri-*) is interpreted as referring to "really existent traversing" (*sadbhūtaṃ gamanam*), "not really existent traversing" (*asadbhūtaṃ gamanam*) and "really and not really existent traversing" (*sadasadbhūtaṃ gamanam*). It is, therefore, to be surmised that according to Candrakīrti vv. 24-25ab deal with the

relation between traversing and a traverser, and that the act of traversing is expressed by a cognate accusative, i. e., "*gamanaṃ gacchati*" ("traverses traversing"). The above may be illustrated by the following two diagrams (Diagram 1: Piṅgala's interpretation; Diagram 2: Candrakīrti's interpretation).

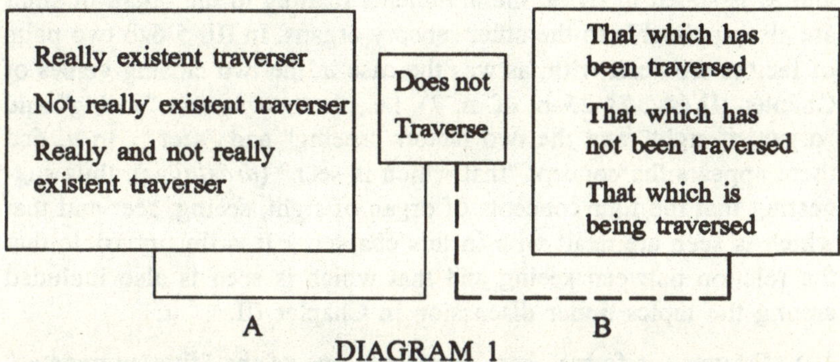

DIAGRAM 1

In Diagram 1 the relation between a traverser and traversing is indicated by a solid line (A) and the relation between that which is traversed and traversing by a broken line (B).

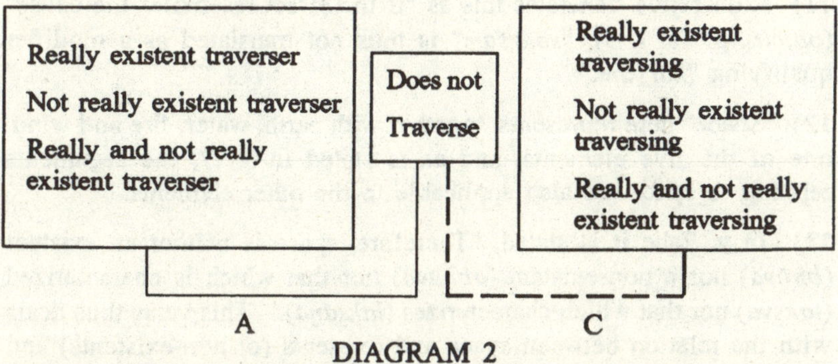

DIAGRAM 2

In Diagram 2 the relation between a traverser and traversing is indicated by a solid line (A) as in Diagram 1, while the relation between really existent traversing, etc., and traversing is indicated by a broken line (C). In the case of this latter relationship, really existent traversing, etc., may be regarded as the object of the act of traversing. A similar relationship also appears in VIII. 9-12, where "really existent action" (*sadbhūtakarman*), etc., represent the object of the verb "performs" (*karoti*).

8) "Seeing" (*darśana*) or the "function of seeing" (*PP*, p. 115, l. 11: *darśanakriyā*, or *ibid*. l. 15: *dṛṣṭikriyā*) is here expressed by the verb "sees" (*paśyati*).

9) "Organ of sight" is here given as one of the six sensory organs, and as is stated in III. 9, the arguments relating to the organ of sight are also applicable to the other sensory organs. In III. 5-6ab two pairs of factors are dealt with, as was the case in the two closing verses of Chapter II (vv. 24-25ab; cf. n. 7), i.e., the two factors "seeing" and "organ of sight" and the two factors "seeing" and "seer." In v. 6cd there appears the concept "that which is seen" (*draṣṭavya*), thus suggesting that the four concepts of organ of sight, seeing, seer and that which is seen are dealt with in this chapter. It is thus possible that the relation between seeing and that which is seen is also included among the topics under discussion in Chapter III.

10) "Matter (or form)" here represents one of the "five aggregates" (*pañcaskandha*) or constituent elements of the body and mind, and as is stated in IV. 7, the arguments relating to matter are also applicable to the other aggregates.

11) Kumārajīva translates this as "if the effect resembles the cause" (*op.cit.*, p. 7a, l. 5); "*sadṛśam*" is thus not translated as a modifier qualifying "*kāryam*."

12) "Space" here represents, together with earth, water, fire and wind, one of the five elements, and as is stated in V. 7, the arguments relating to space are also applicable to the other elements.

13) In v. 7abc it is stated, "Therefore, space is neither an existent (*bhāva*) nor a non-existent (*abhāva*) nor that which is characterized (*lakṣya*) nor that which characterizes (*lakṣaṇa*)." This verse thus deals with the relation between space and existents (or non-existents) and the relation between space and that which is characterized (or that which characterizes). If there should be such a thing as space, it must be either an existent (*bhāva*) or a non-existent (*abhāva*), and it is Nāgārjuna's intention to demonstrate that it is neither. All things are here divided into existents and non-existents in preparation for saying that space is neither, i.e., that it is empty (*śūnya*). Hence the pairs of two factors dealt with here are space and existents, space and non-existents, etc.

14) *Rāga* ("passion") is a noun deriving from the verb √*rañj* meaning "to dye," and it is a general term for "that which dyes [people]," i.e., mental defilements. *Rakta* ("impassioned") means literally "one who has been dyed [with mental defilements]."

15) In this verse "that which exists and does not exist" is expressed as "*sataś cāsataś ca,*" i.e., by the genitive of *sat* ("that which exists") and the genitive of *asat* ("that which does not exist") linked by the conjunction *ca* ("and"), but in the table we have given it in the form of a compound.

16) "Extinction" is expressed by the verb "is extinguished" (*nirudhyate*).

17) See n. 16.

18) In the Chinese translation "*sā avasthā*" is translated as "this *dharma* at this time" (*op. cit.*, p. 11c, l. 11) and "*anyā avasthā*" as "this dharma at another time" (*ibid.* l. 12).

19) "Existing existent" is expressed in v. 30ab not by a compound but by two separate words, i.e., "*sataś* ... *bhāvasya*," and similarly "non-existing existent" is also expressed by two words in v. 31ab.

20) "Performing" is expressed in the form of accusative noun+verb, i.e., "*karma karoti*" ("performs an action").

21) VIII. 1 gives four factors and deals with the four relationships indicated in Diagram 3, i.e., the two relationships between performing really existent action and a really (or not really) existent agent and the two relationships between performing not really existent action and a really (or not really) existent agent.

Really existent agent	Performing really existent action
Not really existent agent	Performing not really existent action

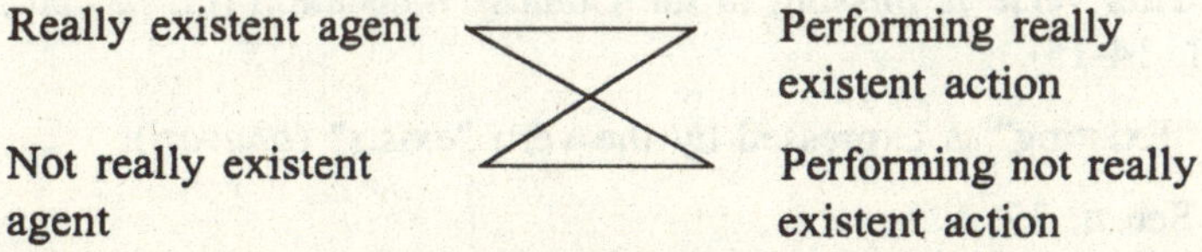

DIAGRAM 3

22) See n. 20.

23) The content of v. 7ab should be considered in conjunction with that of v. 1, for in addition to the four relationships indicated in

Diagram 3, these two verses also deal with the relation between performing both really and not really existent action and a both really and not really existent agent.

24) "Performing" is expressed by a passive verb, i.e., "*kriyate*" ("is performed").

25) See n. 24.

26) "Transmigration" is expressed by the verb "transmigrate" (*saṃsaranti*).

27) "Liberation" is expressed by the verb "is liberated" (*mucyate*).

28) As has already been noted (p. 37), here the present and the future are treated as a single factor.

29) "Past effect" is expressed not by a compound but by two separate words.

30) There are no words corresponding to "present cause" in the Chinese translation.

31) As in the case of "past cause" noted in n. 29, "past cause," etc., are not expressed by compounds in the original text.

32) "Arising" is expressed by the verb "will arise" (*utpatsyate*).

33) "Extinction" is expressed by the verb "will be extinguished" (*nirotsyate*).

34) "Being born" is expressed by the verb "is born" (*jāyate*).

35) See n. 34.

36) This verse is missing in the Chinese translation (cf. *op. cit.*, p. 32, ll. 14-15).

37) "Existing" is expressed by the verb "exists" (*bhavati*).

38) See n. 37.

39) This factor "everything" is given in v. 22.

40) See n. 39.

41) "The fact that I existed" is expressed by the verb "I existed" (*abhūm*), while "the fact that I did not exist" is expressed by the same

verb together with the negative particle "*na*."

42) "The fact that I shall exist" is expressed by the verb "I shall exist" (*bhaviṣyāmi*), while "the fact that I shall not exist" is expressed by the same verb together with the negative particle "*na*."

The pairs of factors listed in the above table and standing in a relationship of dependent co-arising to one another provide the "locus" for the arguments set forth in the *Middle Stanzas*. For example, in Chapter I, dealing with the theme of "things do not arise," the two factors of thing or existent (*bhāva*) and arising (*utpāda*) are the main topics of discussion, while in Chapter II, which demonstrates that "a traverser does not traverse," it is the two factors of "traversing" (*gamana*) and "that which is to be traversed" (*gantavya*), or "traversing" and "traverser" (*gantṛ*), that are the focus of attention. The main subject under consideration in Chapter III is two pairs of two factors, namely, the "function of seeing" (*darśanakriyā*) and "organ of sight" (*darśana*) and the "function of seeing" and "seer" (*draṣṭṛ*), and in Chapter IV the two factors of "matter (or form)" (*rūpa*) and its "cause" (*kāraṇa*), as well as their relationship, are considered.

The relationship between the two factors comprising these pairs, or the nature of dependent co-arising as it obtains between them, is diverse, and it may be one of cause and effect, agent and action, attribute and substance, characteristic and that which is characterized, or *saṃsāra* and *nirvāṇa*, but in the *Middle Stanzas* Nāgārjuna does not offer any single systematic scheme integrating all these pairs of factors. This is doubtless not unrelated to Nāgārjuna's philosophical attitude, in that he renounced propounding any theoretical system of his own and set out to criticize the ideas of others. But if we reconsider the "locus" provided by the above pairs of factors, we come to realize that Nāgārjuna is in fact here presenting a locus that corresponds to nothing less than the totality of the phenomenal world. This will become even clearer when we examine the contents of the individual verses or, more specifically, the propositions to which they give expression. In a word, for Nāgārjuna the phenomenal world (*bhāva*) represented the totality of that which is expressible by means of propositions. For example, the various factors alluded to in propositions such as "all things arise," "an agent acts" and "*saṃsāra* is no different from *nirvāṇa*"—namely, things and arising, agent and action, and *saṃsāra* and *nirvāṇa*–, as well as the relationships obtaining between them, constitute parts of the phenomenal world. When two–and sometimes three or more–terms are incorporated within a single proposition by means of a syntactical connection, these two or more factors become in the *Middle Stanzas* a subject of examination as entities standing in a relationship of dependent co-arising to one another.

CHAPTER FIVE

A SURVEY OF NĀGĀRJUNA'S ARGUMENTS: AN EXAMINATION OF CHAPTER II OF THE *MIDDLE STANZAS*

Chapter II of the *Middle Stanzas*, entitled "An Examination of the Traversed and the Non-traversed" (*Gatāgata-parīkṣā*), embodies within its arguments several pairs of factors and is infused from beginning to end with the spirit of negation, and it is an especially important chapter in that Nāgārjuna himself refers to it in subsequent discussions (e.g., III.3 and VII.14). Let us first review the content of the arguments developed in this chapter and the structure of the negations contained therein.

We shall first explain a number of basic concepts that appear in the arguments of this chapter by means of a commonplace example. Let us suppose that John is on his way home from school. According to the way in which Nāgārjuna analyzes such a situation, it is possible to point out three factors involved in this phenomenon, namely:

(i) the distance to be traversed (*gantavya*),

(ii) the act of traversing (*gamana*), and

(iii) the agent of the act of traversing, i.e., John (*gantṛ*).

Let us call the school point *A*, the point where John is now standing point *B*, and his house point *C*.

John has already completed walking the distance from *A* to *B*. In other words, the distance $\overline{AB}$ has been traversed by him. Nāgārjuna refers to the distance $\overline{AB}$ as "that which has been traversed" (*gata*). The distance that has been traversed and the act of traversing may be understood as standing in the relationship of a locus and the movement that takes place on this locus.

John has not yet walked the distance $\overline{BC}$ from B to C. Nāgārjuna calls this distance $\overline{BC}$ "that which has not been traversed" (*agata*). B is "that which is being traversed" (*gamyamāna*). In addition, Nāgārjuna refers to the sum of the three distances or points consisting of that which has been traversed, that which has not been traversed and that which is being traversed as "that which is to be traversed" (*gantavya*).

Nāgārjuna devotes the whole of Chapter II in the *Middle Stanzas* to the elucidation of the relationships obtaining between these three elements involved in the phenomenon of walking or "traversing." Verses 1-5 deal primarily with the relationship between the act of traversing and the distance that is to be traversed, while verses 6-11 consider the relationship between the traverser and the act of traversing.

Chapter II begins with the following verse:

> That which has been traversed is not being traversed, nor is that which has not been traversed being traversed;
>
> That which is being traversed, [such as is] other than that which has been traversed and that which has not been traversed, is not being traversed (or is not known).
>
> (*gataṃ na gamyate tāvad agataṃ naiva gamyate /*
> *gatāgatavinirmuktaṃ gamyamānaṃ na gamyate //* II.1)

If we substitute X for "that which has been traversed" and X' for "that which has not been traversed," the content of this first verse may be expressed as a conjunction of the following three propositions:

(a) X is not being traversed.

(b) X' is not being traversed.

(c) A point other than X and X', such as is now being traversed, is not being traversed.

Although Nāgārjuna gives no particular reasons for (a), (b) or (c), following the lead of later commentators we may interpret them as follows:

(a) X is not being traversed because the action to be performed there has already come to an end; i.e., it has already been traversed.

(b) X' is not being traversed because the action to be performed there has not yet begun; i.e., it has not yet been traversed.

(c) A point other than X and X', such as is now being traversed, is not being traversed because the sum of that which has been traversed and that which has not been traversed represents the sum total of that which is to be traversed, and the existence of any third distance other than these two distances is inadmissible.

Here the distance to be traversed is subdivided from the perspective of the threefold division of time into the past, future and present, with time being conceived of as resembling a single straight line that has been divided into two by a point. One section of this divided line corresponds to the distance already traversed (X), the other section to the distance not yet traversed (X'), and the point to the spot now being traversed. But this actually represents a division of space, or spatially conceived time, into two complementary parts (X and X'). In other words, the temporal perspective alluded to above is based on a division between A and non-A. In this particular case, the distance already traversed is A and that not yet traversed is non-A ($\tilde{A}$). Therefore, what we have until now designated as X and X' may be designated as X and $\tilde{X}$. Since there exists nothing other than X and $\tilde{X}$ in that which is to be traversed, it turns out that there cannot exist any point other than X and $\tilde{X}$ that is now being traversed.

Let us note that the entire universe of discourse in the present case is not the entire universe, but that which is to be traversed (*gantavya*). Hence the symbol "$\tilde{X}$" would not be suitable to represent that which has not been traversed (*agata*), for the symbol "$\tilde{X}$" would mean the complementary sphere or set of *gata* (that which has already been traversed) with reference to the entire universe, i.e., the entire universe from which *gata* is excluded. The term "*agata*," however, indicates the complementary set of *gata* with reference to *gantavya*. When we put "D" for the entire universe of discourse, *agata* may be more accurately symbolized as "$\tilde{X}/D$," which means the complementary set of X with reference to D (cf. Diagram 4). In the following arguments, however, we will use symbols such as "$\tilde{X}$" rather than symbols such as "$\widetilde{X}/D$" for the sake of brevity unless there is fear of confusion.

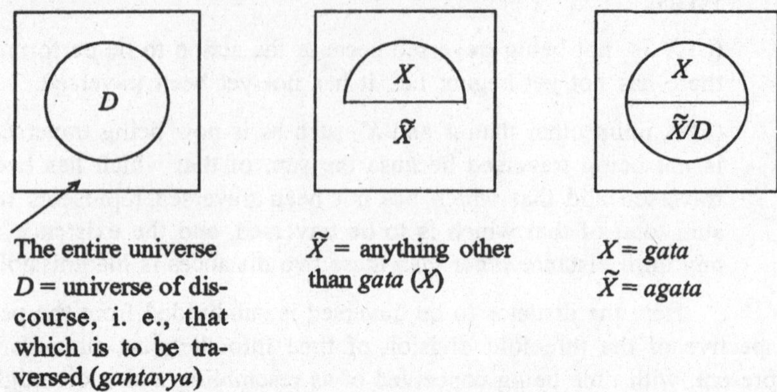

The entire universe
D = universe of discourse, i. e., that which is to be traversed (*gantavya*)

$\widetilde{X}$ = anything other than *gata* (X)

X = *gata*
$\widetilde{X}$ = *agata*

DIAGRAM 4

A further examination of the method of argument employed by Nāgārjuna in verse 1 will enable us to discern a set pattern in his arguments. In verse 1 he considers "the act of traversing" and "the distance to be traversed," namely, a pair of factors standing in the relationship of an action and the locus underlying that action. The entities taken up for consideration by Nāgārjuna in the propositions presented in the *Middle Stanzas* are, as has already been noted, always two things standing in an interdependent relationship to one another. Be they, for example, action and agent (Chapter VIII) or cause and effect (Chapter IV), they are always two entities already intrinsically interrelated in some way, and things such as a dog and a flower or laughter and a stone, which are not necessarily related to one another, are never chosen as the two factors of a proposition.

In expressing the relationship between the two factors in the form of a proposition, Nāgārjuna posits the largest possible instance of either one of them (in this case, the distance to be traversed) and divides it. This division is a distribution into A and the complementary set of $\widetilde{A}$ with reference to the universe of discourse. He then concludes the proposition, which contains a reference to the factor that has been subjected to the operation of distribution, with a negation.

Distributing one of two intrinsically interrelated entities so as to cover all possible instances, expressing the relationship between the two in the form of a proposition, and concluding all such propositions with a negation—this procedure employed by Nāgārjuna in II.1 represents his most common method of argument.

But what, then, in the final analysis is this first verse trying to say? It is saying that no point that is to be traversed is in actual fact traversed. Our everyday way of thinking considers the proposition "that which is to be traversed is traversed" to be quite natural, but Nāgārjuna first demonstrates that this pattern of thinking is in error and thus brings to cessation the linguistic proliferation of "that which is to be traversed is traversed."

In reply to this assertion of Nāgārjuna's, his opponent argues that although there may not be any traversing on the distance already traversed or the distance not yet traversed, the act of traversing must exist on the point where there is now movement. Nāgārjuna had already reached the conclusion in verse 1 that there is no traversing on any point to be traversed, but here he makes a concession to consider the argument of his opponent which is focussing on the point now being traversed. Nāgārjuna replies to this counterargument by using a different method from that employed in verse 1 (vv. 3-5).

Nāgārjuna maintains that the traversing of that which is being traversed requires the premise that the point being traversed and the act of traversing be separate entities. He is asserting, in other words, that the proposition "there is traversing on that which is being traversed" is valid only when there exists as an intrinsic reality a point being traversed that serves as the locus upon which there takes place the separate act of traversing. He is not, of course, subscribing to the view that the point being traversed and the act of traversing are two separate entities; instead, he is giving it as an example of a patent fallacy. His basic view is that the point being traversed can exist only in conjunction with the act of traversing and that there exists no point being traversed that is unconnected to the act of traversing.

Here Nāgārjuna is, in other words, employing a form of *reductio ad absurdum. Reductio ad absurdum* is a method of argument whereby the truth of one's probandum proposition p is demonstrated when the negation of p and assertion of $\tilde{p}$ lead to an obviously false conclusion. In the present context, "there is traversing on that which is being traversed" corresponds to proposition $\tilde{p}$, and the reason that it is "obviously false" is sought in the fallacy that would posit the existence of a point being traversed that is not being traversed or that is separate from the act of traversing (v. 4). Through the use of *reductio ad absurdum* in this manner, it is maintained that the proposition "there is traversing on that which is being traversed" represents a fallacy.

The relationship between the act of traversing and a traverser is examined in the same way as was the relationship between the distance to be traversed and the act of traversing in verse 1. Verse 8 reads as follows:

> A traverser does not traverse, nor does a non-traverser traverse.
> What third person other than a traverser and a non-traverser traverses?
> (*gantā na gacchati tāvad agantā naiva gacchati/*
> *anyo gantur agantuś ca kas tṛtīyo hi gacchati* // II.8)

If the statement "a traverser traverses" is to be true, there are only two possibilities, namely, "a traverser traverses" or "a non-traverser traverses." This is another example of complementary distribution, similar to the division of the distance to be traversed into the distance already traversed and that not yet traversed.

For the first proposition "a traverser traverses" to be true, the traverser must exist apart from the act of traversing, and in the final analysis this means that there exists a traverser unconnected to the act of traversing. This is the same argument as that employed in verses 3-5. The second proposition "a non-traverser does not traverse" is self-explanatory and requires no further comment. And it is inconceivable that there should exist a third person other than a traverser and non-traverser.

What, then, does the statement "a traverser does not traverse, nor does a non-traverser traverse" actually mean? It means that no one at all performs the act of traversing. In this manner the linguistic proliferation of "a traverser traverses" is brought to cessation. It is possible to demonstrate that "no one comes" or even "no one acts" by exactly the same method. One would be able to negate all forms of human activity by this type of proposition.

In the course of our above examination it will have been seen that in Chapter II of the *Middle Stanzas* there first appears a pattern of negation consisting of the complementary distribution of space (and also of time) and the negation of all action on the locus provided by this space (v. 1). Then, in regard to two pairs of two factors, namely, the act of traversing and distance to be traversed and the traverser and act of traversing, there is developed a second pattern of negation which develops the logic of *reductio ad absurdum*, according to which positing the existence of an action on that locus leads to the fallacy of an action and locus (vv. 3-5) or an action and agent (vv.8-10) existing as separate and intrinsically real entities.

Chapter II of the *Middle Stanzas* contains, however, one further important pattern of negation. This is the line of logic developed in verses 18-21, which also correspond to the section demonstrating that two things standing in an interdependent relationship do *not* exist as separate entities, and so they also serve as the basis for the second pattern of negation.

In this section, dealing with the relationship between the act of traversing and the traverser, Nāgārjuna again begins with a complementary distribution of the relationship existing between the two factors in question.

> It is not proper to say that traversing and the traverser are identical.
>
> Nor is it proper to say that the traverser is different from traversing.
>
> (*yad eva gamanaṃ gantā sa eveti na yujyate/*
> *anyo eva punar gantā gater iti na yujyate//* II.18)

After having pointed out that the act of traversing and the traverser are not identical since it is not possible to say that "the act of traversing *is* the traverser" (v. 19), thereby reconfirming the negation in the first half of the above verse, Nāgārjuna goes on to describe the error involved in regarding them both as different.

> If it is falsely considered that the traverser is different from traversing,
>
> There would be traversing without a traverser and a traverser without traversing.

(*anya eva punar gantā gater yadi vikalpyate/*
gamanaṃ syād ṛte gantur gantā syād gamanād ṛte// II.20)

The conclusion to this section is, therefore, "If two things exist neither as one nor separately, how is it possible for them to exist?" (v. 21), thus negating both the traverser and the act of traversing. This pattern of negation appearing in verse 20 serves, in conjunction with the second pattern of negation, as an important weapon in the logic behind the negation of existence in the *Middle Stanzas*.

In the above we have considered three patterns to be seen in the arguments of Chapter II of the *Middle Stanzas*. The first pattern entailed subjecting entities existing in time to a complementary distribution in the same manner as a straight line is divided into two. In the case of the second pattern, insofar that they are expressed as separate terms in a proposition, the referents of these terms must exist separately, but Nāgārjuna maintains that this is incorrect. For an understanding of the third pattern it becomes necessary, as will be seen below, to distinguish carefully between the negation of a term and the negation of a proposition. These three patterns are to be found not only in Chapter II but also in other chapters of the *Middle Stanzas*, and what is even more important is that the arguments concerning the negation of the existence of things in the *Middle Stanzas* always follow one of these three patterns.

CHAPTER SIX

COMPLEMENTARY RELATIONSHIP IN THE *MIDDLE STANZAS*: THE NEGATION OF THE PROFANE (1)

The method whereby the total distance to be traversed, constituting the entire universe of discourse, was distributed into the two spheres of "that which has been traversed" and "that which has not been traversed" in the first verse of Chapter II in the *Middle Stanzas* represents the point of departure for all of Nāgārjuna's arguments.

After having given expression in the form of a single proposition to two factors standing in an interdependent relationship. Nāgārjuna distributes either or both of the two factors, or the relationship itself, into two complementary parts such that the sum of both parts is equivalent to the whole. Either or both of the two factors, or the relationship between them, is established as the fixed locus of the discussion, and this locus is in turn distributed in such a manner that there remains no sphere that is left untouched by Nāgārjuna's arguments. In the propositions describing dependent co-arising in the *Middle Stanzas* there appear a variety of factors that have been subjected to complementary distribution, and although the number varies somewhat depending upon the way in which they are counted, we have been able to list 84 examples in the 450-odd verses of the *Middle Stanzas* (see Table 3, pp. 76-87 below).

The methods of distributing either or both of the two factors are of two types; they are, namely, distributed either into two cases or into three or four cases. (We shall refer to the entities into which a factor is distributed as "cases.") Among our 84 examples, the former type accounts for 58 examples and the latter type for 26 examples. Those representing a relationship of complementary distribution in the strict sense of the term are restricted to the instances of distribution into two cases, while the distribution into three or four cases does not constitute a complementary distribution in any logical sense. The distribution into four cases has traditionally been referred to as the tetralemma (*catuṣkoṭi*), and the distribution into three cases may be regarded as an incomplete tetralemma. But in the arguments developed in the *Middle Stanzas* the distribution is, practically speaking, completed with the distribution into the first and second cases, and any arguments based on the third and fourth cases are not essential to Nāgārjuna's line of reasoning.

We shall first classify the instances of dyadic distribution into a variety of types, and then move on to consider the distribution into three and four cases. The complementary distribution into two cases may be basically conceived of as a distribution of the universe of discourse into set M and set non-M ($\tilde{M}$), but the methods of distribution can be classified into the following five types (A-E).

Type A : The distribution into two cases is indicated either by the modifier of either of the two terms representing the factors or by a prefix affixed to either of the terms. For example, in IV.6 the factor "effect" (*kārya*) is distributed into the two cases of "effect similar to the cause" ("*sadṛśaṃ kāryam*") and "effect dissimilar to the cause" ("*asadṛśaṃ kāryam*").

Type B : The form of the first case is identical with the factor itself, while the second case is indicated by the addition of a negative prefix (*a-*, *an-*) or the negative particle (*na*) to the first case. For example, the two cases in V.7ac are "existent" (*bhāva*) and "non-existent" (*abhāva*). The first case is identical with the factor "existent," while the second case is indicated by adding a negative particle (*a-*) to the first case.

Type C1 : Type C represents instances of the distribution of the relationship between the two factors and, among these, those in which the distribution into two cases is indicated by a gerund are here referred to as Type C1. For example, in X.12 two types of relationship between the two factors in question (fuel and fire) are considered; namely, the case of fuel (or fire) being contingent upon fire (or fuel)—this represents the first case—and that of fuel (or fire) being not contingent upon fire (or fuel)—this represents the second case. Here, the first case "contingent" is expressed by the gerund *apekṣya*, while the second case is indicated by the addition of a negative prefix to this gerund, i. e., *anapekṣya*.

Type C2 : The distribution into two cases is indicated by the locative absolute. For example, when the relationship between form or matter (*rūpa*) and its cause (*rūpakāraṇa*) is considered in IV.4, the two cases of "when form exists" ("*rūpe sati*") and "when form does not exist" ("*rūpe 'sati*") are posited.

Type C3: The distribution into two cases is indicated by indeclinables such as "together" (*saha*) and their negative forms. For example, when the relationship between "passion" (*rāga*) and "one who is impassioned" (*rakta*) is considered in VI.10, the two cases of "when passion exists in conjunction with (*saha*) one who is impassioned" and "when passion exists not in conjunction with (*asaha*) one who is impassioned" are posited.

Type D : The distribution into two cases is indicated by "oneness (or identity)" (*ekatva*) and "otherness (or difference)" (*anyatva*). For example, when the relationship between "cause" (*hetu*) and "effect" (*phala*) is considered in XX.19, the two cases of when the two factors are identical and when they are different are posited.

Type E: The complementary distribution into two cases is expressed without the use of any negative prefix or particle. For example, in XXV.17-18 the "Blessed One" (*bhagavān*) is subjected to a complementary distribution into "the Blessed One after death" ("*paraṃ nirodhād bhagavān*") and "the living Blessed One" ("*tiṣṭhamāno bhagavān*").

The passages where the above five types of complementary distribution appear in the *Middle Stanzas* are given in the following table.

TABLE 2

Type A		I. 6; IV. 6; V. 3; VII. 21; VII.27; VII. 30, 31; VII. 32; VIII. 8 (distribution of agent [*kartṛ*]); VIII. 8 (distribution of action [*karman*]); XVI. 6; XX. 17, 18; XX. 21.
Type B		I. 4ab; I. 4cd; I. 14; III. 5; V. 7a; XIV. 7; XVI. 1; XVI. 8; XVII. 29; XVIII. 6ab; XVIII. 6cd; XIX. 5; XX.24; XXI. 7;XXI. 9; XXI. 12 (distribution of existent [*bhāva*]); XXI. 12 (distribution of being born [*jāyate*]); XXIII. 3; XXIII. 9; XXIII. 24, 25; XXVII. 3, 9; XXVII.14.
Type C	1	III. 6; X. 12; XIX. 1, 3; XXIII. 10ab, 11ab.
	2	IV. 4; VI. 2.
	3	VI. 10; XXI. 1.
Type D		VI. 4; VII. 28; X. 1; XIII. 5; XVII. 28; XVIII.1; XX. 19; XXI. 10; XXII. 1; XXV. 23a; XXVII. 8.
Type E		I. 11; V. 7a; XX. 10; XXV. 17, 18.

CHAPTER SEVEN

SYNTACTICAL RELATIONSHIP IN THE *MIDDLE STANZAS*: THE NEGATION OF THE PROFANE (2)

Now that we have ascertained the patterns of negation and the methods of distributing the universe of discourse in the *Middle Stanzas*, both important stays of its system of logic, we shall next take up for consideration some further propositions describing dependent co-arising in addition to Examples 1 (VIII. 12ab) and 2 (XIX.1) given in Chapter 4 above and attempt to detect a method of argument common to them all.

Example 3

na bhāvo nābhāvo...ākāśam...// (V.7)

(Space is not an existent, nor is it a non-existent....)

The above Sanskrit sentence may be rewritten without any change of meaning as follows:

na ākāśaṃ bhāvo na ākāśam abhāvaḥ. —(a)

If we now substitute "*X*nom" for "*ākāśam*" (space), "*Y*nom" for "*bhāvaḥ*" (existent), and "$\tilde{Y}$nom" for "*abhāvaḥ*" (non-existent), the following formula may be obtained:

$\sim$ (*X*nom *Y*nom) $\cdot\sim$ (*X*nom $\tilde{Y}$nom) —(b)

"$\sim$" is the negation sign and "$\cdot$" the conjunction sign. "*X*nom" means that the term *X* is in the nominative, while "*Y*nom" similarly means that the term *Y* is in the nominative. "$\tilde{Y}$" signifies "non-*Y*," namely, the term *Y* modified by a negative (in this case "*a*-"). Hence "$\tilde{Y}$nom" is a symbol for the term "*abhāvaḥ*" (non-existent). In Example 3 the two interdependently related factors are "space" and "existent (or non-existent)." We may note the following three features in formula (b):

(1) "Existent" (*bhāva*), the referent of "Y," and "non-existent" (*abhāva*), the referent of "$\tilde{Y}$," are complementary to one another. The sum of existents and non-existents constitutes the entire universe of discourse in the present instance, i.e., the entire universe. The content of formula (b) may be also expressed by the following formula:

$(X\text{nom } Y\text{nom}) \cdot (X\text{nom } \tilde{Y}\text{nom})$ $(\text{set}Y \cup \text{set}\tilde{Y} = \text{set}E)$

Set$Y$ = set of existents.

Set$\tilde{Y}$ = set of non-existents.

Set$E$ = entire universe.

The content of the formula (set$Y$ set$\tilde{Y}$ = set$E$), which means that the union of set$Y$ and set$\tilde{Y}$ is the entire universe, is evident. Such an evident formula occurs when the universe of discourse corresponds to the entire universe. In the following analysis we shall omit such self-evident formulae when the universe of discourse corresponds to the entire universe.

(2) The relationship between the two factors, namely, between the referents of "X" and "Y" (or "$\tilde{Y}$"), is expressed by the syntactical connection existing between two nominatives.

(3) The two propositions "(Xnom Ynom)" and "(Xnom $\tilde{Y}$nom)" are both false.

The following verse also represents a proposition describing dependent co-arising.

Example 4

sataś ca tāvad utpattir asataś ca na yujyate /
na sataś cāsataś ceti ... // (VII.20)

(The arising of that which exists, of that which does not exist, and of that which both exists and does not exist is not possible.)

This example consists of three propositions and, as in the case of Example 3, it may be rewritten without any change of meaning as follows:

sataś ca utpattiḥ na yujyate,
asataś ca utpattiḥ na yujyate,
sadasataś ca utpattiḥ na yujyate. —(a)

(The arising of that which exists is not possible,
The arising of that which does not exist is not possible,
And the arising of that which exists and does not exist is not possible.)

It is to be readily seen that "arising" (*utpatti*) and "that which exists" (*sat*) stand in a *dharma-dharmin* relationship (*dharmadharmitva-sambandha*), for the attribute or movement (*dharma*) of arising may be considered to exist upon the locus (*dharmin*) of that which exists. The relationship between arising and that which does not exist (*asat*)—or between arising and that which exists and does not exist (*sadasat*)—may also be tentatively conceived of in a similar manner to that obtaining between arising and that which exists (even though it is impossible for any property to adhere to a locus that does not exist).

Let us now substitute "*X*gen" for "*satas*," "*Y*nom" for "*utpattiḥ*," "*V*" for "*yujyate*" (is possible or proper), "$\tilde{X}$gen" for "*asatas*," and "$X\tilde{X}$gen" for "*sadasatas*." The symbol "*V*" indicates that the word for which it has been substituted is a verb. (a) may now be expressed by means of the following formula:

$$\sim (X\text{gen}\ Y\text{nom}\ V) \cdot \sim (\tilde{X}\text{gen}\ Y\text{nom}\ V) \cdot \sim (X\tilde{X}\text{gen}\ Y\text{nom}\ V) \quad \text{—(b)}$$

As in the case of Example 3, we may point out three features of this formula.

(1) The sum of that which exists and that which does not exist constitutes the entire universe of discourse in the present instance. These two alternatives are, in other words, in a complementary relationship to one another. The concept "that which exists and does not exist" (*sadasat*) may require some explanation. Logically speaking, any such entity is impossible. That *x* should exist and simultaneously not exist is simply a contradiction. Commentators on the *Middle Stanzas* such as Buddhapālita and Candrakīrti were aware of the fact that the simultaneous existence and non-existence of an entity constitutes a contradiction.[1] But it is also possible to interpret "that which both exists and does not exist" (*sataś ca asataś ca*) as referring to the union of the set of that which exists (*sat*) and

1. Max Walleser (ed.), *Buddhapālita. Mūlamadhyamakavṛtti*, *Bibliotheca Buddhica* XVI (St. Petersburg, 1913), p.23, l.2; Louis de la Vallée Poussin (ed.), *Prasannapadā*, *Bibliotheca Buddhica* IV (St. Petersburg, 1913), p.83, l.11.

the set of that which does not exist (*asat*), namely, the entire universe. If we take "*sadasat*" to mean "that which simultaneously exists and does not exist," "$X\tilde{X}$" represents a contradiction. In that case, we may ignore this alternative and concern ourselves solely with the first two propositions. But if we take "*sadasat*" to mean the sum of that which exists and that which does does not exist (i. e., that which exists or that which does not exist), "$X\tilde{X}$" represents the union of set X and set $\tilde{X}$ ($X \cup \tilde{X}$), namely, the entire universe. In either case, however, the argument set forth in this verse ends for all practical purposes with the first two propositions ~(Xgen Ynom V) and ~($\tilde{X}$gen Ynom V), and the third proposition ~($X\tilde{X}$gen Ynom V) adds no new information whatsoever. This third proposition corresponds to the third alternative of the so-called tetralemma, which we shall reconsider in a later chapter.

(2) The relationship between the two factors referred to by "Y" and "X" (or "$\tilde{X}$" or "$\tilde{X}X$") is expressed by the syntactical connection existing between a genitive, nominative and verb.

(3) All three propositions are false.

Example 5

na cāpi viparītasya saṃbhavanti viparyayāḥ/
na cāpy aviparītasya saṃbhavanti viparyayāḥ//
na viparyasyamānasya saṃbhavanti viparyayāḥ/

(XXIII. 17-18ab)

(The errors of one who has erred do not come into existence,
The errors of one who has not erred do not come into existence,
And the errors of one who is erring do not come into existence.)

The two factors dealt with by Nāgārjuna in this verse are "error" (*viparyaya*) and "one who has erred" (*viparīta*) (or "one who has not erred" [*aviparīta*] or "one who is erring" [*viparyasyamāna*]). These two factors stand in a *dharma-dharmin* relationship to one another. If we substitute "Xgen" for "*viparītasya*," "V" for "*saṃbhavanti*" (come into existence), "Ynom" for "*viparyayāḥ*," "X'gen" for "*aviparītasya*," and "X''gen" for "*viparyasyamāna*." Example 5 may be expressed by means of the following formula:

~ (Xgen V Ynom) · ~ (X'gen V Ynom) · ~ (X''gen V Ynom) —(b)

The three features of this formula are as follows:

(1) Nāgārjuna distributes a person who commits an error from the perspective of the three divisions of time, namely, past, future and present. The universe of discourse in the present case is man, not the entire universe. Time is conceived of as a continuum that is divided into two parts by a given point. The past and future represent the two parts of this line, while the point corresponds to the present. Hence it is possible to liken one of the two parts divided by the point to someone who has already erred, the other part to someone who has not yet erred, and the point to someone who is at present erring. "*Viparīta*" is the past participle of the verb "*vipari√i*" (to err), "*aviparīta*" a compound consisting of the negative prefix "*a-*" and "*viparīta,*" and "*viparyasyamāna*" the present participle (middle voice) of "*vipari√i.*"

(2) The relationship between the two factors referred to by "*Y*" and "*X*" (or "*X*'" or "*X*''") is expressed by the syntactical connection existing between a genitive, nominative and verb.

(3) All three propositions are false.

In the above three examples either of the two factors was directly subjected to a complementary distribution. In the following two examples, however, one of the two factors is indirectly distributed. In other words, the complementary distribution is performed by the modifier of either the term *X* or the term *Y*.

Example 6

na kāraṇasya sadṛśaṃ kāryam ity upapadyate /
na kāraṇasya asadṛśaṃ kāryam ity upapadyate // (IV.6)

(It is not appropriate to say that a cause has a similar effect;
It is not appropriate to say that a cause has a dissimilar effect.)

The word "*iti*" ([to say] that...) here indicates that the negative particle *na* modifies not a particular term but the whole proposition. Therefore, the meaning of this verse should become clearer if rewritten as follows:

kāraṇasya sadṛśaṃ kāryam iti na upapadyate /
kāraṇasya asadṛśaṃ kāryam iti na upapadyate //

The translation of this rewritten verse is the same as that given above. In the rewritten version the negative particle *na* is placed after *iti*. In this example the two words "*sadṛśam*" (similar) and "*asadṛśam*" (dissimilar) modify the word "*kāryam*" (effect). Hence the universe of discourse here is all the effects in the world. As in the previous examples, the content of this verse may be expressed by means of the following formula:

$\sim(X\text{gen } M.Y\text{nom}) \cdot \sim(X\text{gen } \tilde{M}.Y\text{nom})\ (\text{set}M.Y \cup \text{set}\tilde{M}.Y = \text{set}Y)$

Xgen = *kāraṇasya* (a cause has; literally, "of a cause" [in Sanskrit possession is frequently expressed by the genitive case alone]).

$M.Y$nom = *sadṛśaṃ kāryam* (a similar effect; "M" [*sadṛśa*] modifies "Y" [*kārya*]).

$\tilde{M}.Y$nom = *asadṛśaṃ kāryam* (a dissimilar effect; "$\tilde{M}$" [*asadṛśa*] modifies "Y" [*kārya*]).

$\sim$ = *na upapadyate* (it is not appropriate).

Set$M.Y$ = set of similar effects.

Set$\tilde{M}.Y$ = set of dissimilar effects.

Set$Y$ = set of effects.

In this case too we may point out three features:

(1) The similar effect referred to by "$M.Y$" and the dissimilar effect referred to by "$\tilde{M}.Y$" are complementary to one another. If an effect should at all exist, it must be either similar or dissimilar to the cause. In this verse Nāgārjuna assumes that there does not exist any third possibility such as a similar and dissimilar effect (*sadṛśāsadṛśakārya*). The union of all similar effects and all dissimilar effects represents the sum of all effects in the world, corresponding to the entire universe of discourse in the present instance.

(2) The relationship between the two factors referred to by "X" and "$M.Y$" (or "$\tilde{M}.Y$") is expressed by the syntactical connection existing between a genitive and a nominative.

(3) Both propositions are false.

Example 7

na svato jāyate bhāvaḥ parato naiva jāyate /
na svataḥ parataś ceti...// (XXIII.20abc)

(An existent is born not from itself, nor is it born from another,
Nor from both itself and another.)

This verse may be rewritten without any change of meaning as follows :

bhāvaḥ svato na jāyate,
bhāvaḥ parato na jāyate,
bhāvaḥ svataḥ parataś ca na jāyate.

(An existent is not born from itself;
An existent is not born from another;
An existent is not born from both itself and another.)

Here the words "*svataḥ*" (from itself), "*parataḥ*" (from another) and "*svataḥ parataś ca*" (from both itself and another) modify the function of the verb "*jāyate*" (is born). This function corresponds to one of the two factors, namely, "being born (or arising)" (*jāti* or *utpatti*). In this case, the two factors are "being born" and "existent," and they stand in a *dharma-dharmin* relationship.

Let us now consider the relationship obtaining between "self" (*sva-*), "other" (*para-*) and "self-and-other" (*svapara-*). "Self" and "other" may here be considered to stand in a complementary relationship, while "self-and-other" represents the union of the sphere of "self" and the sphere of "other." Therefore, we may substitute "M" for "*sva-*," "$\tilde{M}$" for "*para-*" and "$M \cup \tilde{M}$" for "*svapara-*" (or "*svataḥ parataś ca*"). The content of this verse may then be expressed by means of the following formula:

$\sim$ (*X*nom $M.Y$v) $\cdot\sim$ (*X*nom $\tilde{M}.Y$v) $\cdot\sim$ (*X*nom $M \cup \tilde{M}.Y$v) (set$M.Y \cup$ set$\tilde{M}.Y =$ set$Y$)

$M.Y$v = *svato jāyate* (is born from itself; "v" indicates that "Y" is a verb).

$\tilde{M}.Y$v = *parato jāyate* (is born from another).

$M \cup \tilde{M}.Y$v = *svataḥ parataś ca jāyate* (is born from both itself and another).

Set$M.Y$ = set of that which is born from itself.

Set$\tilde{M}.Y$ = set of that which is born from another.

Set$Y$ = set of that which is born.

The three features of this formula are as follows:

(1) The sphere indicated by "$M.Y$" and that indicated by "$\tilde{M}.Y$" are complementary. The third proposition " ~ (Xnom $M \cup \tilde{M}.Y$v)" adds no new information. According to Nāgārjuna, in order to negate the proposition "(Xnom $M \cup \tilde{M}.Y$v)" it suffices to reiterate the reason that "(Xnom $M.Y$v)" and "(Xnom $\tilde{M}.Y$v)" are false.

(2) The relationship between the two factors referred to by "X" and "$M.Y$v" (or "$\tilde{M}.Y$v" or "$M \cup \tilde{M}.Y$v") is expressed by the syntactical connection existing between a nominative, indeclinable and verb.

(3) All three propositions are false.

Example 8

apekṣya indhanam agnir na na anapekṣya agnir indhanam/
apekṣya indhanam agniṃ na na anapekṣya agnim indhanam //

(X.12)

(Contingent upon fuel there is no fire, and not contingent upon fuel there is no fire;

Contingent upon fire there is no fuel, and not contingent upon fire there is no fuel.)

In this verse the relationship between the two factors "fuel" (x) and "fire" (y), which constitute the universe of discourse in the present case, is distributed into the following two complementary instances: (i) that when x (or y) is contingent upon y (or x) and (ii) that when x (or y) is not contingent upon y (or x). Nāgārjuna does not allow for any third possibility. As in the case of the previous examples, the content of this verse may be expressed by means of the following formula:

~ (Mger Xacc Ynom) · ~ ($\tilde{M}$ger Ynom Xacc) · ~ (Mger Xnom Yacc) · ~ ($\tilde{M}$ger Yacc Xnom)

This formula may be rewritten in the following manner so as to make the content of the argument clearer:

((Xacc Mger) Ynom) · ((Xacc $\tilde{M}$ger) Ynom)·

((Yacc Mger) Xnom) · ((Yacc $\tilde{M}$ger) Xnom)

*M*ger = *apekṣya* (contingent; "*M*ger" indicates that "*M*" is given in the form of a gerund ["*apekṣya*" is the gerund of *apa*√*īkṣ*]).

$\tilde{M}$ger = *anapekṣya* (not contingent).

*X*nom = *indhanam* (fuel).

*X*acc = *indhanam* (upon fuel).

*Y*nom = *agnir* (fire).

*Y*acc = *agnim* (upon fire).

The three features of this formula are as follows:

(1) The referents of "*M*" and "$\tilde{M}$" are complementary to one another in the universe of discourse in the present case.

(2) The relationship between the two factors is expressed by the syntactical connection existing between a gerund, accusative (or nominative) and nominative (or accusative).

(3) All four propositions are false.

In the six examples considered above (Examples 3-8) it is possible to point out three salient features.

Feature 1: Either of the two factors, or the relationship between them, is subjected to a complementary distribution. This distribution may be performed "directly," as in Examples 3 and 5, or "indirectly" (i.e., by means of a modifier), as in Examples 6 and 7. Example 4 does not, however, show a complementary relationship in the strict sense of the term, while in Example 8 the relationship between the two factors is distributed into two complementary cases.

Feature 2: In each verse the relationship between the two factors is expressed by a particular syntactical connection.

Feature 3: The propositions comprising the content of each verse are all false.

As has already been pointed out, the very occurrence of linguistic proliferation (*prapañca*) implies the existence of language that assumes the form of sentences or propositions. By demonstrating in almost every chapter of the *Middle Stanzas* that all sentences and propositions contain contradictions and are ultimately invalid, Nāgārjuna attempts to point to a plane on which linguistic proliferation has been extinguished. The reason that the propositions considered in Examples 3-8 above were all false was simply that Nāgārjuna wished to negate propositions in that they embody linguistic proliferation. In Example 6, for instance, the proposition "a cause has an effect (or an effect is born of a cause)" is negated. Regardless of how extensively and frequently such a proposition might be employed as a valid statement in everyday life, for Nāgārjuna it represented linguistic proliferation, which must be negated.

There are, on the other hand, a number of instances in the *Middle Stanzas* where Nāgārjuna not only gives expression to his own standpoint —i.e., does not simply quote the views of his opponents—but also describes the two factors and their relationship in the form of a proposition in the affirmative. One such example is VIII.12, which we have already considered as Example 1 (p. 36).

In Table 3 we have attempted to extract from the *Middle Stanzas* all propositions containing two factors that have been subjected to complementary distribution, and we have added a description of the three aforementioned features as they apply in each case. Complementary distribution was an indispensable part of Nāgārjuna's method, and as may be seen in Table 3, the cases into which a factor is distributed may number two, three or four. We are now left with the task of clarifying the relationship between these factors and then elucidating Nāgārjuna's system of negation from a logical standpoint.

(1) An asterisk (*) indicates that the factors subjected to complementary distribution in the verse in question have already been given in Table 1 (pp. 37-45) together with the Sanskrit of the resultant cases. Verses omitted in Table 1 and mentioned only in Table 3 are instances where the relationship between the factors or the relationship between the cases born of the subsequent complementary distribution is by no means clear and requires explanation.

(2) The letters A, B, C, etc., indicate the types of complementary distribution into two cases described in Chapter 6 (pp. 62-63). Hence in instances of distribution into three or four cases these letters have been omitted. In regard to the first two cases in instances of distribution into three or four cases, however, the above method of classification may be applied.

(3) A bar (–) indicates that the verse in question does not presuppose any relationship based upon complementary distribution.

(4) In the case of verses in which both factors have been subjected to complementary distribution, the cases resulting from the distribution of each of the factors are given in the columns corresponding to Feature 1 and linked by a brace ({)

(5) The abbreviations used in the column corresponding to Feature 2 are as follows:

abl.: ablative; acc.: accusative; gen.: genitive; gr.:gerund; ind.: indeclinable; inf.: infinitive; inst.: instrumental; loc.: locative; nom.: nominative; v.: verb.

(6) Feature 3 has been indicated only in regard to the first case of the tetralemma, etc., for it may be assumed that it will be the same in the remaining cases too. In verses containing more than one type of syntactical connection, these have been separated by a solidus (/).

TABLE 3

Ch.	Verse	Distribution Type	Feature 1	
I	1	* A (Ex. 13)	[Existents] that have arisen from self ("*svataḥ utpannāḥ*")	[Existents] that have arisen from another ("*parataḥ utpannāḥ*")
	4 ab	*	That which has conditions (*pratyayavat*)	That which has non-conditions (*apratyayavat*)
	4 cd	*	That which has functions (*kriyāvat*)	That which has non-functions (*akriyāvat*)
	6	*	Existing entity (*sadartha*)	Non-existing entity (*asadartha*)
	11		That which is particular (*vyasta*)	That which is general (*samasta*)
	14	*	That which is composed of conditions (*pratyayamaya*)	That which is composed of non-conditions (*apratyayamaya*)
II	1	*(Ex.16)	That which has been traversed (*gata*)	That which has not been traversed (*agata*)
	8	(Ex.17)	Traverser (*gantṛ*)	Non-traverser (*agantṛ*)
	12	*	That which has been traversed (*gata*)	That which has not been traversed (*agata*)
	15	*	Traverser (*gantṛ*)	Non-traverser (*agantṛ*)
III	5	* B	Organ of sight (*darśana*)	That which is not an organ of sight (*adarśana*)

		Feature 2	Feature 3
[Existents] that have arisen from both ("*dvābhyām utpannāḥ*")	[Existents] that have arisen without cause ("*ahetutaḥ utpannāḥ*")	ind. + nom. + v.	False
		nom. + nom.	False
		nom. + nom.	False
		gen. + nom.	False
		loc. nom. + v.	False
		nom. + nom.	False
	That which is being traversed (*gamyamāna*)	nom. + v.	False
	Third person other than a traverser and non-traverser ("*anyo gantur agantuś ca ... tṛtīyo*")	nom. + v.	False
	That which is being traversed (*gamyamāna*)	nom. + v.	False
	Third person other than a traverser and non-traverser ("*anyo gantur agantuś ca ... tṛtīyo*")	nom. + v.	False
		nom. + v.	False

	6	C1	Apart from (*tiraskṛtya*)	Not apart from (*atiraskṛtya*)
IV	4	C2	When [matter] exists (*sati*)	When [matter] does not exist (*asati*)
	6	* A (Ex. 6)	That which is similar (*sadṛśa*)	That which is dissimilar (*asadṛśa*)
V	3		That which has characteristics (*salakṣaṇa*)	That which is without characteristics (*alakṣaṇa*)
	7a	B (Ex. 3)	Existent (*bhāva*)	Non-existent (*abhāva*)
	7b		That which is to be characterized (*lakṣya*)	That which characterizes (*lakṣaṇa*)
VI	2		When [passion] exists (*sati*)	When [passion] does not exist (*asati*)
	4	D	When [passion and one who is impassioned] are one (*ekatve*)	When [passion and one who is impassioned] are separate (*pṛthaktve*)
	10	C3	When [passion and one who is impassioned] are together (*saha*)	When [passion and one who is impassioned] are not together (*asaha*)
VII	14	*	That which has arisen (*utpanna*)	That which has not arisen (*anutpanna*)
	20	* (Ex. 4)	That which exists (*sat*)	That which does not exist (*asat*)
	21	*	Existent that is being extinguished (*nirudhyamānabhāva*)	Existent that is not being extinguished (*anirudhyamānabhāva*)
	22	*	Existent that has stood (or abided) (*sthitabhāva*)	Existent that has not stood (*asthitabhāva*)
	26	*	That which has been extinguished (*niruddha*)	That which has not been extinguished (*aniruddha*)

			acc.+gr.+nom.+v.	False
			loc.+ loc.+ nom.	False
			gen. + nom.	False
			loc. + nom.	False
			nom. + v.	False
			nom. + v.	False
			<loc.+loc.+nom.>[1]	False[2]
			loc.+nom.	False
			inst.+gen.+nom.+ind.	False
		That which is arising (*utpadyamāna*)	nom. + v.	False
	That which exists and does not exist (*sadasat*)[3]		gen.+nom. + v.	False
			gen.+nom.+v.	False
		[Existent] that is standing (*tiṣṭhamāna*)	nom.+v.	False
		That which is being extinguished (*niru-dhyamāna*)	nom.+v.	False

	27	* B	Existent that has stood (*sthitabhāva*)	Existent that has not stood (*asthitabhāva*)
	28	*	Because of this state ("*tayā avasthayā*")	Because of another state ("*anyayā avasthayā*")
	30, 31	*	Existing existent (*sadbhāva*)	Non-existing existent (*asadbhāva*)
	32	*	By itself (*svātmanā*)	Because of another (*parātmanā*)
VIII	1,7	*	Really existent agent ("*sadbhūtaḥ kārakaḥ*")	Not really existent agent ("*asadbhūtaḥ kārakaḥ*")
		*	Really existent action ("*sadbhūtaṃ karma*")[4]	Not really existent action ("*asadbhūtaṃ karma*")
	8	*	Existing agent ("*satā kartrā*")	Not existing agent ("*asatā kartrā*")
		*	Existing [action] (*sat*)	Not existing [action] (*asat*)[5]
	9,10,11	*	(same as VIII.1, 7)	
	12	(Ex. 1)	——————————[6]	
IX	5		——————————	
X	1		If [fuel and fire] are identical ("*yad ...sa...*")	If [fuel and fire] are different (*anya*)
	12	* C1 (Ex. 8)	Contingent upon (*apekṣya*)	Not contingent upon (*anapekṣya*)[8]
XI	3, 4, 5		Before (*pūrvam, āditaḥ*)	After (*uttaram, paścāt*)
XII	1		That which is self-produced ("*svayaṃ kṛtam*")	That which is produced by another ("*parakṛtam*")
XIII	5	*	One thing (*tat*)	Another thing (*anya*)

		gen.+gen.+nom.+v.	False
		inst.+inst.+nom.+ nom.+v.	False
		gen.+gen.+nom.+v.	False
		inst.+nom.+v.	False
Really and not really existent agent ("*sada-sadbhūtaḥ kārakaḥ*") Really and not really existent [action] ("*sadasat tat*")		nom.+nom.+acc.+ acc.+v.	False
		inst.+v.+nom.	False
			False
		gr.+acc.+nom.+v.	True
		v.+inst.+nom.	True
		[7]	False
		gr.+acc.+nom.	False
	Simultaneously (*saha*)	3,4: <ind.+nom. +nom.+ind.>[9] 5: inst.+nom.+ ind.+v.	False
That which is produced by both ("*dvābhyāṃ kṛtam*")	That which is without cause ("*ahetukam*")	<nom.+nom.>[10]	False
		gen.+nom.	False

XIV	7	*	That which is other (*anya*)	That which is not other (*ananya*)
XVI	1	*	That which is permanent (*nitya*)	That which is impermanent (*anitya*)
	6	*	One who has attachment (*sopādāna*)	One without attachment (*anupādāna*)
	8	* B	One who is bound (*baddha*)	One who is not bound (*abaddha*)
XVII	28		One who is different from the agent ("*kartur anyo*")	The agent himself ("*sa eva*")
	29	* B	That which has arisen from conditions (*pratyayasamutpanna*)	That which has not arisen from conditions (*apratyayasamutpanna*)
XVIII	1		[When the self is the aggregates][12]	[When the self is] different (*anya*) [from the aggregates]
	6 ab		Self (*ātman*)	Non-self (*anātman*)
	6 ab		Self (*ātman*)	Non-self (*anātman*)
	8	*	That which is true ("*tathyam*")	That which is not true ("*na tathyam*")
XIX	1, 3	C1 (Ex. 2)	Contingent [upon the past] (*apekṣya*)	Not contingent [upon the past] (*anapekṣya*)
	5	B	That which has stood (or abided) (*sthita*)	That which has not stood (or abided) (*asthita*)
XX	10		Extinguished cause ("*niruddhaḥ hetuḥ*")	Present cause ("*tiṣṭhan hetuḥ*")
	12, 13, 14	*	Past effect (*atītaphala*)	Future effect (*ajātaphala*)
		*	Conjunction with a past cause ("*atītena hetunā saha saṃgatiḥ*")	Conjunction with a future cause ("*ajātena hetunā saha saṃgatiḥ*")
	17, 18	* A	Empty effect ("*śūnyaṃ phalam*")	Non-empty effect ("*aśūnyaṃ phalam*")

		loc.+nom.+v.	False
		nom.+v.	False
		nom.+v.	False
		nom.+v.	False
		nom.+gen.+nom.; nom.+ind.+nom[11]	False
		nom.+nom.	False
		[13]	False
		[14]	True
		[15]	False
That which is both true and untrue ("*tathyaṃ cātathyaṃ ca*")	That which is neither true nor untrue ("*naivātathyaṃ naiva tathyam*")	nom.+nom.	True
		[16]	False
		nom.+v.+nom.	False
		[17]	False
	Present effect (*jātaphala*) Conjunction with a present cause ("*jātena hetunā saha saṃgatiḥ*")	gen.+gen.+ind.+ inst.+inst.+nom.+v.	False
		nom.+v.	False

	19	D	Identity [of cause and effect] (*ekatva*)	Difference [of cause and effect] (*anyatva*)
	21	*	Effect with really existent own-being ("*svabhāvasadbhūtaṃ phalam*")	Effect with not really existent own-being ("*svabhāvāsadbhūtaṃ phalam*")
	24	*	That which is produced by conjunction (*sāmagrīkṛta*)	That which is produced by non-conjunction (*asāmagrīkṛta*)
XXI	1		Without [occurrence] (*vinā*)	With [occurrence] (*saha*)
	7	* B	That which is destructible (*kṣaya*)	That which is not destructible (*akṣaya*)
	9	*	That which is empty (*śūnya*)	That which is not empty (*aśūnya*)
	10		[The fact that occurrence and dissolution are] identical (*eka*)	[The fact that occurrence and dissolution are] different (*nānā*)
	12 {	*	Existent (*bhāva*)	Non-existent (*abhāva*)
		*	Being born from an existent (*bhāva*)	Being born from a non-existent (*abhāva*)
	13	*	Being born from self ("*svato jāyate*")	Being born from another ("*parato jāyate*")
XXII	1		[The fact that the Tathāgata and aggregates are] identical	[The fact that the Tathāgata and aggregates are] different
XXIII	3	*	Existence (*astitva*)	Non-existence (*nāstitva*)
	9	*	Purity (*śubha*)	Impurity (*aśubha*)
	10ab, 11ab		Not contingent [upon *x*] (*anapekṣya*)	Contingent [upon *x*] (*apekṣya*)[19]
	10c, 11c		————————	
	17,18	* (Ex. 5)	One who has erred (*viparīta*)	One who has not erred (*aviparīta*)

		gen.+gen.+nom.+v.	False
		acc.+acc.+nom.+v.	False
		nom.+nom.	False
		ind.+v.+nom.+inst.	False
		gen .+nom.+v.	False
		nom.+nom.+ind. + gen.+v.	False
		nom.+nom.+nom.	False
		abl.+nom.+v.	False
Being born from self and another ("*svataḥ parataś caiva jāyate*")		ind.+v.+nom.	False
		nom.+ nom./ nom.+abl.+nom.[18]	False
		gen.+nom.+v.	False
		nom.+loc.+v.	False
		gr.+acc.+v. + nom.[20]	False
		acc.+gr.+nom.[21]	True
	One who is erring (*viparyasyamāna*)	gen.+v.+nom.	False

	20	* (Ex. 7)	Being born from self ("*svato jāyate*")	Being born from another ("*parato jāyate*")
	24,25	* A	Those that already exist by their own-being ("*bhūtāḥ svabhāvena*")	Those that do not already exist by their own-being ("*abhūtāḥ svabhāvena*")
XXV	10,13, 16	* (Ex. 14)	Existent (*bhāva*)	Non-existent (*abhāva*)
	17	* E	Existing ("*bhavati*")	Not existing ("*na bhavati*")
	18	* E	The Blessed One after death ("*paraṃ nirodhād bhagavān*")	The living Blessed One ("*tiṣṭhamāno bhagavān*")[23]
	19		Distinction (*viśeṣaṇa*)	Non-distinction (*aviśeṣaṇa*)[25]
	22	*	That which has a limit (*antavat*)	That which is without a limit (*ananta*)
	23a	*	That very thing ("*tad eva*")	Something else ("*anyat*")
	23bcd	*	Eternalness (*śāśvata*)	Non-eternalness (*aśāśvata*)
XXVII	3,9	*	The fact that I existed ("*abhūm*")	The fact that I did not exist ("*nābhūm*")
	8	D	That which is different [from attachment] (*anya*)	That which is identical [with attachment] (*eva*)
	13	*	The fact that I existed ("*abhūm*")	The fact that I did not exist ("*nābhūm*")
	14	*	The fact that I shall exist ("*bhaviṣyāmi*")	The fact that I shall not exist ("*na bhaviṣyāmi*")

Being born from self and another ("*svataḥ parataś ca [jāyate]*")		ind.+v.+nom.	False
		<nom.+inst.+nom. +gen.+ind.>[22]	False
Existent and non-existent ("*abhāvo bhāvaś ca*")	Neither existent nor non-existent ("*naivābhāvo naiva bhāvaḥ*")	nom.+nom./ nom.+nom. + nom.	False
Existing and not existing ("*bhavaty ubhayam*")	Neither existing nor not existing ("*nobhayam*")	17ab: ind.+abl.+ nom.+nom. <18ab: nom.+nom. + v.>[24]	False False
		gen.+abl.+nom.+ ind.+v.+nom.	False
That which both has a limit and is without a limit ("*anantam antavac ca*")	That which neither has a limit nor is without a limit ("*nāntaṃ nāntavac ca*")	22ab: nom.+nom. 22cd: nom.+nom. + nom.+ind.	False
		nom.+nom.	False
Eternalness and non-eternalness ("*aśāśvataṃ śāśvataṃ ca*")	Neither eternalness nor non-eternalness ("*nobhayam*")	nom.+nom.[26]	False
		v.+acc.+acc.[27]	False
		nom.+abl.+nom./ nom.+ind.+nom.	False
The fact that I both existed and did not exist ("*ubhayam*")	The fact that I neither existed nor did not exist ("*nobhayam*")	loc.+v.	False
		loc.+v.	False

Notes to Table 3

1) The discussion relating to the two factors "passion" and "one who is impassioned" in VI.2cd: *sati vāsati vā rāge rakte 'py eṣa samaḥ kramaḥ//* (Both when passion exists and when it does not exist, the relationship is the same [as before] in regard to [the non-existence of] one who is impassioned) may be rewritten "*sati vāsati vā rāge na raktaḥ.*" This in turn may be understood as a conjunction of the two propositions "*sati rāge na raktaḥ*" (When passion exists, there is no one who is impassioned) and "*asati rāge na raktaḥ*" (When passion does not exist, there is no one who is impassioned), both of which have the syntactical structure loc.+loc.+nom. The angle brackets < > in Table 3 indicate that the corresponding proposition does not appear in this form in the original text, but has been rewritten without any change of meaning in order to bring out more clearly our three features.

2) See n. 1. Although this verse does not contain the negative particle *na*, it is evident from the phrase "the relationship is the same [as before]" that Feature 3 is "false."

3) See n. 15, p. 49.

4) The two factors dealt with in VIII.1, 7ab are "agent" (*kāraka*) and "performing action (*karman*)." The latter factor "performing action" is further distributed into three elements, i.e., really existent action, not really existent action, and really and not really existent action.

5) VIII.8a deals with the two factors "really existent agent" and "not really existent action," while v. 8b deals with the two factors "not really existent agent" and "really existent action." Judging from other passages in the *Middle Stanzas*, it is evident that this verse implies the combination "really existent agent" and "really existent action" and the combination "not really existent agent" and "not really existent action." Furthermore, as in the instance pointed out in n. 4, here too "action," one of the constituent elements of the factor "performing action," is distributed into two cases, i.e., "really existent action" and "not really existent action."

6) As has already been noted in connection with Example 1, no complementary distribution appears in this verse. Instead, the structure "in dependence upon x (action) there is y (agent), and in dependence upon y there is x" suggests an interchangeability of the two factors.

7) X.1: *yad indhanaṃ sa ced agnir ekatvaṃ kartṛkarmaṇoḥ/ anyaś ced*

indhanād agnir indhanād apy ṛte bhavet // (If fuel were fire, then agent and action would be identical; if fire were different from fuel, then fire would exist even without fuel). This verse may be considered to presuppose a proposition such as "Fuel is not fire (*indhanam agnir na*), nor is fire different from fuel (*anyaḥ indhanād agnir na*)," in which case it should also be possible to point to Feature 2 in this verse too.

8) "Contingent upon *x* (fuel) there is no *y* (fire), and contingent upon *y* there is no *x*" again suggests an interchangeability of the two factors. See n. 6.

9) If XI.3ab be understood in a manner similar to X.1 (see n. 7), it may be considered to presuppose a proposition such as "*pūrvaṃ jātir jarāmaraṇam uttaram iti na yujyate*" (It is not possible that there should be life before and old age and death after). The first half of the sentence preceding "*iti*" has the structure ind.+nom.+ind. XI.4ab may be interpreted in a similar manner.

10) XII.1: *svayaṃ kṛtaṃ parakṛtaṃ dvābhyāṃ kṛtam ahetukam* / *duḥkham ity eka icchanti tac ca kāryaṃ na yujyate* // (Some maintain that suffering is self-produced, produced by another, produced by both, or without cause, but it is not proper that [suffering] should be an effect). The basic meaning of this verse may be expressed as "it is not the case that suffering is self-produced....or without cause." Feature 2 in a proposition of this form is the syntactical connection nom.+nom.

11) XVII.28cd: ...*sa ca na kartur anyo na ca sa eva saḥ*// (He is neither different from the agent nor is he [the agent] himself). Leaving aside the indeclinable "*ca*" (and), the first half of this quotation has the structure nom.+gen.+nom., while the second half has the structure nom.+ind.+nom.

12) Here the relationship between the self and the aggregates is distributed into two cases, namely, that when the self is the aggregates and that when the self is different from the aggregates.

13) XVIII.1 may be considered to presuppose two propositions such as "the self is not the aggregates" (*na ātmā skandhāḥ*) and "the self is not different from the aggregates" (*na ātmā skandhebhyo 'nyaḥ*). These two propositions have the structure nom.+nom. and nom.+abl.+nom. respectively.

14) XVIII. 6ab: *ātmety api prajñapitam anātmety api deśitam*/ (It has

been both indicated that the self [exists] and taught that no-self [exists] [or "that it is no-self"]). Here it is to be conjectured that a verb corresponding to "exists" or "is" —e.g., *asti*—has been omitted, in which case it may be said that this verse also implies Feature 2 in the form of the syntactical connection nom.+v. Although the two factors are not patent in this verse, if the above supplementary addition should prove to be admissible, the two factors of "self (or no-self)" and "existence" may be posited.

15) Features 1 and 2 in XVIII.6cd may be considered in the same manner as in v.6ab (see n. 14), but Feature 3 is "false."

16) XIX.1,3 presuppose a proposition to the effect that "the present and past do not exist regardless of whether they are contingent or not contingent upon the past." Here the relationship between the "present and future" and the "past" is distributed into two cases, namely, that when the present and future are contingent upon the past and that when they are not contingent upon the past.

17) XX.10: *janayet phalam utpannaṃ niruddho 'staṃgataḥ katham/ tiṣṭhann api kathaṃ [hetuḥ] phalena janayed vṛtaḥ//* (How should an extinguished [cause] that has disappeared give birth to an already arisen effect? And how should an actually existing cause connected with an effect give birth [to an effect]?). Feature 2 in this verse is basically the syntactical connection nom.+acc.+v.

18) In XXII.1, "*skandhā na...tathāgataḥ*" (The Tathāgata is not the aggregates) has the syntactical structure nom.+nom., while the subsequent "*nānyaḥ skandhebhyo...[tathāgataḥ]*" ([The Tathāgata] is not different from the aggregates) has the syntactical structure nom.+abl.+nom. The method employed in this verse, positing five instances — (i) *x* is not *y*, (ii) *x* is not different from *y*, (iii) *y* is not within *x*, (iv) *x* is not within *y*, and (v) *x* does not possess *y* — and then negating them all, has traditionally been known in China and Japan as the "negation of the five postulates." Among these five instances, Feature 1, i. e., complementary distribution, is to be seen in (i) and (ii). A similar positing of five instances appears also in XVI.2, XXII.8 and XXIII.5, although in these three verses there appears only the word "*pañcadhā*" (in five ways), and the five instances are not mentioned individually as in XXII.1.

19) XXIII.10abc: *anapekṣya śubhaṃ nāsty aśubhaṃ prajñapayemahi/ yat pratītya śubham...//* (We say that not contingent upon purity there is

not impurity (ab) and that in dependence upon that [impurity] there is purity (c)); XXIII.11abc: *anapekṣyāśubhaṃ nāsti śubhaṃ prajñapayemahi/ yat pratītyāśubham...//* (We say that not contingent upon impurity there is not purity (ab) and that in dependence upon that [purity] there is impurity (c)). Vv. 10ab and 11ab have the structure "not contingent upon *x* (or *y*) there is not *y* (or *x*)," and as in the case of X.12 (Example 8) it is probably possible to supplement here also a proposition to the effect that "contingent upon *x* (or *y*) there is not *y* (or *x*)," in which case the relationship between the two factors (*x* and *y*) may be understood as having been distributed into two cases, namely, that when "*y* (or *x*) is contingent upon *x* (or *y*)" and that when "*y* (or *x*) is not contingent upon *x* (or *y*)," with only the second case being given in vv. 10ab and 11ab. Vv.10c and 11c, on the other hand, deal with the relationship expressible as "in dependence upon *x* (or *y*) there is *y* (or *x*)," already discussed in connection with VIII.12 (Example 1), in which there appears no complementary distribution.

20) The syntactical connection appearing in v. 10ab is gr. (*anapekṣya*) + acc. (*śubham*) + v. (*nāsti*) + nom. (*aśubham*), and v. 11ab may be interpreted in the same manner.

21) The syntactical connection appearing in v.10c is acc. (*yat*) + gr. (*pratītya*) + nom. (*śubham*), and v. 11c may be interpreted in the same manner.

22) XXIII.24 may be considered to presuppose the proposition "*na bhūtāḥ svabhāvena kleśāḥ kasya cid*" (The defilements of no one already exist by their own-being), while XXIII.25 may be considered to presuppose the proposition "*nābhūtāḥ svabhāvena kleśāḥ kasya cid*" (The defilements of no one do not already exist by their own-being). In this case Feature 2 may be understood in the manner indicated.

23) In XXV. 17a, 18b the "Blessed One" (*bhagvat*) is distributed into the "Blessed One after death" and the "living Blessed One."

24) XXV.18ab: *tiṣṭhamāno 'pi bhagavān bhavatīty eva nohyate* (It is not held that even the living Blessed One exists). The latter half of the verse from "*bhavatīty*" onwards may be rewritten as "*na bhavati*" without any change of meaning. The syntactical connection in this case is nom.+ind.+nom.+v.

25) XXV.19: *na saṃsārasya nirvāṇāt kiṃ cid asti viśeṣaṇam/ na*

nirvāṇasya saṃsārāt kiṃ cid asti viśeṣaṇam// (There is no distinction whatsoever between *saṃsāra* and *nirvāṇa*; there is no distinction whatsoever between *nirvāṇa* and *saṃsāra*). Here the relationship between the two factors of *saṃsāra* and *nirvāṇa* may be considered to have been distributed into two cases, namely, that when there is a distinction (*viśeṣaṇa*) between them and that when there is no distinction (*aviśeṣaṇa),* with only the former being dealt with in this verse. Although the second case is not explicitly mentioned, judging from the discussion up to this point, it too may be assumed to constitute a premise of this verse.

26) The syntactical connection of each of the four propositions forming the tetralemma in XXV. 23bcd is basically nom.+nom.

27) XXVII.3ab: *abhūm atītam adhvānam ity etan nopapadyate* (It is not appropriate to say that "I existed in a past age"). The part corresponding to "I existed in a past age" has the syntactical structure v.+acc.+acc.

CHAPTER EIGHT

THE NEGATION OF A TERM AND THE NEGATION OF A PROPOSITION: THE NEGATION OF THE PROFANE (3)

Although it is a well-known fact that in the *Middle Stanzas* Nāgārjuna bent his energies upon refuting the views of his opponents, not much attention has been given to the fact that in his arguments he employs two types of negation. The crux of Nāgārjuna's system of negation lies in fact in the combined use of these two types of negation. Let us review these two types of negation by referring back to Example 6 (IV.6), which belongs to distribution type A.

Example 6

na kāraṇasya sadṛśaṃ kāryam ity upapadyate /
na kāraṇasya asadṛśaṃ kāryam ity upapadyate //

(It is not appropriate to say that a cause has a similar effect;
It is not appropriate to say that a cause has a dissimilar effect.)

Here, the second of the two factors of "cause" and "effect" is subjected to a complementary distribution into two cases. But it is unlikely that the opponent's view which Nāgārjuna was criticizing embodied any such distribution. The opponent's assertion would probably have been simply "a cause has an effect" (*kāraṇasya kāryam*). In seeking to demonstrate the invalidity of this proposition, Nāgārjuna's first step was to subject one of its two factors to a complementary distribution. This distribution would have been performed in the following manner:

If a cause has an effect (p),

Either it must be an effect similar to the cause (q),

Or it must be an effect dissimilar to the cause (r). —(a)

In this example all causes have been distributed into either effects similar to the cause or effects dissimilar to the cause, and at least in this verse the existence of any third possibility such as an effect both similar and dissimilar to the cause is not recognized. Nāgārjuna next seeks to demonstrate that neither of the two propositions incorporating the two cases born of the above distribution (*q* and *r*) can be regarded as valid from his standpoint. Namely, he attempts to prove non-*q* and non-*r*. If non-*q* and non-*r* should be true, this implies that the antecedent *p* is false. It means, in other words, that the proposition "a cause has an effect" will never be true regardless of the nature of the effect.

The content of IV.6 (Example 6) may be expressed by means of the following formula:

$$\sim(X\text{gen } M.Y\text{nom}) \cdot\sim (X\text{gen } \tilde{M}.Y\text{nom}) \quad (\text{set}M.Y \cup \text{set}\tilde{M}.Y = \text{set}Y)$$

*X*gen = *kāraṇasya* (a cause has).

*M.Y*nom = *sadṛśaṃ kāryam* (a similar effect).

$\tilde{M}$.*Y*nom = *asadṛśaṃ kāryam* (a dissimilar effect).

In this case, the negative particle *a-* affixed to *sadṛśa* (similar), the referent of *M*, negates not the proposition "a cause has a similar effect" but only the term "similar." In other words, in the expression "$\tilde{M}$.*Y*nom" the term "$\tilde{M}$" modifies only the term "*Y*," and the idea of negativity contained in "$\tilde{M}$" does not determine the truth or untruth of the proposition "(*X*gen *Y*nom)." The term "dissimilar" signifies the postulation of, among all effects, effects dissimilar to the cause. In Sanskrit grammar this type of negative has traditionally been termed "*paryudāsa*" (literally, "exclusion"), and it may be rendered as "affirming negative," signifying implicative (or choice) negation. The negation of a proposition as a whole, on the other hand, such as for example "a cause does not have an effect," is called "*prasajyapratiṣedha*," which we may translate as "non-affirming negative" and corresponds to absolute (or exclusion) negation. This latter type of negative means literally "the negation (*pratiṣedha*) of some thing after having ascertained (*prasajya*) its possible validity." For example, after having ascertained the possible validity of the statement "a cause has an effect" in that it is meaningful or comprehensible, it is then negated. It is not clear when the two terms *paryudāsa* and *prasajyapratiṣedha* became established as technical terms. They are at least not used in Nāgārjuna's extant works. But the complementary distribution with which we are here dealing indicates an awareness of implicative negation (*paryudāsa*), while the question of the truth of a proposition concerns absolute negation (*prasajyapratiṣedha*), and both are clearly differentiated in the *Middle Stanzas*. Although Nāgārjuna does not mention these two types of negation by name, it may thus be assumed that he was fully conscious of the distinction between them, and his selective use of them represents in fact the most important adjunct to his methods of argument in the *Middle Stanzas*.

The results of our above examination of IV.6, which belongs to complementary distribution type A, may also be applied to other verses of distribution type A. Let us next consider, for example, VII.27.

Example 9

sthitasya tāvad bhāvasya nirodho nopapadyate /
nāsthitasyāpi bhāvasya nirodha upapadyate // (VII.27) —(a)

(First, extinction is not possible for an already abiding existent;
Extinction is also not possible for a not yet abiding existent.)

Having excluded the words "first" (*tāvad*) and "also"(*api*), which are not directly related to our discussion, we may in order to facilitate our understanding of the structure of the content of this verse rearrange the word order as follows:

nirodhaḥ sthitasya bhāvasya na upapadyate.
nirodhaḥ asthitasya bhāvasya na upapadyate. —(b)

In accordance with the method employed for Examples 3-8, (b) may then be symbolically expressed as follows:

$\sim(X\text{nom } M.Y\text{gen } Zv) \cdot\sim (X\text{nom } \tilde{M}.Y\text{gen } Zv)$ $(\text{set}M.Y \cup \text{set}\tilde{M}.Y = \text{set } Y)$ —(c)

Xnom = *nirodhaḥ* (extinction).

$M.$ Ygen = *sthitasya bhāvasya* (for an already abiding existent).

$\tilde{M}.Y$gen = *asthitasya bhāvasya* (for a not yet abiding existent).

Zv = *upapadyate* (is possible).

Set$M.Y$ = set of already abiding existents.

Set$\tilde{M}.Y$ = set of not yet abiding existents.

Set$Y$ = set of existents.

In this verse "existent (or thing)" is subjected to a complementary distribution into "(already) abiding" (*sthita*) and "non-abiding (or not yet abiding)" (*asthita*). This distribution takes the form of the modification of "existent" by the two terms "abiding" and "non-abiding" respectively. In our formula this distribution is indicated by "*M. Y*gen" and "$\tilde{M}$*. Y*gen," with the terms "*M*" and "$\tilde{M}$" modifying the term "*Y*." Here again the negative prefix *a-* appearing in "*asthita*" (non-abiding) signifies an implicative negation, and it should be distinguished from the negative particle *na* which negates the two propositions and expresses an absolute negation.

According to present-day transformational grammar, a sentence (S) is considered to be composed of a noun phrase (NP) and a verb phrase (VP), and what is known as a "tree diagram" is used to illustrate this. As is shown in Diagram 5, the noun phrase and verb phrase are each indicated at the end of two diagonal lines that meet to form a chevron. For example, the sentence "a traverser traverses" (*gantā gacchati*; *Middle Stanzas*, Chapter II) is composed of a noun phrase (NP) consisting of the single noun (N) "traverser" and a verb phrase (VP) consisting of the single verb (V) "traverses." This sentence may thus be expressed as in Diagram 6. Negation, however, is dealt with in transformational grammar as a type of verb.[1] For example, "a traverser does not traverse" (*gantā na gacchati*) may be regarded as an intransitive sentence with "a traverser traverses"

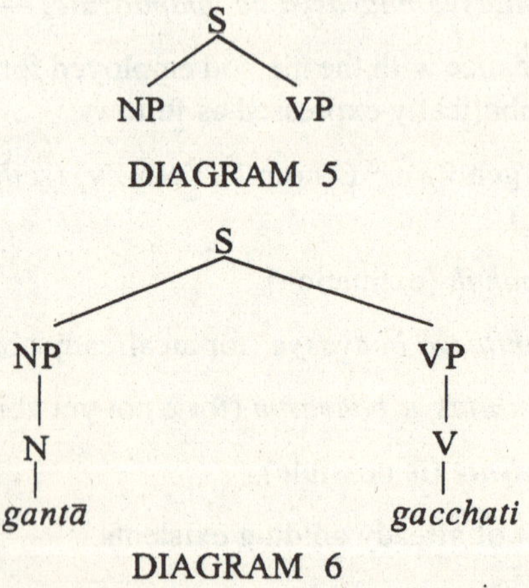

DIAGRAM 5

DIAGRAM 6

1. Imai Kunihiko, *Henkei bunpō no hanashi* (On Transformational Grammar; Tōkyō: Taishūkan, 1979), p. 95.

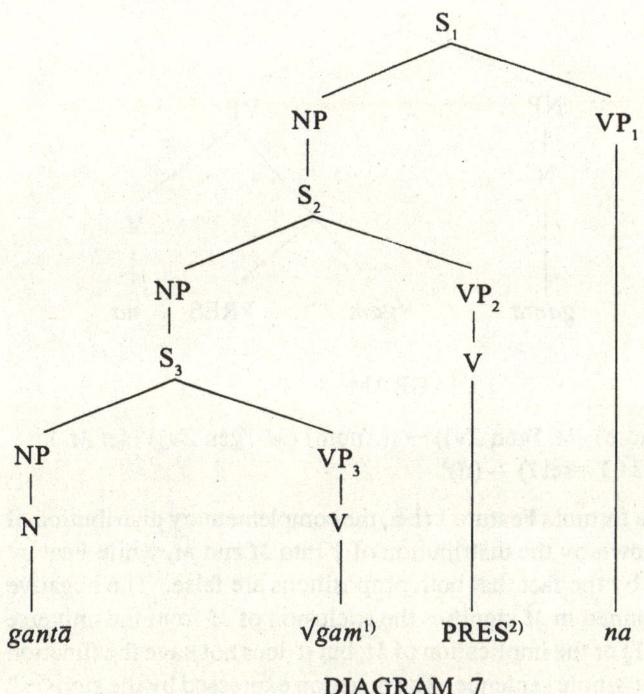

DIAGRAM 7

1) √*gam* is the root of *gacchati* (present tense).

2) "PRES" indicates that the verb *gacchati* is in the present tense.

as its subject and the negative particle "*na*" as its verb. The subject of this sentence constitutes a noun phrase, which in turn contains a noun phrase and a verb phrase. This negative sentence may be illustrated by the tree diagram given in Diagram 7. As a result of operations following the conventions of transformational grammar, this Diagram 7 may in turn be transformed into Diagram 8.[2]

If we divide the proposition in Example 9 (VII.27) above into a noun phrase (NP) and a verb phrase (VP), "*X*nom" becomes the noun phrase and "*M*.*Y*gen *Z*v" (or "$\tilde{M}$.*Y*gen *Z*v") becomes the verb phrase. Hence (c) may be further rewritten as follows:

2. *Ibid*., pp. 95-100.

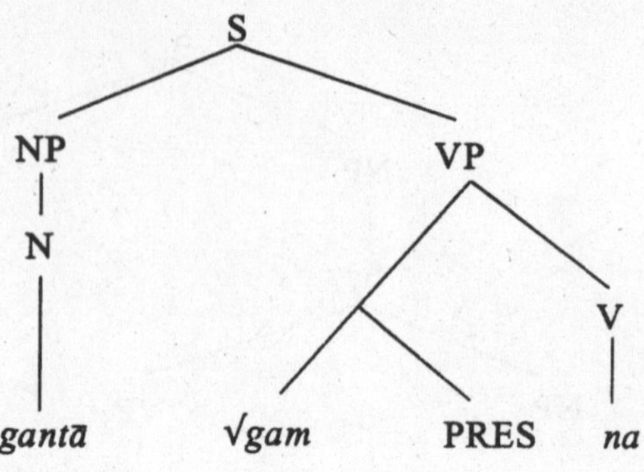

DIAGRAM 8

$\sim((X\text{nom})\ (M.Y\text{gen}\ Z\text{v}))\cdot\sim((X\text{nom})\ (M.Y\text{gen}\ Z\text{v}))\ (\text{set}\ M.Y \cup \text{set}\tilde{M}.Y = \text{set}Y)$ —(d)[3]

In this formula Feature 1 (i.e., the complementary distribution of a factor) is shown by the distribution of Y into M and $\tilde{M}$, while Feature 3 is indicated by the fact that both propositions are false. The negative prefix *a-* contained in $\tilde{M}$ signifies the exclusion of M from the universe of discourse (Y) or the implication of $\tilde{M}$, but it does not have the function of negating the whole sentence. The negation expressed by the sign "~," on the other hand, represents the negation of the whole sentence. Furthermore, the negation of a whole sentence signifies the negation of any connections between the referent of the noun phrase and the referent of the verb phrase. Therefore, in the case of this verse the negative proposition "the extinction (X) of an existent (Y) is *not* possible" means

3. Example 9 may also be read to mean "the extinction of an already abiding existent (or a not yet abiding existent) is not possible." In this case, its content may be symbolically expressed as follows:

$\sim((X\text{nom}\ M.Y\text{gen})\ (Z\text{v}))\cdot\sim((X\text{gen}\ \tilde{M}.Y\text{gen})\ (Z\text{v}))$

In this formula the noun phrase—"the extinction of an already abiding existent (or a not yet abiding existent)"—points to two factors, namely, "an already abiding existent (or a not yet abiding existent)" and "existent." See Tachikawa Musashi, "*Chūron* ni okeru nishu no hitei —*Chūron* no ronrigakuteki kōsatsu (3)—" (The Two Types of Negation in the *Middle Stanzas*: Logical Considerations of the *Middle Stanzas* (3)), in *Nasu Seiryū Hakushi beiju kinen ronbunshū* (Collected Papers in Honour of Dr. Nasu Seiryū's 88th Birthday; Narita: Naritasan Shinshōji, 1984), p. 645.

that any connection between *X* and what is possible for *Y* is found not to hold true. This negative proposition is generally expressed, without any

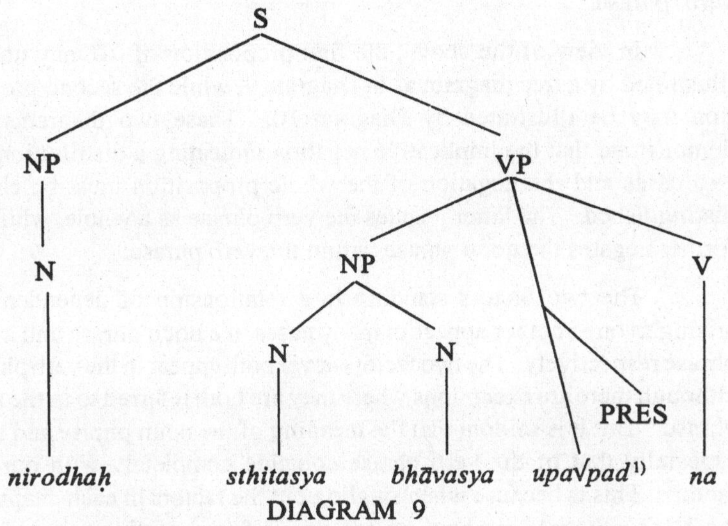

DIAGRAM 9

1) *upa√pad* is the root of *upapadyate*.

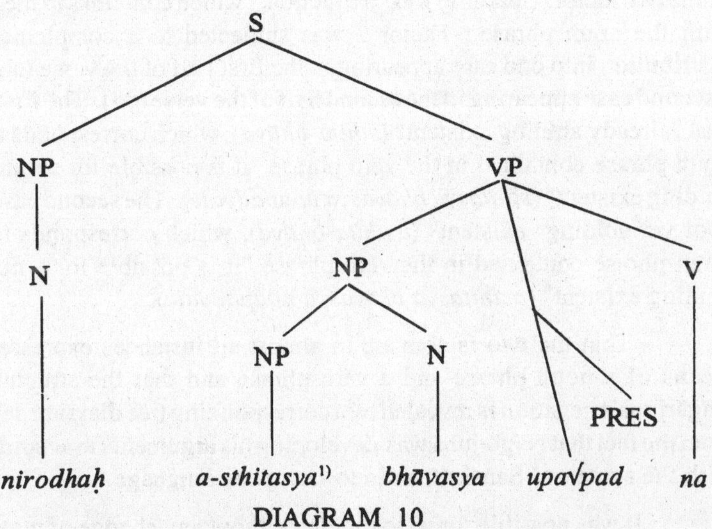

DIAGRAM 10

1) *a-sthita* is a compoumd consisting of *sthita* and the negative particle *a-*. By negating *sthita*, the negative particle *a-* implies the affirmation of *asthita*.

change of meaning, as "*X* is not possible for *Y*," and in this case the negation of the whole sentence assumes the form of the negation of the verb phrase.

In view of the above, the first proposition of (d) may now be illustrated by a tree diagram as in Diagram 9, while the second proposition may be illustrated by Diagram 10. These two diagrams also demonstrate that the implicative negation indicating a distribution into two cases and the negation of the whole proposition must be clearly distinguished. The latter negates the verb phrase as a whole, while the former negates the noun phrase within the verb phrase.

The two factors standing in a relationship of dependent co-arising to one another appear in many cases in a noun phrase and a verb phrase respectively. The two factors never both appear in the verb phrase, although there are exceptions where they are both referred to in the noun phrase.[4] But it is seldom that the meaning of the noun phrase and more especially that of the verb phrase coincide completely with our two factors. This is because when singling out the factors in each chapter of the *Middle Stanzas*, we have treated, with a few exceptions, the referent of the noun in the verb phrase as a factor. In Example 9, for instance, one of the two factors (factor 1) was "extinction," which coincides in meaning with the noun phrase. Factor 2 was subjected to a complementary distribution into one case appearing in the first half of the verse (ab) and a second case appearing in the second half of the verse (cd). The first case was "already abiding existent" (*sthita-bhāva*), which corresponds to the noun phrase contained in the verb phrase "it is possible for an already abiding existent" (*sthitasya bhāvasya upapadyate*). The second case was "not yet abiding existent" (*asthita-bhāva*), which corresponds to the noun phrase contained in the verb phrase "it is possible for a not yet abiding existent" (*asthitasya bhāvasya upapadyate*).

That the two factors are in almost all instances expressed by means of a noun phrase and a verb phrase and that the structure of Nāgārjuna's negation is revealed by a corresponding tree diagram derives from the fact that Nāgārjuna was developing his arguments in accordance with the syntax of Sanskrit, an Indo-European language.

It was possible for us to rewrite without any change of meaning

---

4. See *Middle Stanzas*, XX.19.

the verse "space is not an existent, nor is it a non-existent"(V.7; Example 3), an example of a verse of distribution type B, and express the rewritten proposition by means of the following formula:

~(*X*nom *Y*nom) ·~ (*X*nom $\tilde{Y}$nom)

*X*nom = *ākāśaḥ* (space).

*Y*nom = *bhāvaḥ* (existent).

$\tilde{Y}$nom = *abhāvaḥ* (non-existent).

(The universe of discourse here is the entire universe.)

Here two possibilities–namely, when "space (*X*) is an existent (*bhāva*) (*Y*)" and when "space is a non-existent (*abhāva*) ($\tilde{Y}$) or that which is not an existent"–are posited, and then both are negated. By demonstrating that one can say neither that "space is an existent" nor that "space is a non-existent," Nāgārjuna wished to contend that there is no such thing as space. And what had thus been demonstrated in regard to space could of course also be applied to the other elements (*dhātu*) of earth, fire, water and wind.[5]

The content of V.7ac may be considered in the same manner in which we considered the proposition in VII.27 from the perspective of noun phrase and verb phrase. The two propositions in this verse lack any verb. But in Sanskrit the copula corresponding to the verb "to be" (*asti, bhavati*) is often omitted. If we now supplement the verb "to be" and also take into account the distinction between a noun phrase and a verb phrase, the above formula may be rewritten as follows:

~((*X*nom) (*Y*nom [*Z*v])) ·~ ((*X*nom) ($\tilde{Y}$nom [*Z*v]))

(*X*nom) = space; noun phrase.

[*Z*v] = is; the square brackets indicate a supplementary addition.

((*Y*nom [*Z*v])) = is an existent; verb phrase.

(($\tilde{Y}$nom [*Z*v])) = is a non-existent; verb phrase.

The idea of negativity contained in the term "non-existent" (*a-bhāva*) implies the affirmation of that which stands in a complementary relationship to "existent" (*bhāva*), namely, non-being or nothingness. In

5. See *ibid.*, V.7.

other words, this negation modifies only the single element "*Y*" in the verb phrase "(*Y*nom [*Z*v])" and does not modify the verb phrase as a

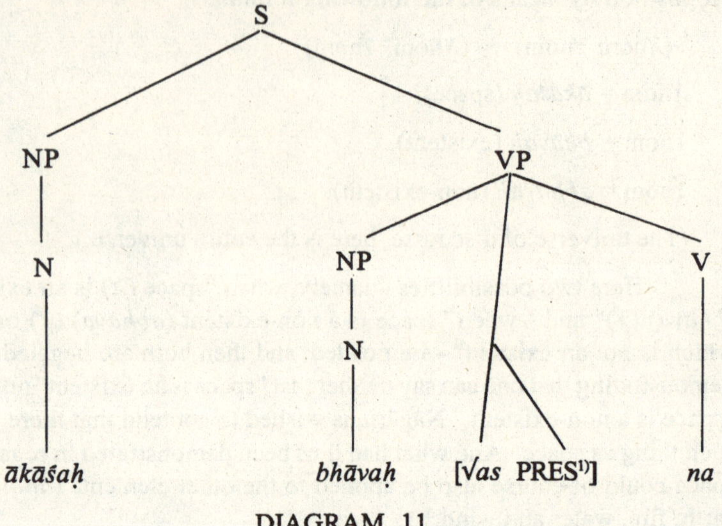

DIAGRAM 11

1) "PRES" indicates that the verb √*as* is in the present tense.

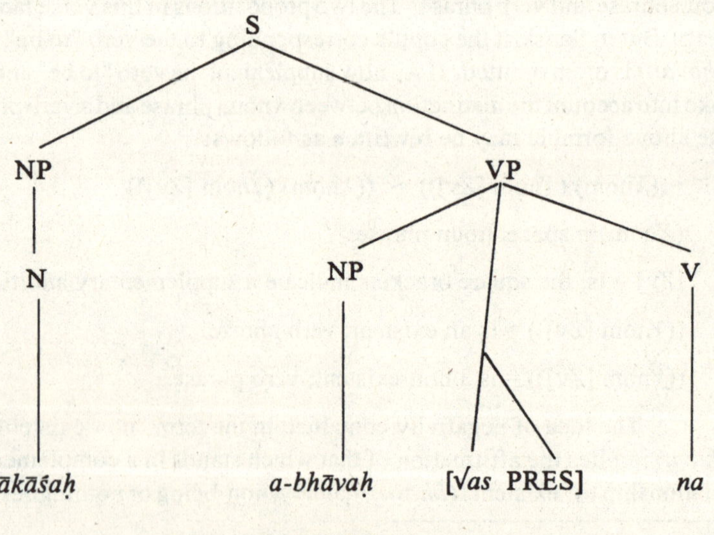

DIAGRAM 12

whole. Thus on no account does the statement "space is not a non-existent" mean that "space exists." This is because of the two possibilities "space is an existent (*bhāva*) " and "space is a non-existent (*abhāva*; that which is not an existent)," the statement "space is not a non-existent" merely negates the latter possibility without implying that "therefore, space is an existent." If Nāgārjuna had said, "it is not the case that space is not an existent (*bhāva*)," this would probably have meant that "space is an existent," but this kind of double negative is not the issue here.

Expressed formulaically, this means that "($\tilde{Y}$nom[*Z*v])" does not signify "~(*Y*nom [*Z*v])," nor does "~((*X*nom) ($\tilde{Y}$nom [*Z*v]))" signify "~~((*X*nom) (*Y*nom [*Z*v]))," i.e., "((*X*nom) (*Y*nom [*Z*v]))."

The first half of this verse is illustrated by Diagram 11 and the second half by Diagram 12. The content of the verse as a whole is shown by the combination of Diagrams 11 and 12. In other words, the factors subjected to complementary distribution are both simply negated. In Diagram 12 it is evident that the negative prefix *a*- used to indicate "*non*-existent" and the negative particle *na* used to negate the proposition in "is *not* a non-existent" do not constitute a double negative. As in our earlier examples, the negation indicating that the proposition is false appears also in Diagrams 11 and 12 in a distinct form on the right-hand side of the verb phrase.

The typical method of argument followed in the *Middle Stanzas* is to first make mention of two interdependently related factors in a single proposition, then subject either or both of the two factors to a complementary distribution, and finally demonstrate that the two propositions each containing one of the cases born of the above distribution are both false. As was noted earlier, the varieties of this distribution can be classified into five types, and the negation employed in this distribution is an implicative negation. In other words, by excluding a subset from the universe of discourse, its complement is implicitly affirmed.

A proposition or sentence is composed of a noun phrase and a verb phrase, and in the *Middle Stanzas* implicative negation is to be found in the noun phrase or the noun phrase contained within the verb phrase. The negation of a proposition as a whole, on the other hand, is indicated by the negation of the verb phrase. In other words, the demonstration of the falsity of a proposition, which was Nāgārjuna's aim, is performed by this latter type of absolute negation.

Among the various types of complementary distribution, we have for reasons of space been able to take up for consideration only propositions of the two distribution types A and B. But even though the other types of distribution are each characterized by specific syntactical features, they too have in common the fact that they involve implicative negation. These different types simply reflect various modes of distribution and as far as the *Middle Stanzas* are concerned the negation of the proposition as a whole is invariably indicated by absolute negation.

In the above we have shown, by taking a number of propositions as examples, that each of these propositions or sentences is divided into a noun phrase and a verb phrase, and that it is in fact this very division of a sentence that constitutes the basic structure of *prapañca*, with its meaning of "extension" or "dichotomy." With his conclusion that all propositions are false, Nāgārjuna was in fact seeking to bring this very *prapañca* itself to extinction.

But at the same time, by enumerating a great many pairs of interdependently related factors, Nāgārjuna was nonetheless admitting the existence of something dependently co-arisen. The means for portraying such a phenomenal world, ultimately to be negated, lay in the "sentence" which embodies from the first a division into two factors, into two cases, and into a noun phrase and a verb phrase.

CHAPTER NINE

"OWN-BEING" IN THE *MIDDLE STANZAS*: FROM THE PROFANE TO THE SACRED

In the *Middle Stanzas* Nāgārjuna makes mention within a single proposition of two entities standing in an inseparable relationship to one another, such as cause and effect or attribute and substance, and then distributes either or both of these "two factors" into two, three or four cases. Distribution into two cases is, in this case, a distribution into two complementary spheres. IV. 6 (Example 6) was one example of such a distribution.

It is not appropriate to say that a cause has a similar effect;
It is not appropriate to say that a cause has a dissimilar effect.

But why is it "not appropriate to say that a cause has a similar effect"? Judging from the commentaries on this verse and from arguments found in other passages of the *Middle Stanzas*, a "similar effect" here signifies an effect completely identical to the cause, while a "dissimilar effect" signifies an effect completely different from the cause. Thus, insofar that he distributed the effect into a similar effect and a dissimilar effect, Nāgārjuna may indeed be considered to have divided all effects in a complementary manner. But in his actual argument the terms "similar effect" and "dissimilar effect" refer to an effect identical to the cause and an effect completely different from the cause respectively. In other words, in the actual arguments of the *Middle Stanzas* the union of the two spheres of "similar effects" and "dissimilar effects" does not correspond to the entire realm of "all effects."

Nāgārjuna considered the reason that "it is not appropriate to say that a cause has a similar effect" to be that a cause could not possibly have an effect identical to itself, and likewise he considered the reason that "it is not appropriate to say that a cause has a dissimilar effect" to be that a cause could not possibly have an effect completely different from or unrelated to itself. The device employed in this verse is that the two distributed spheres that would appear to complement one another do not in fact encompass the entire universe of discourse.

But this device is not limited to the arguments developed in this verse, and it may be observed in the majority of instances in which either or both of two factors standing in an interdependent relationship to one another have been subjected to a complementary distribution into two, three or four cases. Let us consider, for example, X. 12ab once again.

Contingent (*apekṣya*) upon fuel there is no fire,

And not contingent (*anapekṣya*) upon fuel there is no fire.

Here too the situation in which "[*x*] is contingent upon [*y*]" is meant to be understood as one in which *x* and *y* are identical, while that in which "[*x*] is not contingent upon [*y*]" is meant to be understood as one in which *x* and *y* are completely different and unrelated to one another.[1] As far as their mode of expression is concerned, the two instances "[*x*] is contingent upon [*y*]" and "[*x*] is not contingent upon [*y*]" would appear to represent a complementary division of the relationship between *x* and *y*, but the real import of the two phrases "contingent upon" and "not contingent upon" does not lie in the indication of any complementary relationship. Thus the two spheres resulting from a distribution into a complementary relationship represent in actual fact only two extreme instances, while the union of these two spheres does not correspond to the entire universe of discourse. This constitutes an important distinguishing feature of the arguments of the *Middle Stanzas*.

Although the expressions "similar effect" and "dissimilar effect" would appear to suggest a complementary relationship, the fact that in Nāgārjuna's actual arguments these two expressions refer to only two extreme cases is possible because the meaning of the word "similar" in the expression "similar effect" and its meaning in the expression "dissimilar effect" are different. If one takes the word "similar" to mean "identical," it would be normal to take the meaning of "similar" in the word "dissimilar" to also mean "identical." In this case, the union of "identical effects" and "non-identical effects" would correspond to "all effects." But in the *Middle Stanzas* the word "similar" in the expression "dissimilar effect" is used not in the sense of "identical" but in the sense

1. This has already been pointed out by Ueda Yoshifumi in *Daijō Bukkyō shisō no konpon kōzō* (The Basic Structure of Mahāyāna Buddhist Thought; Kyōto: Hyakkaen, 1957), p. 77 ff.

of "having the slightest similarity." Interpreting the same word in different ways, as in this case, was an indispensable part of Nāgārjuna's methods of argument. The third pattern of negation in Chapter II of the *Middle Stanzas* is a case in point, for the statement that the action of traversing and the traverser are "one" means that they are completely identical, while the statement that they are "different" means not that they are "not completely identical" but that they are "completely unrelated and different from one another."

Here we would like to consider the term "*svabhāva*" (own-being), a basic concept that plays an important role in the arguments in which linguistic proliferation is negated in the *Middle Stanzas*. This word appears in the *Middle Stanzas* 37 times in 30 verses. In addition, the word "*niḥsvabhāva*" (without own-being) appears three times in three verses.[2] Although the term *svabhāva* appearing in these passages has a basic meaning common to all instances in which it is used, its sphere of meaning changes in accordance with the context and it serves as the driving force, as it were, behind Nāgārjuna's negation of linguistic proliferation.

The first verse in Chapter XV of the *Middle Stanzas*, entitled "An Examination of Own-being" (*Svabhāva-parīkṣā*), reads as follows:

> The occurrence of own-being through conditions and causes is not possible;
>
> An own-being born of causes and conditions would be something that had been created.
>
> (*na saṃbhavaḥ svabhāvasya yuktaḥ pratyayahetubhiḥ/*
> *hetupratyayasaṃbhūtaḥ svabhāvaḥ kṛtako bhavet //*)

The argument of the second half of this verse is based on a kind of *reductio ad absurdum* in that it is based on the reasoning that if own-being or intrinsic reality were born of causes and conditions, this would lead to the unacceptable conclusion that "own-being is something created," and therefore its antecedent cannot be true. In the following second verse the irrationality of this conclusion and the reason therefor are indicated.

---

2. See *Daijō Bukkyō no seiritsushiteki kenkyū* (Studies in the History of the Development of Mahāyāna Buddhism; Tōkyō: Sanseidō, 1954), Appendix 2 (by Saigusa Mitsuyoshi and Kuga Sunao): "Chūron, Bon-Kan-Zō taishō goi" (Comparative List of Sanskrit, Chinese and Tibetan Terms in the *Middle Stanzas*), p. 42.

But how could own-being be something that has been created?

For own-being is something uncreated and non-contingent upon another.

(*svabhāvaḥ kṛtako nāma bhaviṣyati punaḥ katham /*
akṛtrimaḥ svabhāvo hi nirapekṣaḥ paratra ca //)

"Uncreated and non-contingent upon another" is the most basic meaning of the word "*svabhāva*" as used in the *Middle Stanzas*.

Nāgārjuna also makes frequent mention of *svabhāva* or "own-being" in other chapters of the *Middle Stanzas* apart from Chapter XV, and according to these allusions anything that exists as own-being is "eternal" (XVII. 22), "its non-existence is not possible" (XXI.17), and "its extinction is not admissible" (XXIV. 23), and if it were to exist as own-being it would "not arise" (XXIV. 22) and would be "without causes and conditions" (XXIV. 16). When described in such terms, anything existing by its own-being is found to be free from birth and death, permanent, not created by causes and conditions, not non-existent and, in a word, eternal and immutable. The existence of any such own-being could on no account be admitted in Nāgārjuna's system of logic which sought to negate the existence of things.

The content of the above verses relating to own-being may be summarized as follows:

If something exists by its own-being (*svabhāva*), it is without change (*anyathābhāva*) or birth-and-death. —(a)

This represents one aspect of the meaning of *svabhāva* in the *Middle Stanzas*.

The word *svabhāva* also serves an important purpose in the two propositions in XX. 21, which have a structure similar to the propositions in IV. 6 (Example 6).

Example 10

phalaṃ svabhāvasadbhūtaṃ kiṃ hetur janayiṣyati /
phalaṃ svabhāvāsadbhūtaṃ kiṃ hetur janayiṣyati // (XX. 21)

(Would a cause produce an effect that is really existent by its own-being?

Would a cause produce an effect that is not really existent by its own-being?)

In these two sentences "cause" represents the noun phrase, while the remaining parts constitute the verb phrase. Here all effects are subjected, at least formally, to a complementary distribution into those "really existent by their own-being" and those "not really existent by their own-being." In other words, as is explained by Candrakīrti in the *Prasannapadā*, his commentary on the *Middle Stanzas*, if a cause is to produce an effect, the effect must be either an effect that is really existent by its own-being or an effect that is not really existent by its own-being.[3] Yet Nāgārjuna maintains that neither is possible. As in the case of the "similar effect" and "dissimilar effect" in IV. 6, "effects that are really existent by their own-being" and "effects that are not really existent by their own-being" do not signify two spheres that together constitute the entire realm of all "effects"; instead they actually refer merely to two types of effects far removed from one another, one effects that are eternal and immutable entities and the other effects that are without any shadow of existence and are equivalent to nothing. In the case of the former, "own-being" (*svabhāva*) refers to something eternal and immutable, whereas in the case of the latter it signifies not only something eternal and immutable, but everything existent, including that which is subject to change. It is impossible for anything eternal to change into an effect, nor can something non-existent change. Nāgārjuna negates both these "really existent effects" and "not really existent effects," but when considered only from their mode of expression, they of course cover the entire realm of all effects, and so Nāgārjuna's negation becomes a negation of "all effects."

XVII. 21ab refers to the relationship between the state of being without own-being or "own-beinglessness" (*niḥsvabhāvatva*) and the non-arising of action in the following manner:

Example 11

karma notpadyate kasmāt/ niḥsvabhāvaṃ yatas tataḥ /

(XVII. 21ab)

(Why does action not arise? Because it is without own-being.)

This may be rewritten without any change of meaning as follows:

Because it is without own-being, action does not arise. — (b)

3. *Prasannapadā*, p. 404, ll. 9-10.

If "action" is understood as just one example of an existent, the content of Example 11 as rewritten in (b) may then be logically expressed as follows:

If *x* is without own-being, *x* is without change or birth-and-death. —(c)

We have, however, already obtained the following formula:

If something exists by its own-being, it is without change or birth-and-death. —(a)

As was noted earlier, the meaning of "own-being" differs in (a) and (c). In the case of (c) it signifies anything endowed in the slightest degree with the quality of something "created," while in (a) it refers to that which exists as something immutable and "uncreated." Here lies the nub of Nāgārjuna's argument. But these two formulae are not always contradictories, for when change and birth-and-death do *not* exist, the conjunction of (a) and (c) is true. It is to be surmised, therefore, that Nāgārjuna was attempting to prove that, regardless of the existence or non-existence of own-being, there is no such thing as change.

In Example 11 and also for instance in I.10 it is maintained that "if there is no own-being, there is no arising or change." But there are also some passages in the *Middle Stanzas* where the very *existence* of change (*pṛthaktva*) constitutes the basis of own-beinglessness. For example, XIII. 3ab reads as follows:

Example 12

bhāvānām niḥsvabhāvatvam anyathābhāvadarśanāt /

(XIII. 3ab)

(Because of the observation of change in existents, they are without own-being.)

The gist of this verse may be expressed as follows:

Because there is change, things are without own-being. —(d)

In this case, "things are without own-being" refers to the entire realm of things that lack eternal and immutable substantiality and are subject to change. This means that Nāgārjuna here recognizes the existence and mutability of some sort of entity, even though it may not be an eternal and substantial entity.

"Change" is in this case regarded as an established fact, and it constitutes the basis of the consequent. In the case of (a), (c) and Example 10, on the other hand, change (or birth-and-death) is negated regardless of the existence or non-existence of own-being.

In the *Middle Stanzas* it is thus maintained on the one hand that change (or birth-and-death) is impossible and on the other hand that there is change. How are we to interpret this "contradiction" in Nāgārjuna's system?

In Chapter XXIV there appear a number of verses stating that even from the standpoint of emptiness birth and death are possible. For example, verse 14 says that "for whom emptiness is befitting, everything is befitting" (*sarvaṃ ca yujyate tasya śūnyatā yasya yujyate /*). "Everything" here naturally includes change and birth-and-death, and so Nāgārjuna is in some way or another recognizing change and birth-and-death and even the existence of the so-called phenomenal world.

One background factor in Nāgārjuna's statements that at times totally negate the phenomenal world and at other times appear to recognize it would seem to be a change in perspective that supports his use of the same word in different meanings. We began by saying that Nāgārjuna develops his arguments by means of a method of distribution that would appear to be a distribution into a complementary relationship. But in actual fact his is a distribution into two extreme cases, and this results from the fact that he takes up for consideration only the smaller of the two spheres indicated by each of two valid complementary relationships.

For example, in IV. 6 he selects from two possible methods of distribution, namely, the complementary distribution into things "completely similar" and things "not completely similar" and that into things "completely dissimilar" and things "not completely dissimilar," the two former alternatives and links them together as if they represented a complementary distribution. Likewise, in XX. 21 he has chosen only one alternative of each of the two distributions into "that which really exists as something eternal and immutable" and "all else" and "that which does not exist at all" and "all else."

Thus, while confuting his opponents by simultaneously using two perspectives as it were and thereby negating everything, when it comes to discussing own-beinglessness and the possibility of change,

Nāgārjuna would appear to attain a new field of vision through a time shift that utilizes these two perspectives. He is, of course, clearly employing a subtle device in doing so.

When Nāgārjuna declares, as in Example 10, that there is no change even if there is own-being and no change even if there is no own-being, he is pointing to the movement leading towards the cessation of linguistic proliferation, namely, the movement from the profane to the sacred (the first vector), while when, as in Example 12, he says that "because there is change, things are without own-being," he would seem to be pointing to the movement in which the same linguistic proliferation that had been brought to cessation is reborn as provisional designation, namely, the movement from the sacred to the profane (the second vector). This corresponds to the resurrection of the phenomenal on the plane of emptiness in Chapter XXIV.

The immediate purpose of this device in Nāgārjuna's arguments whereby he utilizes two extreme interpretations of the sphere of meaning indicated by the basic term "own-being" was to effectively refute the views of his opponents. But it also serves over and beyond this as an effective means to reveal his own religious universe. Nor was this kind of device limited to the case of "own-being," and it was to function as a potent method supporting his use of *reductio ad absurdum* in all fields of discussion.

This term "own-being" (*svabhāva*) as used in the *Middle Stanzas*, which allows us to gain a glimpse of the secret of a device in Nāgārjuna's arguments that would appear to cast doubt on his adherence to the principles of logic and his strictly methodological manner of argumentation, is also important in that it leads us to a realm in which linguistic proliferation has been brought to cessation. It is probably only those who, guided by this term, have obtained a plurality of perspectives together with Nāgārjuna that will be able to comprehend the structure of his theory of "emptiness" in which the many negative propositions of the *Middle Stanzas* commingle with a small number of affirmative propositions.

CHAPTER TEN

THE AFFIRMATION OF THE PHENOMENAL WORLD: FROM THE SACRED TO THE PROFANE

The *Middle Stanzas* contain a number of passages in which Nāgārjuna gives expression to his own standpoint instead of quoting the views of his opponents and in which he furthermore makes mention of the "two factors" and their relationship in an affirmative proposition. One such example is VIII. 12, which has already been referred to in Chapter 3 and discussed as Example 1 in Chapter 4.

Example 1

pratītya kārakaḥ karma taṃ pratītya ca kārakam /
karma pravartate... // (VIII. 12)

(In dependence upon an action there arises an agent,
And in dependence upon an agent there arises an action.)

This verse may be rewritten without any change of meaning as follows:

pratītya karma kārakaḥ pravartate.
pratītya kārakaṃ karma pravartate. —(a)

And as in the case of our earlier examples, it may be formulaically expressed in the following manner:

(*M*ger *X*acc *Y*nom Zv) · (*M*ger *Y*acc *X*nom *Z*v) —(b)
*M*ger = *pratītya* (depending, in dependence).
*X*acc = *karma* (upon an action).
*Y*nom = *kārakaḥ* (an agent).
*Y*acc = *kārakaṃ* (upon an agent).
*X*nom = *karma* (an action).
Zv = *pravartate* (arises).

As was noted towards the end of Chapter 3, Nāgārjuna here

admits that something does arise. If we consider this verse in relation to the three features that were pointed out in Examples 3-8 in Chapter 7, it will be found that Feature 1 does not apply in this case, while Feature 2—syntactical connection—is quite explicit, for the two factors referred to by "*X*" and "*Y*" are indicated within the context of the connection between a gerund, accusative, nominative and verb. But the fact that both propositions in Example 1 are true is directly contrary to Feature 3. These points indicate that propositions such as this Example 1 serve a purpose in the arguments of the *Middle Stanzas* differing from that of the propositions in Examples 3-8.

Nāgārjuna's radical negation of the phenomenal world generally took the form of a critique of the realist views of his opponents, and in such cases negative propositions such as those in Examples 3-8 were appropriate. But at the same time Nāgārjuna also sought to redeem the profane phenomenal world as it is. In this case, the "sacralized profane"—namely, all dependently co-arisen things and their interrelationships—is presented in the form of affirmative propositions.

Propositions that describe dependent co-arising in affirmative terms are to be found, in addition to Example 1 (VIII. 12), also at IX. 5ab, XVIII. 6ab, XXIV. 10c, XXIV. 11c, etc. IX. 5ab reads as follows:

A certain thing (*y*) is indicated by a certain thing (*x*),

And a certain thing (*x*) is indicated by a certain thing (*y*).

(*ajyate kena cit kaś cit kiṃ cit kena cid ajyate/*)

This verse has the same structure as Example 1 in that the relationship between two things (*x* and *y*) is not subjected to a complementary distribution and the relationship between the two, whereby "( ) is indicated by ( )," is affirmed.

There are also instances of a proposition being affirmed—that is, Feature 3 being "true"—even when subjected to complementary distribution. XVIII. 8 is one such example, but this we wish to consider in Chapter 11. In order to understand the significance of these affirmed propositions in the *Middle Stanzas*, one has to understand the doctrine of dependent co-arising, which forms the core of Nāgārjuna's thought in the *Middle Stanzas*.

Although the doctrine of dependent co-arising constitutes the very crux of Śākyamuni's teachings, today it is extremely difficult to determine in detail the exact nature of his teaching relating to dependent co-arising. Instead of searching for the fundamental cause of the endless transmigration of living beings in some eternal entity such as Brahman or a cosmic self, dependent co-arising seeks it in various elements of the phenomenal world, such as human ignorance, cognition and action, and in the relations of cause and effect obtaining between them. In the closing period of what is known as Primitive (or Early) Buddhism, the doctrine of dependent co-arising came to be expressed in a systematic form that is referred to as the "twelvefold chain of dependent co-arising."

In the doctrine of dependent co-arising belonging to the period of Early Buddhism, the question of whether or not the individual members of the causal nexus possess any perduring and immutable reality (*svabhāva*) hardly arose. This was because when considered from the viewpoint of the early doctrine of dependent co-arising, maintaining as it did that the "world" had not been created by some eternal and imperishable god or similar entity, it was only natural that human ignorance, cognition and action, all pertaining to the world of transmigration, should be impermanent and without any intrinsic reality.

But by the time of Nāgārjuna the doctrine of dependent co-arising, with its denial of any eternal and immutable reality, was no longer fulfilling its purpose. This was because, as a result of the emphasis placed on the reality of the individual constituent elements of the world in the course of developments within Abhidharma philosophy in the period succeeding that of Early Buddhism, the doctrine of dependent co-arising, which ought to have been an expression of the negation of own-being (*svabhāva*), had become an expression of the affirmation of own-being. According to Abhidharma philosophy, dependent co-arising means that a certain constituent element of the world (or a combination of elements) (*x*) arises—or is arising—from another constituent element (or combination of elements) (*y*) in accordance with a consistent relationship obtaining between cause and effect. In other words, dependent co-arising in Abhidharma philosophy represents the causal relationship obtaining among a limited number of constituent elements of the world. In this case, *x* is considered to act as the cause from which *y* is born, and this presupposes the fact that *x* and *y* must exist each with their separate own-being. In Abhidharma philosophy a certain thing (*x*), possessing within itself its own existential base, enters into a relationship with another thing (*y*), different from itself (*x*) and also possessing within itself its own existential base. Thus the causal relationship posited by Abhidharma philosophy is a relationship between a certain thing (*x*) endowed with own-being and another thing (*y*) also endowed with own-being. On the basis of such ideas, Abhidharma philosophy further systematized and disseminated the doctrine of the twelvefold chain of dependent co-arising.

In the view of Nāgārjuna, this interpretation of causal relationships in Abhidharma philosophy ran counter to the spirit of Early Buddhism. Although it was true that Abhidharma philosophy was following a tradition going back to Early Buddhism in denying the existence of any creator-god or cosmic self and seeking to explain the origins of the world in terms of the causal relationships obtaining among constituent elements within the realm of experience, it had come to look upon the causes and effects themselves, the constituent members of these causal relationships, as being endowed with a perduring and immutable reality. Although Abhidharma philosophy had not abandoned the basic thesis of Buddhism which declared that "all things are impermanent," in the view of Abhidharma philosophy it was "man" (*pudgala*: the centre of personality considered to reside within the individual) as a complex of constituent elements that was impermanent, and the individual elements constituting "man" were eternal and unchanging. Nāgārjuna, on the other hand, held not only "man" but also the individual elements (*dharma*) of which he is composed to be impermanent. This is why Nāgārjuna's standpoint has been defined as advocating that "both *pudgala* and *dharma* are without self." Seeking as he did to attain to emptiness through the radical negation of the profane, he could not admit the reality of the constituent elements.

In Nāgārjuna's *Middle Stanzas* the doctrine of dependent co-arising also occupies a central position. But his theory of dependent co-arising, grounded on a critique of Abhidharma philosophy, incorporated a number of new ideas not to be found in earlier Buddhist traditions. In the first place, he extended the sphere of the members interrelated through dependent co-arising, and secondly he linked dependent co-arising and emptiness, which had until then constituted two separate currents of thought.

Many modern scholars have interpreted dependent co-arising as it is set forth in the *Middle Stanzas* as "interdependence." "Interdependence" means in this case that all things exist in interdependence upon one another, so that the existence (or arising) of *y* is possible only in dependence upon *x* and the existence (or arising) of *x* is possible only in dependence upon *y*, and that neither *x* nor *y* possesses within itself any permanent and unchanging existential base.[1] It is indeed true that one of the major distinguishing features of the *Middle Stanzas* lies in the fact that, compared with the doctrine of dependent co-arising in Early Buddhism and the early schools which, with a few exceptions, was explained as a one-directional relationship leading from one member (*aṅga*) *x* of the relationship to another member *y*, they emphasize a mutual relationship such that "*y* arises in dependence upon *x*" ($x \rightarrow y$) and "*x* arises in dependence upon *y*" ($y \rightarrow x$). This perspective of Nāgārjuna's was born of a more penetrating observation of the "dependently co-arising" phenomenal world, and it also served as the starting point for his negation of the independent existence of the constituent elements of the phenomenal world.

The meaning of dependent co-arising in the *Middle Stanzas* is

---

1. There is also an interpretation that would understand "interdependence" not simply as the interdependent relationship obtaining between two factors, but would maintain that the identity of *x* and *y* be a prerequisite for the interdependence of *x* and *y*. According to this interpretation, when standing in a "reciprocal relationship" such that *y* is incorporated by *x* when *y* is without own-being and *x* is incorporated by *y* when *x* is without own-being, "the identity of the two is established. If one conceives of interdependence as the mutual relationship existing between two independent entities that are not identical in this sense, it becomes impossible for them to be 'established through mutual dependence' " (Ueda Yoshifumi, *op.cit.*, p. 90). Ueda declares that "there exist simultaneously mutual exclusiveness and identity between fire and fuel" (*ibid.*, p. 91) and other factors. Historically speaking, this way of thinking in which the negation of one factor signifies the affirmation of the other factor belongs to the tradition of interpreting emptiness on the basis of implicative negation (*paryudāsa*) rather than that of interpreting it by means of absolute negation (*prasajyapratiṣedha*). In the history of Indian Mādhyamika thought the interpretation based on absolute negation is believed to have represented the main current of thought at least until the time of Candrakirti, after which there began to appear in India and also in Tibet people who interpreted emptiness on the basis of implicative negation. In the Yogācāra school, on the other hand, it may be assumed that emptiness was understood on the basis of implicative negation by the time of Bhāvaviveka (?-*ca.* 570). Cf. Saigusa Mitsuyoshi, "Ryūju no kū ni tsuite" (On Nāgārjuna's Emptiness), in *Daijō Bukkyō no seiritsushiteki kenkyū* (*op. cit.*), p. 286.

not, however, exhausted by interdependence alone. In the interpretation that would equate dependent co-arising with interdependence, the existence of the two or more members interrelated through dependent co-arising and the relationship obtaining between the members is affirmed. Dependent co-arising (*pratītya-samutpāda*) does in fact signify the arising (*samutpāda*) of a certain thing in dependence upon (*pratītya*) another thing, and it represents the affirmation of a relationship between two or more members. But in the case of dependent co-arising as elaborated in the *Middle Stanzas*, not only the existence of the two or more members involved in this relationship, but also the very relationship itself is negated. In other words, dependent co-arising as described in the *Middle Stanzas* has, in addition to the meaning of interdependence, also the meaning of "cessation of linguistic proliferation (*prapañca*)." In this latter case, dependent co-arising refers to a "sacred" state in which the "profane" in the form of linguistic proliferation has been annihilated. These two meanings of dependent co-arising are not, however, applicable simultaneously, for interdependence requires two or more members, while the cessation of linguistic proliferation means that the members participating in an interdependent relationship no longer exist. The members making up a relationship based on dependent co-arising are nothing other than a part of linguistic proliferation. If a certain relationship in the form of interdependence is held to be possible, then the existence of the various members making up that relationship must also be recognized. When linguistic proliferation has, on the other hand, ceased, no relationship whatsoever exists, nor do its constituent members. The absence of both a relationship and its constituent members means that there are also no words to express this relationship, and when language has ceased to function, there is also no arising of mental images. It is intimated in the *Middle Stanzas* that the world of words and images and that of dependent co-arising in which these have been extinguished are mutually exclusive.

But at the same time the single term "dependent co-arising" is used to refer both to the appearance assumed by this dependently co-arising mundane world and to the sacred that transcends the mundane world. This fact in itself indicates the proximity in which the two religious poles of the sacred and the profane stood to one another in the eyes of Nāgārjuna.

Dependent co-arising in its capacity as the sacred is, however, predicated in the *Middle Stanzas* only in negative terms. The view that the sacred is unchanging and that it is both unborn and imperishable is by no means unusual. For the Vedānta school the cosmic principle is unborn and undying, while in the *Bhagavadgītā*, a Hindu scripture, it is stated that although living beings die, the godhead is immortal,[2] and in Abhidharma philosophy too the constituent elements of space and *nirvāṇa* are held to be unborn and imperishable.[3] Even in the *Middle Stanzas* dependent co-arising or Dharma-nature (*dharmatā*) is held to be unborn and undying. But at the same time it is also impermanent. By way of contrast, in the Vedānta and other similar schools the cosmic principle, etc., were considered to be unborn and undying for the very reason that they are permanent. In other words, in the *Middle Stanzas* dependent co-arising rejects, with one or two exceptions, all predication, whereas in the Vedānta and other schools the sacred may be qualified in terms of existence and permanence. In the case of this latter standpoint the sacred exists as something different in nature from the profane that is to be negated, and in negating the profane the act of negation does not violate the realm of the sacred. But in the *Middle Stanzas* the force that negates the profane also impinges on the realm of the sacred, and the sacred can no longer be held to really exist. When considered in regard to the question of the distance between the two poles of the sacred and the profane, Abhidharma philosophy may be said to emphasize the distance separating them, whereas Vedānta thought and the conception of emptiness as represented by the *Middle Stanzas* both assert the identity of these two religious poles. But there is also a marked difference between these latter two currents of thought. In the *Middle Stanzas* the two poles are brought infinitely close to one another, but their very existence is itself negated, at least at the point when the profane is negated and the sacred manifests itself. In Vedānta thought, on the other hand, the profane merges with the really existent sacred and relinquishes its independent existence.

It is nevertheless true that the sacred is not adequately described

---

2. *Bhagavadgītā*, II. 18, XI. 18, etc.

3. In his *Conception of Buddhist Nirvāṇa* (Leningrad, 1927), Th. Stcherbatsky writes that the reality of the elements posited by the Sarvāstivādins "is very similar to the reality of the Sāṃkhya's undifferentiated matter (*prakṛti*), it is eternal, absolute death" (p. 32).

in the *Middle Stanzas*. Attempts to define in explicit terms the sacred, which appears in the *Middle Stanzas* under a variety of names such as "ultimate truth" (*paramārtha*), "thusness" (*tattva*), "emptiness" (*śūnyatā*) and "*nirvāṇa*," were not welcomed from the very beginnings of Buddhism. The view that no form of predication whatsoever can do full justice to the godhead or the fundamental cosmic principle is frequently encountered not only in Buddhism but also in Indian thought in general and even in the thought of regions outside of India. On the subject of the ultimate cosmic principle, the sages of the Upaniṣads said only "It is not so, it is not so" (*neti neti*). Nāgārjuna was also heir to this agnostic tradition, and W. Ruben considers him to have pushed this agnosticism as exemplified by the Upaniṣads to its very limits.[4]

As was noted above, the term "dependent co-arising," corresponding to the sacred, is in the *Middle Stanzas* qualified by a great many negative modifiers. But among the dozen or so modifiers given in the verses of salutation at the start of the *Middle Stanzas* there is one that does not have any negative connotations. This is the word "auspicious" (*śiva*), and it is worth taking note of the fact that, alongside modifiers with negative connotations such as "[dependent co-arising] which has no ceasing, no arising,... is quiescent of linguistic proliferation," Nāgārjuna applied to dependent co-arising a modifier lacking any negative affix. But in all three instances in which this word "*śiva*" appears in the *Middle Stanzas* it is employed in conjunction with the term "*upaśama*" (cessation), which has a negative connotation. Namely, the verses of salutation have "dependent co-arising which...is quiescent (*upaśama*) of linguistic proliferation, and is auspicious," V. 8 has "the cessation of that which is to be seen (i.e., objects of sight), which is auspicious," and XXV.24 has "the cessation of all objects, the cessation of linguistic proliferation is auspicious."

In the *Middle Stanzas* (VIII. 5ab) Nāgārjuna states that "when there is no action, etc., both *dharma* and non-*dharma* do not exist" (*dharmādharmau na vidyete kriyādīnām asaṃbhave/*). But in saying this he did not mean to imply that "therefore action, etc., really exist for the world at large and Mādhyamikans." Nor was he resting on the premise that neither *dharma* nor non-*dharma* exist in any sense of the

---

4. Walter Ruben, *Die gesellschaftliche Entwicklung in alten Indien*, IV, *Die Entwicklung der Philosophie* (Berlin: Akadamie-Verlag, 1971), p. 193.

word whatsoever. *Dharma* and non-*dharma* do exist even in Nāgārjuna's system, although it is a moot point in just what sense they exist. From this premise and the statement that "when there is no action, etc., both *dharma* and non-*dharma* do not exist" is drawn the conclusion that "action, etc., do exist." Here the exact nature of their "existence" comes into question. It is not existence in the sense of the existence of a perduring and immutable entity. In what manner, then, was it possible in the view of Nāgārjuna for action and also *dharma* and non-*dharma* to exist?

As noted in the previous chapter, it is stated in the *Middle Stanzas* (XXIV. 14) that "for whom emptiness is befitting, everything is befitting." This may be taken to mean that someone who has understood emptiness is able to understand why things arise and disappear. In this case "everything is befitting" does not refer to the arising and disappearance of things as they are observed in general everyday life. It is only with the premise that emptiness is befitting, or understood, that one can say that everything is possible, but not the reverse. Some modern scholars have been seen to adopt the interpretation that since it may be observed in everyday linguistic activity that things arise and disappear, things are therefore without own-being and empty. In this interpretation the mutations of the everyday world would appear to represent the basis of own-beinglessness. But if one posits the own-beinglessness of things in order to explain the arising and disappearance of things in the everyday world, it no longer becomes necessary to propound a mode of dependent co-arising in which linguistic proliferation has ceased. It is only in regard to changes in the conventional world (*saṃvṛti*) as seen through the eyes of someone who has understood emptiness or the cessation of linguistic proliferation that Nāgārjuna acknowledges the existence of change in the everyday world. As far as the *Middle Stanzas* are concerned, the question of the nature of the structure of things or of the world itself is virtually meaningless. It is through whose eyes the world is seen that matters. Therefore, even though the world seen by an ordinary person and that seen by an enlightened person who has comprehended emptiness may, objectively speaking, be identical, for the Mādhyamikan in pursuit of an understanding of emptiness they differ from one another.

Let us now return to the verse quoted above. In exactly what sense is "everything befitting"? It cannot mean that everything exists with its own-being, as was advocated in Abhidharma philosophy, for once emptiness has been understood, the non-existence of own-being must also be admitted. Verse 18 of the same chapter informs us of the manner in which "everything is befitting."

> Whatever is dependent co-arising, that we declare to be emptiness. (ab)
>
> It (emptiness) is appropriating [an object] to make [its existence] known (i.e., provisional designation) and it is the middle way. (cd)

By declaring dependent co-arising, namely, this dependently co-arising world, to be emptiness, Nāgārjuna first asserts that the phenomenal world that has evolved as the conventional is, properly speaking, the sacred in the form of emptiness.[5] This expression tallies with the expression "form is emptiness" in the Prajñāpāramitā scriptures. Verse 18ab describes the experience of a person "for whom emptiness is befitting (or established)," alluded to in verse 14a.

In verse 18cd emptiness is identified with provisional designation, by which it is meant that by appropriating, or in dependence upon (*upādāya*) an object one incorporates it into one's sphere of cognition and "makes" its existence provisionally "known" (*prajñapti*) by means of language. The entity whose existence is thus provisionally made known by means of language is of course not an entity the constituent elements of which really exist as in the case of Abhidharma philosophy. Immediately after it has been declared that dependent co-arising is emptiness (18ab), emptiness is now once again described in positive terms (18cd). This tallies with the expression "emptiness is form" in the Prajñāpāramitā scriptures. What is described in positive terms, corresponding to provisional designation, manifests itself in concrete form as linguistic proliferation, namely, individual phenomena. This may appear—at least as far as can be surmised by an ordinary person—to be almost identical with the world of linguistic proliferation as observed by ordinary people. But the conventional that has attained to emptiness and has then been reborn—that is, has reentered linguistic proliferation—is no longer the same as the world experienced by the ordinary person through the medium of everyday linguistic activity (*vyavahāra*). It is the profane that has once

5. Here "dependent co-arising" probably refers to the profane negatee, i.e., linguistic proliferation, although when it is stated that "dependent co-arising is emptiness," dependent co-arising is already being viewed by an enlightened person and it represents the sacralized profane.

died and been reborn, and it is qualitatively different in some way or other from the profane that has undergone no self-negation whatsoever.

Chapter XXVI of the *Middle Stanzas* is devoted to an examination of the twelvefold chain of dependent co-arising. This chapter and the final chapter entitled "An Examination of [False] Views" that immediately follows it occupy a unique position in the *Middle Stanzas*, and Dr. Ui Hakuju has opined that, practically speaking, the arguments of the *Middle Stanzas* end with Chapter XXV, and Chapter XXVI should be regarded as a sort of appendix.[6] It is indeed true that the development of the arguments in the final two chapters does differ from that of the foregoing chapters, and so it would seem to be incumbent upon us to reconsider here whether or not these two chapters, particularly Chapter XXVI which is so important for our present inquiry, should be looked upon as actually standing apart from the arguments of the preceding chapters.

In the *Middle Stanzas*—at least in the form in which they are preserved today—dependent co-arising is at the very outset said to be "quiescent of linguistic proliferation," and in Chapter XXIV it is stated that "dependent co-arising is emptiness" (v. 18), after which it is taken up for consideration once again in Chapter XXVI. But dependent co-arising as expounded in the first twenty-five chapters represents the ultimate truth (*paramārtha*) that transcends language, whereas dependent co-arising as described in Chapter XXVI is expressed in terms of Abhidharma philosophy, which Nāgārjuna had until then been criticizing. In other words, it is not the dependent co-arising of non-arising but the dependent co-arising of arising that is set forth in this Chapter XXVI.

Commentators of the *Middle Stanzas* have long been aware of the fact that the doctrine of dependent co-arising developed in Chapter XXVI differs in nature from that of the foregoing chapters. According to the *Akutobhayā*, "Here [the opponent] advocates as follows: '[Until now] you [the Mādhyamikan] have taught the entry into ultimate truth (*paramārtha*) by means of the teaching of the Mahāyāna, but now you

---

6. Ui Hakuju, "*Kokuyaku Chūron*" (Japanese Translation of the *Madhyamakakārikā*), *Kokuyaku Daizōkyō* (Japanese Translation of the Tripiṭaka), Ronbu (Treatises), Vol. 5 (1920), p. 240, n. 127; cf. Hatani Ryōtai, *Kokuyaku Issaikyō* (Japanese Translation of the Tripiṭaka), Chūganbu (Mādhyamika), Vol. 1 (1925), p . 233, n. 1.

should teach the entry into ultimate truth by means of the teaching of the Śrāvaka'," whereupon the twelve verses of Chapter XXVI are given in reply.[7] Thus the author of the *Akutobhayā* was also aware of the fact that the doctrine of dependent co-arising in Chapter XXVI was that of the Śrāvaka Vehicle, and it is evident that "the teaching of the Śrāvaka" alluded to here represents the doctrines of Abhidharma philosophy.

Piṅgala also identifies the doctrine of dependent co-arising in Chapter XXVI of the *Middle Stanzas* with the "Śrāvaka Dharma": "Question: [Until now] you have been expounding the path to ultimate truth in accordance with the Mahāyāna Dharma. Now we wish to hear you expound how the Śrāvaka Dharma enters the path to ultimate truth." In reply to this question, the twelve verses of Chapter XXVI are then given.[8] Piṅgala's commentary on this section has many points of similarity to that of the *Akutobhaya*. In his Japanese translation of the *Akutobhayā*, Teramoto Enga makes the following comment: "Nāgārjuna adopted the Sarvāstivādin doctrine of the twelvefold chain of dependent co-arising as it was, and without undertaking any examination of the doctrine of dependent co-arising in Fundamental Buddhism, namely, the pristine view of dependent co-arising prior to the division into the Theravāda school and the Mahāsāṃghika school, he transmitted as it was the traditional doctrine of dependent co-arising based on karma in the Hīnayāna teachings inherited from the past and did nothing more than simply sublate karmic dependent co-arising by means of the idea that everything is empty."[9]

But was this in fact the case? From the very opening chapter of the *Middle Stanzas* Nāgārjuna had been directing his criticism primarily at the doctrine of dependent co-arising in Abhidharma philosophy. Hence it is inconceivable that at the end of the same work he should have presented with no modification whatsoever the Abhidharma doctrine of dependent co-arising which he had until then been criticizing. There must have been some other reason for introducing the traditional doctrine of

7. Tibetan Tripiṭaka (Peking Edition), Vol. 95, p. 44, f. 4, l. 4.

8. Taishō Tripiṭaka, Vol. 30, p. 36b, l. 18.

9. Teramoto Enga (transl. and annotated), *Ryūju-zō Chūron Muisho* (The Commentary *Akutobhayā* on the *Madhyamakakārikā* by Nāgārjuna; Tōkyō : Kokusho Kankōkai, 1974 [repr.]), p. 529.

dependent co-arising. Is it perhaps not possible to regard it as the result of his having attempted to incorporate—or having succeeded in incorporating—the Abhidharma doctrine of dependent co-arising into his own system of thought?

It has already been pointed out by many researchers that Nāgārjuna does not simply reject Abhidharma philosophy. For example, after having shown by means of the example of "passion" (*rāga* = mental defilements) and "one who is impassioned" (*rakta*) in Chapter VI that in Nāgārjuna's doctrine of dependent co-arising the arising of a certain member *y* in dependence upon another member *x* is negated, Saigusa Mitsuyoshi adds the following comment: "But Nāgārjuna, who does not make light of the doctrinal concepts of the Abhidharma, does not by any means ignore the twelve members [of the causal nexus]. The whole of Chapter XXVI is devoted to them, and in XXIII. 23 (v. 22 of Kumārajīva's [Chinese] translation), the extinction of delusion→the extinction of ignorance→the extinction of the formative forces [*saṃskāra*] is expounded."[10] It is indeed true that in the *Middle Stanzas* Nāgārjuna not merely criticizes Abhidharma philosophy, but also seeks out the basic concepts for building his own system in this same Abhidharma philosophy. For example, the four types of causes and conditions negated in Chapter I have their basis in the philosophic system of the Abhidharma. If Nāgārjuna's positive evaluation of Abhidharma philosophy in Chapter XXVI does not represent a compromise, for what reason then did he criticize the Abhidharma doctrine of dependent co-arising and yet at times appear to "affirm" it?

In the *Prajñāpradīpa*, a commentary on the *Middle Stanzas* by Bhāvaviveka, the author explains that Chapter XXVI was written "in order to expound dependent co-arising in its form as everyday linguistic activity (*vyavahāra*)."[11] He too points out that Chapter XXVI describes not dependent co-arising in which linguistic proliferation has ceased, but dependent co-arising that has assumed the form of linguistic proliferation. He makes the following comment in regard to verse 9cd ("in this

10. Saigusa Mitsuyoshi, "Engi no kōsatsu" (A Consideration of Dependent Co-arising), *Indogaku Bukkyōgaku Kenkyū*, Vol. 6, No. 2 (1958), p.355, n. 44.

11. Tibetan Tripiṭaka (Peking Edition), Vol. 95, p. 257, f. 2, 1. 2; Kajiyama Yūichi, "Chūganha no jūnishi engi kaishaku" (The Interpretation of the Twelvefold Chain of Dependent Co-arising in the Mādhyamika School), in *Bukkyō shisōshi* (The History of Buddhist Thought), Vol. 3 (1980), p. 121.

manner this aggregate of suffering alone arises" [*kevalasyaivam etasya duḥkhaskandhasya saṃbhavaḥ//*]):

> That this aggregate [of suffering] pertaining to the truth of everyday linguistic activity arises refers to the dependent co-arising of everyday linguistic activity. As was explained in the chapters that [demonstrated that dependent co-arising or things] do not arise as ultimate truth, [the dependently co-arisen] does not exist.[12]

Thus Bhāvaviveka posits two types of dependent co-arising, that of ultimate truth and that of conventional truth (or the truth of everyday linguistic activity). The relationship and distinction between these two truths in Bhāvaviveka's system requires further inquiry,[13] but here we simply wish to use his comments as an approach to Nāgārjuna's thought. It should at any rate be evident that Bhāvaviveka also understood dependent co-arising as it is described in Chapter XXVI to represent conventional truth (*saṃvṛtisatya*).

The fact that dependent co-arising as set forth in Chapter XXVI is that which has assumed the form of linguistic proliferation is also recognized by Candrakīrti in his commentary, the *Prasannapadā*. But, unlike the author of the *Akutobhayā* and Piṅgala, he does not equate the content of Chapter XXVI with the teachings of the Śrāvaka Vehicle. According to Candrakīrti, Chapter XXVI was composed in response to the question "What is the nature of dependent co-arising as it is mentioned in XXIV. 18 (which represents, as it were, the conclusion to the *Middle Stanzas*)?," and it elaborates upon the content of provisional designation alluded to in this verse. Nevertheless, Candrakīrti's explanation of dependent co-arising in his commentary on Chapter XXVI

---

12. Tibetan Tripiṭaka (Peking Edition), Vol. 95, p. 258, f. 5, ll. 8ff; Kajiyama Yūichi, *op. cit.*, p. 131.

13. In his commentary on the *Middle Stanzas* Sthiramati writes as follows: "All that has been expounded [in the above] is like a dream or an illusion. It all exists on account of harmonious interaction [and is without any immutable substantiality]. The distinctions between and discrimination of the various modes of existence are [non-existent] like a *gandharva*-castle. All things that have arisen are born of conditions. Explaining these in detail is the method for negating birth from conditions [i.e., dependent co-arising] pertaining to the conventional." (Manji Tripiṭaka, Sec. 26, Vol. 1, p. 73) Thus according to Sthiramati, in Chapter XXVI all dependently co-arisen things, which resemble dreams and illusions, are negated.

contains a considerable number of positive expressions. Quoting the *Āryaśālistamba-sūtra*, he explains the twelvefold chain of dependent co-arising in the following manner:

> Thus the twelvefold chain of dependent co-arising (*dvādaśaḥ pratītyasamutpādaḥ*) is such that [the members] become causes for one another, [the members] become conditions for one another, it is not impermanent (*anitya*), not permanent (*nitya*),... it is not something that is perishable (*kṣayadharma*), it is not something that is imperishable (*akṣayadharma*),... it has been active (*pravṛtta*), it is uninterrupted (*anucchinna*), and it continues (*anupravartate*) like the current of a river.[14]

In the latter part of this quotation from the *Āryaśālistamba-sūtra* dependent co-arising is expressed in positive terms. A more detailed examination of Candrakīrti's interpretation of dependent co-arising will be undertaken in Chapter 13, but in a word he may be said to be emphasizing that aspect of dependent co-arising pertaining to the conventional and to the phenomenal world of everyday experience.[15] But needless to say, for him too the conventional remains to the last the world as it appears to Buddhists—namely, as seen through the eyes of an enlightened person—and it is not the everyday world that his opponents such as the adherents of the Sāṃkhya and Vaiśeṣika schools claim really exists.

The existence or arising of the members interrelated through dependent co-arising as described in Chapter XXVI is not mentioned for the first time in the *Middle Stanzas* in Chapter XXVI. As an expression of his own viewpoint, Nāgārjuna states in VIII.12 that "in dependence upon (*pratītya*) an action there arises an agent, and in dependence upon (*pratītya*) an agent there arises an action." Here the existence of the members (agent and action) interrelated through dependent co-arising,

---

14. *Prasannapadā*, p. 566, l. 3ff. In the *Śālistamba-sūtra* it is stated that "internal (*adhyātmika*) dependent co-arising is to be examined in regard to five causes." Among these five causes, the fourth is "the birth of a large effect from a minor cause" and the fifth is "the continuation of something similar to it (i.e., the cause)." In these two cases too dependent co-arising is expressed not in terms of cessation (*nivṛtti*) but as something positive.

15. Cf. *Prasannapadā*, p. 54, l. 11; p. 189, l. 2.

as well as their interrelationship (the arising of [ ] in dependence upon [ ]), is clearly acknowledged.[16] But the twelvefold chain of dependent co-arising described in Chapter XXVI lacks this aspect of "*inter*relationship" to be seen in Chapter VIII. In other words, the twelvefold chain of dependent co-arising is not such that *y* arises in dependence upon *x* and *x* arises in dependence upon *y*. In the view of Nāgārjuna, however, the members interrelated through dependent co-arising include not only those such as ignorance, formative forces and consciousness, etc., which have a fixed orientation, but also those such as action and agent or traverser and traversing, which are interdependently related. Therefore, as far as Nāgārjuna's doctrine of dependent co-arising is concerned, the distinction of whether *y* arises in dependence upon *x* or *x* arises in dependence upon *y* is not of such great importance as it is in an inquiry into the thought of Early Buddhism and Abhidharma philosophy.

In XVIII. 5 Nagarjuna writes, "Mental defilements and action arise from discriminating thought (*vikalpa*); [discriminating thought] arises from linguistic proliferation (*prapañca*)," and he thus recognizes a causal relationship between these entities. In this case the direction of the moment whereby "mental defilements and action arise from discriminating thought" is fixed, and the reverse is not possible. The causal relationship consisting of "linguistic proliferation→discriminating thought→ mental defilements and action" may be described as Nāgārjuna's "threefold chain of dependent co-arising." Just as the evolution of the world was described in terms of the twelvefold chain of dependent co-arising, so does this threefold chain of dependent co-arising in the *Middle Stanzas* also describe the evolution of the world. And in this case "dependent co-arising" is described in positive terms.

It should now be evident that the existence or arising of the members interrelated through dependent co-arising is recognized not only in Chapter XXVI. Dependent co-arising as the ultimate truth in which linguistic proliferation has ceased and dependent co-arising which has assumed the form of linguistic proliferation coexist in the *Middle Stanzas*. But it is hardly conceivable that they should have been simply mentioned side by side without the presumption of some kind of

16. See Tachikawa Musashi, "*Chūron* ni okeru sezoku to shōgi" (The Conventional and Ultimate Truth in the *Middle Stanzas*), *Tōyō Gakujutsu Kenkyū*, Vol. 16, No. 5 (1977), p. 15. For examples in which Nāgārjuna's own views are expressed in an affirmative form in the *Middle Stanzas*, see Table 3 (pp. 80-81).

relationship between them. It is to be assumed that Nāgārjuna had an explicit reason for expounding these two versions of dependent co-arising and that they are in some way linked to one another in the *Middle Stanzas*.

Is it perhaps not possible to interpret the various aspects of dependent co-arising in the *Middle Stanzas* as indicating the basic structure of religious praxis, which is such that when the profane has been negated the sacred manifests itself and then operates through the medium of the profane? It is, namely, the way of thinking behind Abhidharma philosophy that is being criticized when Nāgārjuna negates the arising of the dependently co-arisen, and this corresponds to the extinction of the profane (a). In defining dependent co-arising as "quiescent of linguistic proliferation" in the verses of salutation and elsewhere, Nāgārjuna is seeking to describe by negative means dependent co-arising as ultimate truth (b). But when he says, "dependent co-arising is auspicious," he is now attempting to describe it as something positive (b'). And the positive interpretation of the traditional twelvefold chain of dependent co-arising, i.e., "conditioned by ignorance there are the formative forces, conditioned by the formative forces there is consciousness, etc.," represents one facet of linguistic proliferation when dependent co-arising as conceived of in Abhidharma philosophy has been recaptured through the eyes of an enlightened one. The profane that has been brought to "death" —or led to cessation—has, namely, been "reborn" (a').[17] In the case of the *Middle Stanzas*, the manifestation and functioning of the sacred within the profane takes place through the sacralization of the phenomenal world. The profane in the form of everyday linguistic activity first moves towards cessation (*nivṛtti*), and once the agent of religious praxis—the "cultivation" (*bhāvanā*) mentioned in XXVI.11 may be given as an example of this religious praxis—has fathomed the meaning of emptiness, it is reborn before the eyes of the enlightened one who has understood linguistic proliferation and begins to function. The sacred itself does not show itself; it merely lends its power to what was formerly the profane and makes its presence felt in the background. The profane that has been reborn vested with the power of the sacred represents the sacralized profane.

---

17. See Nagao Gajin, "Bukkyō no shisō to rekishi" (The Thought and History of Buddhism), in *Sekai no meicho, Daijō butten* (Famous Books of the World: Mahāyāna Scriptures; Tōkyō: Chūō Kōronsha, 1967), p. 47.

Dependent co-arising as described in Chapter XXVI of the *Middle Stanzas* should probably be described as sacralized everyday linguistic activity. The fact that when he came to the end of his *Middle Stanzas* Nāgārjuna employed a mode of expression borrowed from the Sarvāstivādins, who had in fact been the main target of his criticism, does not mean that he adopted it uncritically; rather, it is to be surmised that he composed Chapter XXVI because he considered his own criticism to have been concluded and the views of his opponents to have also been incorporated within his own thesis.

Insofar that they both negate any eternal and immutable cosmic principle and the substantiality of all things, the concepts of emptiness and dependent co-arising have much in common. In this sense they together constituted a powerful antithesis to orthodox Brahmanism. But in another sense these two concepts are incompatible with one another, for dependent co-arising is at any rate something positive in that it implies arising and coming into existence, whereas emptiness refers to an unremitting process of negation or the state resulting from such a process. Thus, although both emptiness and dependent co-arising are grounded on the major premise of Buddhism that both the world and all individual entities in the world are impermanent and by no means eternal and immutable, they point in the opposite directions of negation and affirmation. Emptiness represents the negation of the existence of the profane, while dependent co-arising implies in some sense or another an affirmation of the existence of the world and its constituent elements, namely, the profane or the conventional.

If we consider religious praxis in general, it will be found to embody three elements, namely, (i) the recognition that one's activities and very existence, as well as the group to which one belongs, must be negated on account of the fact that they are profane; (ii) praxis as a method to remedy this situation; and (iii) the goal or result that is attained or obtained by means of this praxis. Emptiness corresponds to the goal or result of (iii), while dependent co-arising in the sense described above is the profane world as it is understood in the recognition of (i) and the existence of which must be negated . This world that is to be negated is regarded as the cause in relation to the result in the form of emptiness. The means or "path" for leading from this cause to the result is nothing other than the process of negating the profane world, a world which in the

Middle Stanzas Nāgārjuna considers primarily from its aspect of linguistic proliferation (*prapañca*).

As has already been seen in the foregoing chapters, the greater part of the *Middle Stanzas* is devoted to the task of negating the profane. The theoretical basis for the execution of this task was the thesis that things do not have any permanent intrinsic reality and that they exist interdependently. Dependent co-arising as it is comprehended in the causal stage (i) also serves in the *Middle Stanzas* as the theoretical basis for the method in (ii). Furthermore, when Nāgārjuna says, "Whatever is dependent co-arising, that we declare to be emptiness," " dependent co-arising" refers to the profane that has been reborn on coming in contact with the sacred as the result of a continuous process of negation. The dependent co-arising that is alluded to in the verses of salutation when it is said that "dependent co-arising is quiescent of linguistic proliferation" is also this same dependent co-arising which is synonymous with emptiness. Dependent co-arising in the *Middle Stanzas* thus has an extremely structured and multifaceted character. And by interpreting dependent co-arising in this manner, Nāgārjuna linked the concept of dependent co-arising with that of emptiness. As we have already noted on more than one occasion, XXIV.18ab quoted above represents a succinct expression of the immediate contiguity of the sacred to the profane, namely, the sacralization of the phenomenal world, which lies at the crux of the thought of the *Middle Stanzas*.

CHAPTER ELEVEN

TETRALEMMAS IN THE *MIDDLE STANZAS*

Either or both of the two factors in the propositions whereby Nāgārjuna describes dependent co-arising in the *Middle Stanzas* are distributed into two, three or four cases. Among these different modes of distribution, that into three or four cases has traditionally been called the "tetralemma" (*catuṣkoṭi*). The negation that occurs in all types of distribution, namely, the negation of one of the resultant cases (non-...), represents the negation of the term that appears in the noun phrase constituting one element of the proposition and it is not the negation of the main verb in the verb phrase. In the case of the *Middle Stanzas*, the former—i.e., the negation of a term—is unrelated to the truth value of the proposition as a whole, which is determined by the latter form of negation.[1] But in a number of later interpretations of the tetralemma this distinction between the negation of a noun phrase and the negation of a verb phrase would not appear to have been strictly observed.

The tetralemma in the *Middle Stanzas* is expressed in either one of the following two forms:

I. A certain thing is neither *M*, nor non-*M*, nor both *M* and non-*M*, nor neither *M* nor non-*M*.

II. A certain thing is either *M*, or non-*M*, or both *M* and non-*M*, or neither *M* nor non-*M*.

(Let us assume here that the universe of discourse is the entire universe.)

In the case of the former (I), the four propositions, each incorporating one of the cases resulting from the distribution, are expressed in the negative and form as a whole a conjunctive proposition. In the case of the

1. Cf. *Middle Stanzas*, XXV. 14.

latter (II), on the other hand, each of the four propositions is expressed in the affirmative and together they form a disjunctive proposition. The tetralemma is to be found in Buddhist literature ever since the Early Canon, but it does not appear in Hindu literature—at least not in the literature of the orthodox Brahmanical schools—and so it has long attracted attention as being indicative of a distinctive feature of Buddhist thinking. Yet the logical structure of this formula has to this day not been clarified.

What does the third case of the tetralemma—"both *M* and non-*M*"—actually mean? To say that something is simultaneously both *M* and non-*M* is, according to formal logic, a contradiction. Did the Buddhists present this third case in full awareness of the fact that it represented a contradiction? Or did they possess a "special logic" of their own that did not recognize (or "transcended") the law of contradiction? "Neither *M* nor non-*M*" in the fourth case is also difficult to comprehend. Generally speaking, a thing is either *M* or non-*M*. Yet the tetralemma would have that a certain thing is neither *M* nor non-*M*. Does this not represent a violation of the law of the excluded middle?

The tetralemma would thus at first sight appear to contain aspects incompatible with the basic rules of formal logic. It is perhaps for this reason that among modern Buddhist scholars there are some who consider the germs of a logic differing from traditional so-called formal logic of the West to be embodied in the tetralemma, especially in the form in which it appears in the *Middle Stanzas*. But as will become evident in the course of our inquiries below, the tetralemma in the *Middle Stanzas* does observe basic rules of logic such as the laws of contradiction and the excluded middle. The reason that these rules would appear to have been violated is that the *Middle Stanzas* were in later ages interpreted on the basis of a confusion between the two types of negation alluded to above.

In the approximately 450 verses of the *Middle Stanzas* the distribution of one of the two factors of a proposition into two, three or four cases appears about eighty times, and among these a distribution into three or four cases occurs a little less than thirty times. (The distribution into three cases may be regarded as an incomplete tetralemma.) As was noted above, tetralemmas may be divided into two major groups: those expressed in negative form and conjunctive (Group I) and those expressed in affirmative form and disjunctive (Group II). Group I is further divided into three types. The first type (Type 1) represents a complete tetralemma in that it has four cases, and it is again subdivided into two types. The first (Type 1-1) may be referred to as the "self, other, both and no cause" type, while in the second subtype (Type 1-2) the four cases are expressed as "*M*, non-*M*, both *M* and non-*M*, and neither *M* nor non-*M*." In regard to content, the former has the same basic structure as the latter, but since it plays an important role in the arguments of the *Middle Stanzas*, appearing for example at the start of Chapter I, it is here dealt with separately.

Type 2 has the first three cases of Type 1 but lacks the fourth case. As with Type 1, Type 2 may also be subdivided into two further types, namely, that in which the three cases are expressed as "self, other, and both" (Type 2-1) and that in which they are expressed as "*M*, non-*M*, and both *M* and non-*M*" (Type 2-2).

Type 3 represents the type with the first, second and fourth cases, and it too is subdivided into two further types. The basic structure of the first type (Type 3-1) is similar to that of the first, second and fourth cases of the type expressed as "*M*, non-*M*, both *M* and non-*M*, and neither *M* nor non-*M*" (Type 1-2), but it is characterized by a syntactical feature. The first case is, namely, expressed by a past passive participle, the second by a negative prefix and past passive participle, and the fourth by a present participle. Type 3-2 is that expressed as "*M*, non-*M*, and a third party other than *M* and non-*M*."

Group II is also divided into Type 1 and Type 2. As was noted above, Type 1 has all four cases, while Type 2 lacks the third case. The distinguishing features of each of the above types may be summarized as in Table 4 (pp. 136-137).

I.1 is an example of Type 1-1 of the tetralemma as it appears in the *Middle Stanzas* (namely, the type that is expressed in the negative form, is conjunctive, has all four cases, and may be referred to as the "self, other, both, and no cause" type).

Example 13

na svato nāpi parato na dvābhyāṃ nāpy ahetutaḥ/
utpannā jātu vidyante bhāvāḥ .....// (I.1)

(Things are born neither from self, nor from another, nor from both

both [self and another], nor without cause.)

The content of Example 13 may be rewritten as a conjunction of the following four negative propositions:

a) Things are not born from self, and

b) Things are not born from another, and

c) Things are not born from both [self and another], and

d) Things are not born without cause.

In other words, things are not born with themselves as the cause, nor are they born with others as the cause, with both themselves and others as the cause, or without any cause. In short, they are not born at all.

In this example "self" and "other" are considered to be contradictories, and the union or sum of the sphere of self and the sphere of other represents the entire universe of discourse (i. e., the cause of all things), while the intersection of these two spheres is the null set (ϕ). If the universe of discourse is confined to the cause of all things, then self and other may be said to represent the result of a complementary distribution. Therefore, if the sphere of self is symbolized by "M," the sphere of other may be expressed as "$\tilde{M}/D$," which means the set complementary to M with reference to the entire universe of discourse (D), namely, the cause of all things. The third case "both [self and other]" indicates the union of the spheres of self and other. The fourth case "without cause" signifies an absence of any cause, with neither self nor other acting as a cause.

Let us now represent the sphere of self (M) by means of an upturned semicircle and the sphere of other ($\tilde{M}$) by means of a downturned semicircle. Then the union of self and other ($M \cup \tilde{M}$), namely, "both," may be represented by joining these two semicircles to form a complete circle. This circle represents the universe of discourse. In this third case the existence of both the sphere of self and that of other is recognized. "Without cause" in the fourth case means "neither self nor other," and since it indicates a sphere standing apart from both the sphere of self (M) and the sphere of other ($\tilde{M}$), it may be said to represent the complement of the union of M and $\tilde{M}$ with reference to the universe of discourse "D" (the cause of all things). Therefore, the fourth case may be symbolized as "$(M \cup \tilde{M})/D$." If we represent the non-existence of the sphere of self and

TABLE 4

Group	Type		First Case	Second Case	Third Case	Fourth Case
Group I	Type 1 (with 4 cases)	1	From self	From other	From both	Without cause
		2	*M*	Non-*M*	Both *M* and non-*M*	Neither *M* nor non-*M*
	Type 2 (with 1st, 2nd and 3rd cases)	1	From self	From other	From both	
		2	*M*	Non-*M*	Both *M* and non-*M*	
	Type 3 (with 1st, 2nd and 4th cases)	1	*M* (past participle)	Non-*M* (negative prefix + past participle)		*M′* (present participle)*
		2	*M*	Non-*M*		Third party other than *M* and non-*M*
Group II	Type 1 (with 4 cases)		*M*	Non-*M*	Both *M* and non-*M*	Neither *M* nor non-*M*
	Type 2 (with 1st, 2nd and 4th cases)		*M*	Non-*M*		Neither *M* nor non-*M*

* The present participle *M′* refers to something other than *M* and non-*M*.
(In this table the question of whether or not the universe of discourse corresponds to the entire universe is not treated.)

TABLE 4

Negative/ Affirmative	Conjunctive/ Disjunctive	Chapters and Verses in *Middle Stanzas*
Negative	Conjunctive	I.1; XII.1; XII.9; XII.10.
Negative	Conjunctive	XXII.12; XXV.10,13,16; XXV.17; XXV.18; XXV.22; XXV.23; XXVII.13; XXVII.20.
Negative	Conjunctive	XXIII.20.
Negative	Conjunctive	I.7; II.24-25; VII.20; VIII.7,8,9,10,11.
Negative	Conjunctive	II.1; II.12; VII.14; VII.22; XI.3,4,5; XXIII.17-18.
Negative	Conjunctive	II.8; II.15.
Affirmative	Disjunctive	XVIII.8.
Affirmative	Disjunctive	XVIII.6.

the sphere of other by describing the two semicircles with dotted lines, the fourth case may be depicted by joining the two dotted semicircles to form a complete circle. The universe of discourse for each of the four cases is illustrated in Diagram 13.

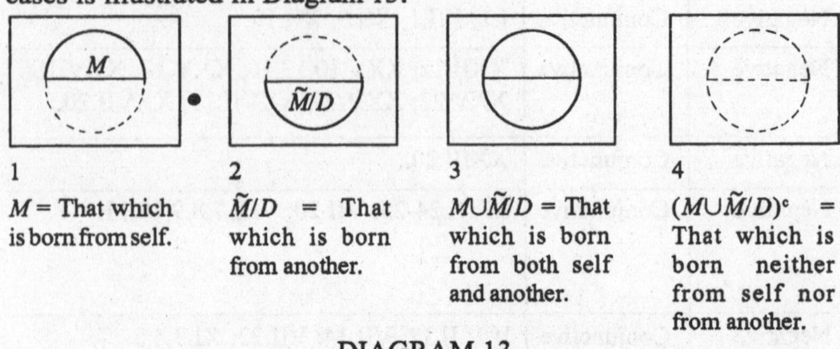

1 M = That which is born from self.

2 $\tilde{M}/D$ = That which is born from another.

3 $M \cup \tilde{M}/D$ = That which is born from both self and another.

4 $(M \cup \tilde{M}/D)^c$ = That which is born neither from self nor from another.

DIAGRAM 13

Diagram 13 shows us that in the case of Example 13, which has all four cases, the demonstration of the fact that "things are not born from anywhere" is in practice completed with the first two cases. It is also evident from the diagram that the third case is no more than a confirmation of what was stated in the first two cases. And since the dotted lines indicate the non-existence of any corresponding sphere, the fourth case requires no demonstration. (The Chinese Hua-yen and some other schools give a different interpretation which will be discussed in the next chapter.)

Examples of the tetralemma other than the "self, other, both, and no cause" type but still containing all four cases (Type 1-2) appear in the *Middle Stanzas* mainly towards the end. One such example reads as follows:

Example 14

...na bhāvo nābhāvo nirvāṇam iti yujyate // (XXV. 10cd)

(It is not proper to say that *nirvāṇa* is an existent nor that it is a non-existent.)

bhaved abhāvo bhāvaś ca nirvāṇam ubhayaṃ katham / (XXV. 13ab)

(How could *nirvāṇa* be both an existent and a non-existent?)

naivābhāvo naiva bhāvo nirvāṇam ... vidyate / (XXV. 16ab)

(The fact that *nirvāṇa* is neither an existent nor a non-existent is unacceptable.)

The sum of existent things (*bhāva*) in the first case and non-existent things (*abhāva*) in the second case constitutes the entire universe of discourse, and the intersection of the sphere of existent things and that of non-existent things is the null set. Therefore, the sphere of existent things may be symbolized as "*M*" and that of non-existent things as "$\widetilde{M}$." Nāgārjuna himself states that "[the union of] the existent and non-existent is conditioned (*saṃskṛta*), whereas *nirvāṇa* is unconditioned (*asaṃskṛta*)" (XXV. 13cd).

Judging from the fact that in verse 14 of the same chapter Nāgārjuna writes, "How should both the existent and the non-existent exist in *nirvāṇa*? The fact that these two are not found in the same place is as in the case of light and dark," the third case, which suggests that a certain thing may be "both an existent and a non-existent," must be regarded as a contradiction. In Example 13 the third case could be interpreted as the union of the spheres of self and other, but in Example 14 the subject of each of the propositions is *nirvāṇa*, which is an indivisible single unit, and hence it is not possible to conceive of one part of *nirvāṇa* as being an existent and the other part as being a non-existent. What we have here is nothing more than the formal application of the tetralemma, a traditional formula of expression, and thus one could say that the discussion has in substance ended with the first and second cases. The intersection of the spheres corresponding to the first two cases is the null set (exclusive), while the union of the two spheres covers all conditioned things (exhaustive). Therefore, the negation of the first two cases amounts to the termination of all discussion concerning the existence of the conditioned. Although the conditioned may be distributed among what is existent and what is non-existent, *nirvāṇa* cannot be said to be either existent or non-existent. In other words, *nirvāṇa* cannot be identified as something conditioned.

In that case is it possible to say that *nirvāṇa* is something that is neither existent nor non-existent? This brings us to the question of the fourth case. But Nāgārjuna maintains that this statement is also untenable. In verse 15, coming together with verse 14 between the propositions constituting the third and fourth cases, he says, "If it is to be recognized as neither existent nor non-existent, then [the existence of] both the existent and non-existent must be established." But for him the existence of neither the existent nor the non-existent has been established. What he found unacceptable in the first and second cases was the whole predicate, namely, the proposition that *nirvāṇa* "*be* an existent" or "*be* a non-existent."

Example 14 can be rewritten as follows:

a) It cannot be accepted that x is *nirvāṇa* and that x belongs to M/D, which is the existent.

b) It cannot be accepted that x is *nirvāṇa* and that x belongs to the complement of M with reference to the universe of discourse (D), which is in this case the conditioned (*saṃskṛta*).

c) It cannot be accepted that x is *nirvāṇa* and that x belongs to both M, which is the existent, and its complement ($\tilde{M}$), which is the non-existent.

d) It cannot be accepted that x is *nirvāṇa* and that x belongs neither to M, which is the existent, nor to its complement ($\tilde{M}$), which is the non-existent.

Let us now replace "x is *nirvāṇa*" by "$f(x)$," "x belongs to M" (x is an element of M) by "$x \in M$," and "x belongs to its complement ($\tilde{M}/D$)" by "$(x \in \tilde{M}/D)$." "$(\exists x) f(x)$" means "there exists a thing (x) that can fulfill $f(x)$," while "$\sim(\exists x) f(x)$" means "there does not exist a thing (x) that can fulfill $f(x)$." The contents of Example 14 may then be symbolized as follows:

a) $(x \in M) \supset \sim(\exists x)\, f(x)$

b) $(x \in \tilde{M}/D) \supset \sim(\exists x)\, f(x)$

c) $(x \in M)\,(x \in \tilde{M}/D) \supset \sim(\exists x)\, f(x)$

d) $\sim(x \in \mathrm{M}) \sim(x \in \tilde{M}/D) \supset \sim(\exists x)\, f(x)$

The crux of the tetralemma concerns the question of to which sphere x belongs, namely, whether x is an element of M or an element of $\tilde{M}/D$, and it is not directly related to the truth value of the propositions themselves. The statement that something may be "both an existent and a non-existent" is regarded as a contradiction by Nāgārjuna himself, as is indicated by XXV. 14 quoted above. Therefore, c) may be rewritten as "$(x)\,(f(x) \cdot x = \phi)$" (where ϕ signifies the null set). Consequently, the third case of Example 14 cannot be illustrated diagrammatically as was the third case of Example13 in Diagram 13. Tetralemmas possessing the same structure as Example 14 appear only after Chapter XXII in the

Middle Stanzas, and while some of them (e. g., XXVII. 20) have the same structure as Example 14 in terms of content and may be illustrated as in Diagram 13, with others (e.g., XXV.17) the third case cannot be illustrated, as is also the case with Example 14.

The only example in the *Middle Stanzas* of a tetralemma of the type possessing the three cases of self, other, and both, but lacking the fourth of no cause (Type 2-1), is as follows:

Example 15

na svato jāyate bhāvaḥ parato naiva jāyate /
na svataḥ parataś ceti.... // (XXIII. 20abc)

(A thing is not born from self, nor is it born from another,
Nor from both self and another.)

This may be regarded as having the same structure as Type 1-2, with the fourth case omitted. As an example of Type 2-2, embodying the first three cases but not in the form "self, other, and both," Example 4, which we have already examined, may be given.

Example 4

The arising of that which exists, of that which does not exist, and of that which both exists and does not exist is not possible. (VII. 20abc)

Here too the first three cases of the tetralemma are given, while the fourth case, which would have been "that which neither exists nor does not exist," has been omitted.

The first two cases of Example 4 may be equated with the first two cases of Examples 13 and 14. What, then, is the meaning of "that which both exists and does not exist" in the third case? It is impossible for a certain thing (*x*) to exist and not exist at the same time. Nāgārjuna himself acknowledges this fact in the *Middle Stanzas*, and his followers also declare that it is impossible for one and the same thing to exist and not exist at the same time.[2]

If that be the case, was Nāgārjuna giving an obvious contradiction merely for the sake of form, which he then went on to negate? Judging from the statements of Nāgārjuna and his followers, however, it may be assumed that, unlike the cases of self and other, this third case

2. Cf. *Mūlamadhyamakavṛtti*, p. 23, l. 2, and *Prasannapadā*, p. 83, l. 11.

embodies an awareness of the notion of contradiction itself. But this is not all. In Example 13 "both" signified the union of "self" and "other," and did not mean that a certain thing was simultaneously both self and other. Likewise, it is perhaps possible to interpret the expression "that which exists" (*sat*) as meaning the sphere of existent things, "that which does not exist" (*asat*) as meaning the sphere of non-existent things, and "that which both exists and does not exist" (*sadasat*) as meaning the union of these two spheres. It is conceivable for a certain part of a whole to exist while another part does not exist. Taking the universe as an example, one can say that certain parts of the universe exist while other parts do not. The union of that which exists and that which does not exist constitutes the whole, and this corresponds to the entire universe of discourse in Example 4.

In regard to the question of how to interpret the third case of Example 13, namely, the question of whether all things are born from both self and other, commentators of later ages merely repeat why the first case of this example is untenable and why the second case is also untenable. Likewise, when interpreting the third case of Example 4, they simply reiterate why that which exists does not arise and why that which does not exist does not arise. On the basis of this one could conjecture that "that which both exists and does not exist" points to the union of the sphere of existents and that of non-existents, as we have already suggested in Chapter 7. Thus the third case of Example 4 may be interpreted in at least two different ways. In the first instance it may be regarded as a contradiction, while secondly it may be interpreted as representing the union of the sphere of existents and that of non-existents (see Diagram 14).[3]

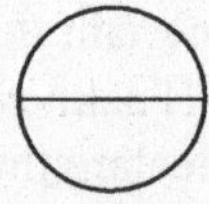

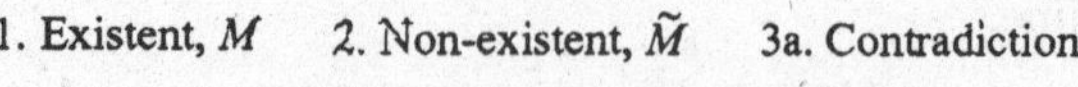

1. Existent, M 2. Non-existent, $\tilde{M}$ 3a. Contradiction 3b. Existent and non-existent, $M \cup \tilde{M}$

DIAGRAM 14

3. R. Robinson rephrases the third case as "some x is A, and some x is not A," which is an example of this latter interpretation. See his *Early Mādhyamika in India and China* (Delhi: Motilal Banarsidass, 1976 [repr.]), p. 57.

It is difficult to determine which of these two possible interpretations Nāgārjuna had in mind when writing the *Middle Stanzas*. But we shall leave this issue aside for the time being since it does not greatly affect the arguments of the *Middle Stanzas*. This is because the main focus of their arguments concerns the first and second cases, while the third and fourth cases are merely ancillary to these. In fact the main discussions of the *Middle Stanzas* are concerned with the propositions relating to the first and second cases of each tetralemma.

Along with the arguments centred on the "self, other, both, and no cause" type of tetralemma in Chapter I of the *Middle Stanzas*, the discussion in Chapter II, already dealt with in Chapter 5 above, is typical of the arguments developed in the *Middle Stanzas* and belongs to Type 3 in our classification of the tetralemma.

Example 16

gataṃ na gamyate tāvad agataṃ naiva gamyate /
gatāgatavinirmuktaṃ gamyamānaṃ na gamyate // (II. 1)

(That which has been traversed is not being traversed, nor is that which has not been traversed being traversed;

That which is being traversed, [such as is] other than that which has been traversed and that which has not been traversed, is not being traversed (or is not known).)

The three negative propositions dealing with "that which has been traversed" (*gata*), "that which has not been traversed" (*agata*) and "that which is being traversed" (*gamyamāna*) may be considered to correspond respectively to the first, second and fourth cases of the tetralemma. Here the compound "*a-gata*" (that which has not been traversed), composed of the past passive participle "*gata*" (traversed) and the negative prefix "*a*-," does not signify the non-existence of that which has been traversed, but refers rather to the existence of that which has not been traversed, which is complementary to that which has been traversed with reference to the universe of discourse, namely, the distance to be traversed (*gantavya*). The union of that which has been traversed and that which has not been traversed corresponds to the whole of the distance to be traversed. That which is being traversed, such as is other than that which has been traversed and that which has not been traversed, represents the sphere that remains after that which has been traversed and that which has not been traversed have been excluded from the distance to be traversed, but such a sphere does not exist.

If we express that which has been traversed by means of "*M*,"

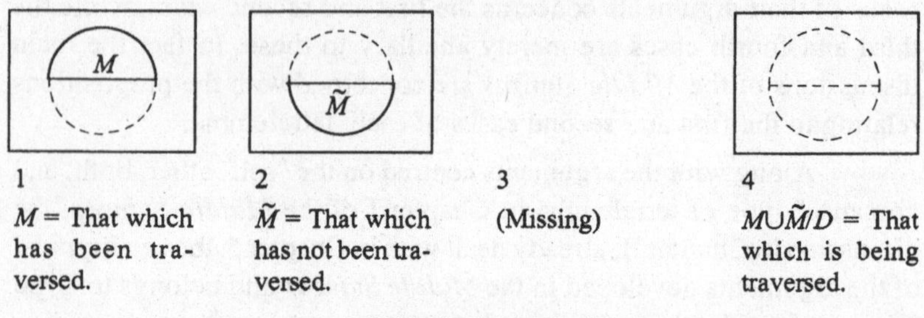

1 M = That which has been traversed.

2 $\tilde{M}$ = That which has not been traversed.

3 (Missing)

4 $M \cup \tilde{M}/D$ = That which is being traversed.

DIAGRAM 15

then that which has not been traversed may be expressed by "($\tilde{M}/D$)." In the fourth case, which may then be expressed as "neither *M* nor $\tilde{M}/D$," "other than that which has been traversed" corresponds to "neither *M*" and "other than that which has not been traversed" corresponds to "nor $\tilde{M}/D$." The universe of discourse in Example 16 may be illustrated as in Diagram 15.

In this diagram, the upturned dotted semicircle (4) indicates that that which is being traversed is not to be equated with that which has been traversed, while the downturned dotted semicircle indicates that it is not to be equated with that which has not been traversed. This method of argument used in Example 16 is typical of the arguments employed in the *Middle Stanzas*, and Nāgārjuna himself refers to the discussion centring on this verse in four other places in the *Middle Stanzas* (III. 7, III. 14, X.13 and XVI. 7). This type of tetralemma (Type 3-1) appears a further five times in the *Middle Stanzas* (see Table 4).

An example of Type 3-2 ("*M*, non-*M*, and that which is neither *M* nor non-*M*") may be found at II. 8.

Example 17

gantā na gacchati tāvad agantā naiva gacchati /
anyo gantur agantuś ca kas tṛtīyo hi gacchati // (II. 8)

(First a traverser does not traverse, nor does a non-traverser traverse. What third person other than a traverser and a non-traverser traverses?)

The third proposition in this example is usually understood to mean that someone who is neither a traverser nor a non-traverser does not traverse, in which case it corresponds to the fourth case of the tetralemma. But Buddhapālita interprets it as meaning that someone who is both a traverser and a non-traverser does not traverse.[4] If interpreted thus, it should be considered to correspond to the third case of the tetralemma, and this example must then be classified as belonging to Type 2-2.

Alongside the first, second and last several chapters of the *Middle Stanzas*, Chapter XVIII is also of considerable importance. The following proposition appearing in this chapter belongs to Group II, Type 1.

Example 18

sarvaṃ tathyaṃ na vā tathyaṃ tathyaṃ cātathyam eva ca /
naivātathyaṃ naiva tathyam etad buddhānuśāsanam // (XVIII. 8)

(Everything is either true, or not true, or both true and untrue,
Or neither true nor untrue: This is the teaching of the Buddhas.)

All of the propositions in Examples 13-17 declare that a certain statement "cannot be accepted." But the first proposition in Example 18 clearly means that something "can be accepted," for the subject "everything" is qualified by the affirmative predicate "is true." In all of our previous examples Nāgārjuna declared that propositions such as "things are born from self or from another" and "arising is possible for that which exists" are untenable during the process of bringing language or linguistic proliferation (*prapañca*) to cessation. Yet here in Example 18 he presents a positive proposition saying that "everything is true." This may be interpreted as the "rebirth" of profane linguistic activity in the form of the teachings of an enlightened person who has returned to the profane world after having brought to extinction the "profane" linguistic activity that had to be negated and having attained to "sacred" ultimate truth. The statement "This is the teaching of the Buddhas" which closes Example 18 would appear to support such an interpretation, as has already been noted in our earlier overview of the arguments of the *Middle Stanzas* (p. 27).

Although the second proposition in Example 1—"everything is not true"— is given in the form of a negative proposition, it too may be

4. Cf. *Mūlamadhyamakavṛtti*, pp. 40-41.

treated in the same manner as the first proposition. In the second case of Example 13 the meaning of "non-self" was expressed by the single word "*para*" (other), while in the second proposition of our succeeding examples the predicate was negated by means of the negative prefix "*a*-," namely, *a-gata* (that which has not been traversed), *a-sat* (that which does not exist), and *a-bhāva* (non-existent). In other words, the particle *na* used for negating propositions was not used to form the second case in these examples. In the second case of Example 18, on the other hand, the negative particle *na* is used, resulting in the expression "*na tathyam*" (is not true) instead of "*atathyam*" (is untrue).[5] Therefore, although this second proposition may be read as "everything is not true," it should not be interpreted to mean "it *cannot* be accepted that everything is true." The reason for this is that Nāgārjuna is here asserting that "it *can* be accepted that everything is *not* true," and it is possible to rewrite the second proposition as "[it can be accepted that] everything is untrue" (*sarvam atathyam*). The word "untrue" (*atathya*) does in fact appear in the third and fourth propositions of Example 18, where the subject "everything" is qualified in the affirmative by the predicates "is both true and untrue" and "is neither true nor untrue."

When the first proposition of Example 18 is true, the second proposition ought to be false, and when the second proposition is true, the first proposition ought to be false. So what does it mean then to assert that both of these propositions are true at the same time? Although the *Middle Stanzas* provide no direct answer to this question, the various commentators have attempted to answer it by taking into account the difference between the plane of conventional truth and that of ultimate truth. For example, in the *Akutobhayā*, the oldest extant commentary on the *Middle Stanzas*, it is stated that the first proposition is based on conventional truth, the second on ultimate truth in which everyday linguistic activity has ceased, the third on both of these truths, and the fourth on the standpoint of a practitioner of *yoga* who has attained the deepest stage of meditation.[6] Bhāvaviveka gives a similar interpretation in his *Prajñāpradīpa*.[7] When interpreted in this manner, there is no logical

5. Further instances in which the negative particle *na* is used instead of the negative prefix *a-/an-* in the second case of the tetralemma appear in the *Middle Stanzas* at XXV. 17-18 and XXVII. 13.

6. Tibetan Tripiṭaka (Peking Edition), Vol. 95, p. 35, f. 3, l. 6.

7. *Ibid.*, Vol. 95, p. 226, f. 5, l. 2.

contradiction in Example 18 since its propositions belong to different planes. The fourth case—"[everything] is neither true nor untrue"—corresponds to the situation of one who has attained to the wisdom of enlightenment, for it is considered possible for him to qualify the subject "everything" with both the predicate "is not true" and the predicate "is not untrue." If everything is not true, then it ought to be untrue. But such an assertion is possible only if the referent of the subject "everything" in this proposition is held to exist. On the plane of the fourth proposition in Example 18, however, it is assumed that everything does not exist. That which does not exist cannot be said to be true, nor can it be said to be untrue.

The content of Example 18 can be rewritten in a manner similar to Example 14. The universe of discourse in Example 18 is the entire universe. Let "$f(x)$" represent "x is an element of everything," "$(x \in M)$" represent "x is an element of the set M (that which is true)," and "$(x \in \tilde{M})$" represent "x is an element of the set $\tilde{M}$ (that which is untrue)." Example 18 may then be symbolically expressed as follows:

a) $(x \in M) \supset (x) f(x)$
b) $(x \in \tilde{M}) \supset (x) f(x)$
c) $\{(x \in M) \vee (x \in \tilde{M})\} \supset (x) f(x)$
d) $\{\sim (x \in \mathrm{M}) \sim (x \in \tilde{M})\} \supset (x) f(x)$

In Example 14 "$f(x)$" represented *nirvāṇa*, but here "$f(x)$" does not mean that "x is everything" but rather that "x is one of the elements comprising the universe." This is because *nirvāṇa* is not a set of different elements, whereas the universe is composed of various elements. Just as in Example 14, "x" as given in the first proposition belongs to the set M, while "x" in the second proposition belongs to set $\tilde{M}$. The third proposition means that "an element belonging to the set 'everything' is either an element of that which is true or an element of that which is untrue." The reason for the use of the sign "v" in this third proposition instead of "." as in the third case of Example 14 is that the universe is here considered to represent a set of various elements. This third case is interpreted in the *Akutobhayā* to mean "that which comprises the universe is true according to conventional truth and untrue according to ultimate truth." But if this interpretation were expressed as "everything is both true and untrue" without any indication of the difference between the two kinds of truth, it would then be impossible to express its content by means of formula c), and a) and b) would represent conventional truth and ultimate truth respectively.

The content of Examples 13-17 was expressed by the conjunction of four (or three) propositions, whereas the content of Example 18 is expressed by a disjunction of four propositions. This tallies with the fact that in the former the tetralemma takes a negative form, whereas in the latter it takes an affirmative form. Generally speaking, the content of the tetralemma in the *Middle Stanzas* is expressed either by a conjunction of negative propositions (Group I) or by a disjunction of affirmative propositions (Group II). The tetralemma in the affirmative form is, however, rare and, apart from Example 18, it appears only in incomplete form in XVIII. 6 (Group II, Type 2).[8]

Every tetralemma appearing in the *Middle Stanzas* may be classified into one of the types considered above. Although there is the difference between negative and affirmative, Examples 13, 14 and 18 are typical examples of tetralemmas with four cases. Thus it is evident that typical tetralemmas are used at important points in the arguments of the *Middle Stanzas*. The method whereby we have indicated the universe of discourse for each of the four cases of the tetralemma by means of a semicircle or circles in Diagrams 13-15 may be applied to every tetralemma in the *Middle Stanzas*. Furthermore, the formulae used in Examples 14 and 18 are based on the same method and are therefore also applicable to any of the other tetralemmas appearing in the *Middle Stanzas*.

By taking up for consideration within a single proposition two entities closely interrelated (*x* and *y*; e.g., existent and arising or the distance to be traversed and the act of traversing), Nāgārjuna examined the relationship obtaining between them. One of the necessary procedures of Nāgārjuna's demonstration of his thesis was the distribution of

---

8. The tetralemma of Example 18 has on occasion been symbolically represented as "*a*, ~*a*, *a* ~*a*,~*a* ~ (~ *a*)." Following this interpretation, the fourth case may be rewritten as "~*a*·*a*," i. e., "*a*~*a*." Consequently the distinction between the meaning of the third case and that of the fourth case, which should be clearly distinguished, is no longer expressed. This kind of symbolic representation probably results from interpreting the negative (*na* or *a*-) in this type of tetralemma as negating the proposition as a whole instead of serving to distribute the universe of discourse.

the sphere of either x or y in a complementary manner (expressed as M/D and $\tilde{M}/D$ in this chapter) or into four further cases (M, $\tilde{M}$, $M \cup \tilde{M}/D$, and $(M \cup \tilde{M}/D)^c$). The tetralemma is essentially the method whereby Nāgārjuna, who wished to effect the extinction of the entire phenomenal world by means of the extinction of linguistic proliferation, sought to distribute in an exhaustive fashion the entire universe of discourse. This distribution is, at least formally, conducted by observing the laws of contradiction and the excluded middle. Furthermore, his arguments developed in this context adhere to the rules of formal logic, even if in a manner peculiar to Nāgārjuna.

Although heir to the traditions of the Prajñāpāramitā scriptures, Nāgārjuna did not employ the famous paradox "form is emptiness." Instead he tried to give expression to the spirit of the Prajñāpāramitā scriptures in as logical a manner as possible. It is true that emptiness may be something transcending language. But Nāgārjuna did not abandon logic to seek refuge in paradoxes. Rather, he pursued "emptiness" in which language had come to cessation while remaining within the bounds of logic. Nāgārjuna's emptiness, corresponding to the culmination of transcendence, is indeed supported by persistent logical inquiry exemplified by the method centring on the tetralemma. But it should go without saying that he was driven to pursue such logical inquiries to their utmost limits by the conviction that emptiness was to be found at their termination.

CHAPTER TWELVE

NĀGĀRJUNA'S TETRALEMMA IN COMPARISON WITH THAT OF THE HUA-YEN SCHOOL IN CHINA

The tetralemma has a long history. In the Early Canon and *Abhidharmakośabhāṣya* it had already been established as a fixed form of expression, and we have seen that it also represented an important method of argument in the *Middle Stanzas*. The tetralemma, or its incomplete form (consisting of the first three cases or propositions), is also to be frequently met with in works such as the *Mahāyānasūtrālaṃkāra* and *Mahāyānasaṃgraha* of the early Yogācāras, always with considerable importance attached to it. But in India it was not employed in later treatises on logic or in the age of Tantrism to the same extent that it had been in early Mahāyāna Buddhism.

In China, on the other hand, the tetralemma assumed an even more important meaning than in India. In Chinese Buddhism it was especially the Hua-yen school that adopted the tetralemma as a particularly important tool in its speculations, and the interpretation of the tetralemma as evidenced in Hua-yen doctrine has also been widely accepted in Japan. Since the understanding of Buddhism in Japan has, at least traditionally, been moulded through the medium of Chinese Buddhism, the understanding of the tetralemma in Japan has also tended to be based on the tetralemma of Hua-yen doctrine rather than on that to be found in the *Middle Stanzas* themselves.

It is sometimes asserted that Buddhism possesses a special form of logic, or the germs of a special form of logic, not to be found in the West. In most cases, this claim implies a positive evaluation of Buddhist thought, namely, that Buddhist logic contains some superior elements absent in Western logic. But in order for such an assertion to be made on an academic level, it is necessary to ascertain whether or not Buddhism does in fact have a *discipline* of logic able to rival the *logos* of the West.

It is probably true that the philosophy of "emptiness" represents a form of thought or religious praxis absent in Christianity and Islam, and that there exists here something that Buddhism may propound with confidence to the world at large. But in the present context it is not a question of whether or not there does exist some quality peculiar to Buddhism as a religion; rather, it is a question of whether or not there is to be found in Buddhism a form of logic "transcending" traditional logic or symbolic logic. It is often claimed that this "special logic" does not observe the general rules of logic (i.e., the laws of identity, contradiction, and the excluded middle). But can any such system actually constitute a form of logic? Surely such a system can be nothing more than a form of "poesy," conveying images of contradiction and the impossible and seeking to evoke some sort of emotion or mental state.

Since the goal of Buddhism is the realm of "thusness" (*tathatā*) which transcends language, it is perhaps only natural that at a certain stage the general rules of logic should be negated, for what Nāgārjuna undertook to do in the *Middle Stanzas* was directed at the negation of language and the experience of an emptiness in which all language has been extinguished. But to date the fact that in the *Middle Stanzas* Nāgārjuna observed the basic laws of logic with extreme consistency would appear to have been unduly disregarded. Nāgārjuna did not deviate from his stance of negating language, and therefore the world, while yet remaining in the realm of language and observing the rules of logic. Rather, by faithfully applying the mechanisms of logic to their utmost limits, he brought about the breakdown of the application of language. Such was the nature of Nāgārjuna's negation, and this attitude of his also represents the basis and starting point of Indian Mahāyāna Buddhism.

The argument "*A* is non-*A*; therefore it is *A*" appears close to twenty times in the *Vajracchedikā Prajñāpāramitā*. But this logical schema, apparently "transcending" the law of identity, does not in itself immediately mean that Buddhism has a special logic of its own, for it represents in fact a form of rhetoric and not a system of logic. If one is going to use the term "logic" at all, one should probably call it a "logic of praxis." The *Vajracchedikā Prajñāpāramitā* is not asserting that in the realm of thusness *A* and non-*A* are identical within an autonomous system (—logic always becomes autonomous once it is systematized). Rather, it is attempting to say that if a person in the process of "accumulating merit" should *think* that he is now "accumulating merit," he is *not* "accumulating merit" in any true sense. It is a form of expression that seeks to convey with force the "*logic* of self-negation." It is true that the act of self-negation is essentially self-contradictory since the self does not wish to be negated and is always seeking recognition, aggrandizement and expansion. But in the context of religion such a self must be put to death at least once, for if the "profane" does not die, it is not possible for it to gain the assistance of the "sacred" and be reborn. The *Vajracchedikā Prajñāpāramitā* is describing the process whereby the profane is sacralized and reborn after having been negated. The profane that has been sacralized continues to exist in the profane world as something that has been sacralized and is yet still profane. In such a situation, "*A* is non-*A*; therefore it is *A*."

Religious practice is by nature a contradictory activity—but not in itself a contradiction. For example, for a living being to relate directly to its own death is similar to the act of someone who, faced with the impossible and possessing no means of rendering it possible, still continues to confront it. It is not possible for anyone to successfully complete the task of self-negation. But it is rather for this very reason that religion continues to emphasize self-negation, and it is important to note that when discussing the most basic aspects of religion, such as one's relationship with death and self-negation, people still use language. As long as one uses language, one has no choice but to follow a system possessing logic, as did Nāgārjuna who employed language in order to negate language.

In trying to give expression to a world transcending language, Buddhism and also other religions and philosophies have, at crucial points, used forms of expression such as paradoxes which transcend the realm of logic. The *Middle Stanzas* are also not without modes of expression such as paradoxes. The question to be considered in such cases is in what circumstances and how frequently paradoxes in this sense are used within a particular system. The *Vajracchedikā Prajñāpāramitā* repeatedly makes conscious use of such paradoxical expressions as a form of rhetoric, and as a result this scripture has come to assume, rather than logical consistency, a paradoxical and rhetorical nature. By way of comparison, the *Middle Stanzas* may be said to have attached considerable importance to logical consistency.

One distinguishing feature for measuring the logical consistency of a system is the plane (or time span) of the universe of discourse. For example, the two propositions "*x* is born from another" and "*x* is not born from another" are contradictories. Both cannot be true *simultaneously*. If, however, they concerned two different points in time, it would be possible for both of these propositions to be true. The fact that *x* is born from another at time "*a*" and the fact that *x* is not born from another at time "*b*" (differing from time "*a*") belong to two different systems of logic. When considering the *logical* structure of the tetralemma in Buddhism, it is necessary to take into account these "time shifts" between systems of logic, for, as will be shown below, there are instances in Buddhism where systems of logic belonging to different time spans are made to appear, even if unconsciously, as if they were systems of logic belonging to the same time span. Not only must we consider the significance of such outward appearances, but we should also take heed of how many planes (or time spans) of logic are employed within a single discussion.

One reason that the logical structure of the tetralemma has still not been fully elucidated lies in the fact that to date we have not clearly distinguished between the traditional "rhetoric" and "logic" of Buddhism and that we have not been consciously aware of the time shifts between different systems of logic. In the following we would like to consider the tetralemma of the *Hua-yen wu-chiao chang* in this light and compare it with that of the *Middle Stanzas*. The understanding of the tetralemma in the former work represents one example of the understanding of the tetralemma prevalent in Japan, and it has also been a major inspiration behind hopes entertained for the existence of a "special logic." Furthermore, although the content of the tetralemma in the *Middle Stanzas* and that in the *Hua-yen wu-chiao chang* are almost totally different, so far this difference has not been accurately pinpointed. The difference between these two may be explained primarily on the basis of the time shift between different systems of logic.

The *Hua-yen i-ch'êng chiao-i fên-ch'i chang* (Essay on the Position of the Hua-yen One-Vehicle Teachings) or *Hua-yen wu-chiao chang* (Essay on the Hua-yen Five Teachings; abbreviated below as *Wu-chiao chang*) by Fa-tsang (642-712) not only represents an outline of Hua-yen doctrines, but is also an introduction to Buddhism,[1] and in China

1. Taishō Tripiṭaka Vol. 45; the text of the *Wu-chiao chang* used here is that to be found in Yutsugi Ryōei, *Kegon gokyōshō kōgi* (Lectures on the *Hua-yen wu-chiao chang*; Kyōto: Hyakkaen, 1927 [repr. 1975]).

and Japan it has been used as the most important introductory work or textbook on Hua-yen doctrines. There exist a text preserved in Japan and a Sung version, differing in their chapter divisions, and towards the end of the work there is a chapter entitled "The Teaching of the Six Meanings of the Causal Gate of Dependent Co-arising." The "six meanings" (*liu-i*) here represent a sixfold division of the modes of being assumed by a cause, and will hereafter be referred to as the "six causal cases." This chapter thus describes the six modes of being assumed by a certain thing when it acts as a cause from which something arises. As will be explained below, the number "six" is in this case closely connected with the number "four" in the tetralemma.

In his consideration of the subject of "cause," Fa-tsang employs the perspective provided by the concepts of *t'i* and *yung* in traditional Chinese thought. "*T'i*" represents the material locus necessary for a certain thing to exist, and it may be said to correspond to "substance" or "entity." "*Yung*" refers to the function operating in *t'i* or the locus. Two kinds of entities are posited in the case of a cause, namely, those that are "empty" and those that are "existent." An "empty causal entity" refers to a causal entity when considered in the light of the fact that anything dependently co-arisen is without own-being and empty, while an "existent causal entity" refers to a causal entity when considered in the light of the fact that anything dependently co-arisen is caused to exist provisionally through the medium of language. As for function (or efficacy), there are held to be two kinds, namely, "existent" and "non-existent." The statement "function is existent in the causal entity" means that the cause alone has sufficient potential to produce an effect or that the cause and conditions both cooperate to produce an effect, while the statement "function is non-existent" means that the cause does not have the potential to produce an effect. There is a further division based on the distinction between whether the cause is dependent or non-dependent on some other entity or condition (including the effect). In the latter case the cause produces an effect without relying upon any other entity, while in the former case the cause and condition cooperate to produce the effect.

Thus the "six causal cases" describe the cause as considered from the six standpoints of the emptiness or existence of the substance (or locus), the existence or non-existence of function, and dependence or non-dependence on conditions. These are expressed as follows in the *Wu-chiao chang*:

1. Empty, efficacious (i.e., with function), and non-dependent on conditions. (a)
2. Empty, efficacious, and dependent on conditions. (b)
3. Empty, non-efficacious (i.e., without function), and dependent on conditions. (c)
4. Existent, efficacious, and non-dependent on conditions. (d)
5. Existent, efficacious, and dependent on conditions. (e)
6. Existent, non-efficacious, and dependent on conditions.[2] (f)

Simply stated, the first three cases (a-c) represent the three cases obtaining when the substance (locus) of the cause is empty and without own-being, while the last three (d-f) represent the three cases obtaining when the substance of the cause has been provisionally hypothesized. Fa-tsang explains each of these six causal cases, giving a name to each.

The first case (a) is called "momentariness." All things are arising and disappearing from one moment to the next. Under such circumstances the cause has not immutable substance (own-being) and is, namely, without own-being and empty. Since it is able to produce an effect unassisted, its function is existent and it is not dependent on any conditions.

The second case (b) is called "simultaneity with the effect," corresponding to a cause accompanied by an effect. Since it is accompanied by an effect, its function is considered to be existent, but insofar that the substance of the cause would not exist if unaccompanied by the effect, its substance is held to be empty. As the effect in this case also represents a condition in relation to the cause, the cause is dependent on conditions.

The third case (c) is called "dependence on conditions," meaning that when something arises, it does not arise from any cause but is dependent on various conditions. In this case, the substance of the cause is empty, its function non-existent, and it is dependent on conditions.

The fourth case (d) is called "determined status of nature." A cause may be by nature either good or wholesome, evil or unwholesome, or morally indeterminate, and from a particular cause there arises a particular effect "determined by nature," as for example in the case of a wholesome effect arising from a wholesome cause. The mode of being

2. *Ibid.*, p. 525.

of a cause in such circumstances, when the causal relationship is determined, is referred to as "determined status." Since this presupposes the existence of the cause itself and since its "nature" remains unchanged, the substance of the cause in this case is held to be existent, it is capable of producing an effect, and it does not depend on any conditions or on the assistance of another entity.

The fifth case (e) is called "attraction of a specific effect." In Abhidharma philosophy, the basic discipline dealing with the Buddhist world view, the world is broadly divided into two major categories, namely, that of physical entities and that of mental entities. A physical cause will invariably produce a physical effect and will never give rise to a mental effect. This relationship, in which a particular cause produces an effect of the same category, is referred to as the "attraction of a specific effect." Since the cause produces a homogeneous effect, its substance is existent, and since it has the potential to produce an effect, its function is also existent. Because in this case the cause relies on a "dominant condition" (*adhipati-pratyaya*: a condition that functions as a condition in the sense that it does not actively obstruct the production of the effect), the cause is dependent on conditions.

The final sixth case (f), called "sequential continuity," refers to the situation in which a cause continues to exist subsequent upon something else. Things which appear through dependent co-arising before our eyes as if they existed have substance insofar that they do exist, even if only provisionally. Furthermore, although the cause is dependent on conditions in that it exists in dependence upon various other entities such as "seeds" (*bīja*) and ignorance, its function is non-existent since it does not in itself possess any immutable and eternal substance.

The basic authority for the above six modes of being of a cause is sought by Fa-tsang in the *Mahāyānasaṃgraha*,[3] in the second chapter of which there appear the "six causal cases" of momentariness, simultaneity, sequential continuity, determined status, dependence on conditions, and attraction of a specific effect.[4] Thus the six forms of a cause, although not identical with the six causal cases of Fa-tsang, had already been conceived of among the Yogācāras in India, and Fa-tsang may be said to have reinterpreted them within the framework of the Chinese

3. *Ibid.*, pp. 526-530.

4. Taishō Tripiṭaka, Vol. 31, p. 389.

categories of substance and function.

It will be noticed that among the six causal cases there are four cases where the function of the cause is efficacious (a, b, d and e) and two cases where it is not (c and f). Needless to say, four cases are also conceivable for when the function is non-efficacious, and this means that the two cases of "empty, without function, and non-dependent on conditions" (g) and "existent, without function, and non-dependent on conditions" (h) have been excluded in the six causal cases. The reason for this given by Fa-tsang is that "when the function of a cause is non-efficacious and the cause does not depend on any conditions, it does not constitute a cause."[5] It is indeed true that regardless of whether the substance of the cause be empty or existent, if its function is non-efficacious and if it does not depend on any conditions, it would not be considered to constitute a cause in Fa-tsang's system. The crux of Fa-tsang's understanding lies in the very fact that for this reason he posited not "eight causal cases" but "six causal cases," and the fundamental difference between the tetralemma in the *Middle Stanzas* and that of the *Wu-chiao chang* is also to be found here.

After having explained the six modes of being of a cause on the basis of his own original interpretation of the six causal cases in the *Mahāyānasaṃgraha*, Fa-tsang next correlates the six causal cases with the tetralemma, and his textual authority in doing so is given as the two forms of the tetralemma appearing in the *Daśabhūmi-śāstra* (by Vasubandhu) and *Abhidharmasamuccaya* (verses by Asaṅga, commentary by Siṃhabodhi).

The tetralemma of the *Daśabhūmi-śāstra* as quoted in the *Wu-chiao chang* is as follows:

1. It is not born of a condition because it is born of its own cause. (Case of non-birth from another)
2. It is not born of a cause because it is born of a condition. (Case of non-birth from self)
3. It is not born of both because there is no knower and because it does not abide while being produced. (Case of non-birth from both)

5. *Kegon gokyōshō kōgi* (*op.cit.*), p. 532.

4. It is not without cause because it exists subsequent upon conditions. (Case of non-birth from causelessness)

(The wording of the *Daśabhūmi-śāstra*, fasc. 8 [Taishō Tripiṭaka, Vol. 26, p. 170b] differs, but the logical structure is identical.)

These four cases or propositions have traditionally been referred to by the names given in parentheses. For convenience' sake, the order of the first two cases of the *Daśabhūmi-śāstra* as quoted in the *Wu-chiao chang* has been reversed. In order to clarify the logical structure of this tetralemma, we may rephrase the four cases in the following manner:

1. Since [a certain thing (*x*)] is born of its own cause, it is not born of a condition. (Case of non-birth from another)
2. Since [a certain thing (*x*)] is born of a condition, it is not born of a cause. (Case of non-birth from self)
3. [A certain thing (*x*)] is not born of the dyad [of cause and condition] because there is no knower and because it does not abide while being produced. (Case of non-birth from both)
4. [A certain thing (*x*)] is not [born] of no cause because it exists subsequent upon conditions. (Case of non-birth from causelessness)

The tetralemma of Fa-tsang's second textual authority, namely, that appearing in the *Abhidharmasamuccaya*, is as follows:

1. Since its own seed exists, it does not follow upon another. (Case of non-birth from another)
2. Since it depends on various conditions, it is not self-produced. (Case of non-birth from self)
3. Since it is without any function, it is not born of both. (Case of non-birth from both)
4. Since it has efficacy, it is not without cause. (Case of non-birth from causelessness)

(*Abhidharmasamuccaya*, fasc. 4 [Taishō Tripiṭaka, Vol. 31, p. 712c])

These four cases have also traditionally been referred to by the same names as those given to the four cases of the tetralemma appearing in the *Daśabhūmi-śāstra*, and it is evident that the above two tetralemmas are logically of an identical structure. In the first proposition of the *Daśabhūmi-śāstra* and *Abhidharmasamuccaya*, "birth from self" is given as the reason for "non-birth from another," while in the second proposition "birth from conditions (another)" is given as the reason for "non-birth from self."

These first two propositions, however, differ in structure from the first two propositions of the corresponding tetralemma in the *Middle Stanzas*, which are as follows:

Things are not born from self.

Things are not born from another.

Although Nāgārjuna offers a reason for both of these propositions, he does not, in contrast with the *Daśabhūmi-śāstra* and *Abhidharmasamuccaya*, give the affirmative form of the second proposition as the reason for the first proposition and the affirmative form of the first proposition as the reason for the second proposition.

As far as wording is concerned, there is no great difference between the third proposition of the tetralemma in the *Daśabhūmi-śāstra* and *Abhidharmasamuccaya* on the one hand and the *Middle Stanzas* on the other, but there is once again a considerable difference in the content of the fourth proposition. The *Daśabhūmi-śāstra* and *Abhidharmasamuccaya*, as well as the *Wu-chiao chang*, take it to mean that since the function of the cause is operating, it cannot be said that there is no cause; in other words, a cause does exist. The *Middle Stanzas*, on the other hand, state simply that nothing is born without a cause. This difference arises from the fact that whereas Nāgārjuna has in mind an identical "time span" for the system of logic in the first two propositions (and in fact for all four propositions), the *Daśabhūmi-śāstra* and *Abhidharmasamuccaya* posit different "time spans." This is because the two propositions "not born of self" and "born of another" can never actually be both valid simultaneously. In addition, for us to posit a "special system of logic" in which the first and second propositions were simultaneously valid would only render the ancient modes of thought current at the time as reflected in the *Daśabhūmi-śāstra* and *Abhidharmasamuccaya* more complex than they actually were. Of course, it is probably correct to assume that Buddhist thinkers at the time did seek, even if unconsciously, to give the impression that these two propositions were simultaneously valid. But just because there are to be found traces of such an attempt, permissible in ancient times, this does not mean that it would necessarily embody a special form of logic able to vie with that of Hegel.

The above two forms of the tetralemma appearing in Indian Yogācāra texts are correlated by Fa-tsang with the six causal cases. The points that have a direct bearing on this correlation with the tetralemma are whether or not the function of the cause is efficacious and whether or not it depends on conditions; whether the causal entity is empty or existent is not of direct concern. This latter point of whether the causal entity is empty or existent relates to the tetralemma as a whole, and the *Wu-chiao chang* presents two kinds of tetralemma, one in the case of the causal entity being empty and the other in the case of the causal entity being existent.

In regard to the two cases of the function of the cause being either efficacious or non-efficacious and the two cases of it either depending on conditions or not depending on conditions, there are four possible combinations. They are as follows:

1. The cause is efficacious and non-dependent on conditions.
2. The cause is non-efficacious and dependent on conditions.
3. The cause is non-efficacious and non-dependent on conditions.
4. The cause is efficacious and dependent on conditions.

These four cases are correlated in this order with the tetralemma in the *Daśabhūmi-śāstra*, etc. However, as has already been pointed out, Fa-tsang considered the third case, in which the cause neither has the power to produce an effect nor depends on anything else, to correspond to none of the six causal cases since it does not function as a cause. As for the remaining three cases (1, 2 and 4), there exist for each two cases, one in which the causal entity is empty and the other in which it is existent, and this results in a total of six cases. Fa-tsang classified causes into six types on the basis of the premise that a cause must fulfill the functions of a cause, and hence he naturally did not consider anything that did not fulfill the functions of a cause to correspond to any of the four propositions of the tetralemma. This means that Fa-tsang understood the tetralemma as being grounded in the premise that "all things are born of causes," and it is here that the source of the difference from the tetralemma in the *Middle*

Stanzas lies. The basic premise of the *Middle Stanzas*, a premise that rejects general common understanding, is that "causes do not produce effects," and when considered from this standpoint, it was in fact the very thesis that "a cause does not fulfill the functions of a cause" that the *Middle Stanzas* were seeking to propound.

The statement in the *Wu-chiao chang* that "the cause is efficacious" refers to "birth from self" and that that "the cause is non-efficacious" to "non-birth from self," while "dependent on conditions" and "non-dependent on conditions" refer to "birth from another" and "non-birth from another" respectively. The correspondences between the tetralemma of the *Daśabhūmi-śāstra* and *Abhidharmasamuccaya*, the six causal cases of the *Wu-chiao chang*, and the six causal cases of the *Mahāyāna-saṃgraha* may be illustrated by means of Table 5.[6]

This table clearly shows that the case given as the third proposition in the *Daśabhūmi-śāstra* and *Abhidharmasamuccaya* has been rejected in the *Wu-chiao chang* as a case that does not fulfill the functions of a cause. The tetralemma in the *Daśabhūmi-śāstra* and *Abhidharmasamuccaya*, based on the traditions of the *Middle Stanzas* and the Early Canon, sought to demonstrate that "things are not born." In the *Wu-chiao chang*, on the other hand, causes were classified on the basis of the premise that, in some way or another, "things *are* born." As is indicated in Table 5, the "case of birth from non-causelessness" (*pu wu yin shêng chü*), which originally represented the fourth proposition of the tetralemma and in the traditions of the *Middle Stanzas* signified "non-birth from causelessness" (i.e., *x* is not born without a cause), has in the *Wu-chiao chang* been adopted as the general designation for all four propositions (including the third proposition, which is not considered to constitute a cause). In other words, in the *Wu-chiao chang* this phrase was interpreted as "*x* is born not without a cause, i.e., it is born from a cause," with the initial negative *pu* modifying not "born" (*shêng*) but the *wu* of "cause*less*ness" (*wu yin*) and thereby implying the existence of a cause.

As we have already mentioned on more than one occasion, the *Middle Stanzas* clearly distinguish between the type of negation that by modifying a particular term establishes by implication the contradictory

6. Cf. *ibid.*, p. 522.

of the negatee (*paryudāsa*: implicative negation) and the type of negation that negates a proposition as a whole without implying anything else (*prasajyapratiṣedha*: absolute negation). Furthermore, the division into four propositions in the tetralemma of the *Middle Stanzas* concerned the subject (or the referent of the noun phrase) of each of the propositions constituting the tetralemma, and it was unrelated to the affirmation or negation of the proposition as a whole.

But in the *Wu-chiao chang*—and this tendency is apparent in the *Daśabhūmi-śāstra* and *Abhidharmasamuccaya* too—these two types of negation were not clearly differentiated as in the *Middle Stanzas*, and there are instances, as in the above case, in which what represented in

TABLE 5

Daśabhūmi-śāstra (fasc. 8)	*Abhidharmasamuccaya* (fasc. 4)	Order in the *Wu-chiao chang*
It is not born of a condition because it is born of its own cause.	Since its own seed exists, it does not follow upon another.	Cause is efficacious and non-dependent on conditions.
It is not born of a cause because it is born of a condition.	Since it depends on various conditions, it is not self-created.	Cause is non-efficacious and dependent on conditions.
It is not born of both because there is no knower.	Since it is without any function, it is not born of both.	Cause is non-efficacious and non-dependent on conditions.
It is not born without cause because it exists subsequent upon conditions.	Since it has efficacy, it is not without cause.	Cause is efficacious and dependent on conditions.

the context of the *Middle Stanzas* a propositional negation was understood as the negation of a particular term. This resulted in the implicative positing of an affirmative content for each of the propositions. In the past there have also been instances in which the *Middle Stanzas* were interpreted from such a Hua-yen viewpoint, and it may be for this reason that it came to be considered that the arguments of the *Middle Stanzas* embodied a special form of logic or at least the germs thereof.

The meaning of the tetralemma as understood by Fa-tsang on the basis of the *Daśabhūmi-śāstra*, etc., and articulated in his *Wu-chiao chang* may in the final analysis be expressed in the following terms:

1. Since [x] is born from self, [x] is not born from another.
2. Since [x] is born from another, [x] is not born from self.

TABLE 5

(causal entity)	(function)	(conditions)	*Mahāyāna-samgraha* (fasc. 2)	Four cases in the *Wu-chiao chang*	
(a) Empty	Efficacious	Non-dependent on conditions	Momentariness	Case of non-birth from another	Case of birth from non-causelessness
(d) Existent	Efficacious	Non-dependent on conditions	Determined status of nature		
(c) Empty	Non-efficacious	Dependent on conditions	Dependence on conditions	Case of non-birth from self	
(f) Existent	Non-efficacious	Dependent on conditions	Sequential continuity		
				[Does not constitute a cause]	
(b) Empty	Efficacious	Dependent on conditions	Simultaneity with effect	Case of non-birth from both	
(e) Existent	Efficacious	Dependent on conditions	Attraction of a specific effect		

3. [x] is not born from self, nor is it born from another.
4. [x] is born from self and born from another.

If "a" is substituted for "born from self" and "b" is substituted for "born from another," "not born from self" may be expressed as "$\tilde{a}$" and "not born from another" as "$\tilde{b}$." The above tetralemma may then be symbolically expressed as follows:

1. a, therefore $\tilde{b}$.	$a \supset \tilde{b}$	(1)
2. b, therefore $\tilde{a}$.	$b \supset \tilde{a}$	(2)
3. $\tilde{a}$ and $\tilde{b}$.	$\tilde{a}\tilde{b}$	(3)
4. a and b.	ab (or $\sim\tilde{a}\sim\tilde{b}$)	(4)

As was noted earlier, the first two propositions of this tetralemma differ considerably from those of the tetralemma in the *Middle Stanzas*. In the *Middle Stanzas* "not born from another" is never given as the reason for "born from self," nor is "born from another" ever given as the reason for "not born from self." In the *Middle Stanzas* it is possible for both "not born from self" and "not born from another" to be simultaneously true, but they can never be simultaneously true in the *Wu-chiao chang*.

The third proposition as formally posited in the *Wu-chiao chang* was "non-efficacious and non-dependent on conditions." "Non-efficacious" means that "x is not born from self," while "non-dependent on conditions" means that "x is not born from another." Therefore, the content of the third proposition in the *Wu-chiao chang* may be expressed by the conjunction of "x is not born from self" ($\tilde{a}$) and "x is not born from another" ($\tilde{b}$), i.e., ($\tilde{a}\tilde{b}$). In the case of the tetralemma of the *Middle Stanzas*, starting with "things are not born from self," the third proposition signified that "x is not born from the sum sphere of self and other." In other words, the *Middle Stanzas* here deny birth from the sphere comprising the sphere of self and the sphere of other.

As has already been mentioned, in the fourth proposition in the *Wu-chiao chang* "not without a cause" was interpreted as a double negative and understood to mean "with a cause." In this case the word "cause" is being used in a broader sense, embracing "conditions" as well, and therefore the statement "efficacious and dependent on conditions" in the *Wu-chiao chang* may be expressed by the conjunction of a and b ($a \cdot b$). In other words, the final proposition becomes in the *Wu-chiao chang* an affirmative one meaning "x is born from self and also born from another."

But in the *Middle Stanzas* it was simply stated that "*x* is *not* born from something that is *neither* self *nor* other (—and therefore non-existent)," and it is not implied that "therefore, it is born from self and also born from another."

In the *Wu-chiao chang*, which adopts the premise that "things *are* born," it is considered that either "born from self" or "born from another" must be true, and this means that "$a \vee b$" (a or b) must be true for each of the four propositions. "$a \vee b$" is false only when both a and b are false. Thus "$a \vee b$" is true when a is true and b is false, when a is false and b is true, and when both a and b are true. Stated simply, each of the propositions in the tetralemma of the *Wu-chiao chang* is based on the premise "$a \vee b$." Hence (1) to (4) may be rewritten in the following manner:

1. $(a \vee b) \cdot (a \supset \widetilde{b})$
2. $(a \vee b) \cdot (b \supset \widetilde{a})$
3. $(a \vee b) \cdot \widetilde{a}\,\widetilde{b}$
4. $(a \vee b) \cdot a\,b$

On the condition that either a or b must be true, it is impossible for the first and second propositions to be simultaneously valid. Likewise, it is obvious that the third proposition can never be valid. In the case of the *Middle Stanzas*, on the other hand, there exists no premise such as $(a \vee b)$, i.e., "a or b." At best one might say that they presuppose the premise $(\widetilde{a}\,\widetilde{b})$, i.e., "$\widetilde{a}$ and $\widetilde{b}$."

In the tetralemma of the *Wu-chiao chang* the causal entity is differentiated according to whether it is existent or empty. This corresponds to the tetralemmas in the *Middle Stanzas* expressed either negatively or positively. Although repeatedly stating on the one hand by means of the tetralemma in negative form that all things are empty because they are dependently co-arisen, the *Middle Stanzas* also express on two occasions by means of the tetralemma in affirmative form the fact that the existence of what is dependently co-arisen is a provisional designation—namely, it *exists* as something dependently co-arisen.[7] Fa-tsang sought to express these two aspects by distinguishing between whether the causal entity was empty or existent. But this distinction in the

7. Cf. Table 4, p. 137.

Wu-chiao chang as to whether the causal entity be empty or existent is not directly related to the content of the tetralemma. In the case of the tetralemma in the *Middle Stanzas*, on the other hand, a distinction is made, depending on whether each of the propositions is expressed in the negative or the affirmative, as to whether the tetralemma in question is for the purpose of negating linguistic proliferation (*prapañca*) or for the purpose of affirming language and the world subsequent to "sacralization."

In the case of the tetralemma in the *Middle Stanzas* expressed in the negative form, the arguments relating to each of the propositions take place in the same time span or on the same plane, as a result of which the propositions are held to be false, while the propositions in the tetralemma expressed in the affirmative express arguments that do not relate to an identical time span. This fact is to be readily understood if one reads the *Middle Stanzas* with care. In the case of the *Wu-chiao chang*, on the other hand, the tetralemma (although in fact consisting of only three propositions) is expressed as if it related to a single time span. This was probably one of the factors that led to the demand for a "special form of logic transcending formal logic."

As Buddhists, both Fa-tsang and Nāgārjuna were pursuing "emptiness in which language has been extinguished." In order to make such assertions while observing, each by his own methods, the rules of formal logic, they added rhetorical elements and made it appear as if they were employing special forms of logic. In doing so, Nāgārjuna sought to minimize any such special features, while Fa-tsang, wishing to emphasize a certain aspect of religious praxis, sought to maximize this "semblance" (here not meant in any derogatory sense). It was this difference that gave rise to the difference in the content of the tetralemma in the *Wu-chiao chang* and the *Middle Stanzas*.

The tetralemma in negative form as appearing in the *Middle Stanzas* represents a method employed by Nāgārjuna for the purpose of encompassing the entire universe of discourse, and in order to carry out this process of negation throughout the entire universe of discourse it had to take place within a single time span. Whereas the tetralemma of the *Middle Stanzas* thus possesses a system of logic in which all language becomes simultaneously false, the *Wu-chiao chang*, *Daśabhūmi-śāstra* and also the *Abhidharmasamuccaya* would seem to have been avoiding any such logic of total negation. In other words, the *Middle Stanzas* aspired to the total negation of the profane, but the *Wu-chiao chang*, etc., did not carry this task of negating the profane through to the very end. The emptiness of the *Middle Stanzas* represents a "rebirth" that follows on from total negation. In the *Wu-chiao chang*, etc., on the other hand, the "remnants" of the profane negatee form the world of provisional designation. This way of thinking, which was absent in Early Buddhism and the early Mādhyamika school, was later to gradually develop in the Yogācāra school, Tathāgatagarbha thought, Tantrism and the Hua-yen and T'ien-t'ai schools in China. The "existence of the cause," which was preserved as the precondition for the six causal cases in the *Wu-chiao chang*, may be regarded as a representative example of such a "remnant."

CHAPTER THIRTEEN

LATER INTERPRETATIONS OF "DEPENDENT CO-ARISING": THE SIGNIFICANCE OF THE PROFANE

1

It is a well-known fact that the Mādhyamika school founded by Nāgārjuna and Āryadeva split in later times into the Prāsaṅgika school established by Buddhapālita and Candrakīrti and the Svātantrika school initiated by Bhāvaviveka, and that the adherents of these two schools criticized one another's views. The names of these two schools, which are the appellations most commonly used when dividing the history of Indian Mādhyamika thought, are believed to have been first used by the Tibetans. Although there were other methods of dividing Indian Mādhyamika thought known to the Tibetans, that dividing the Mādhyamika school into the Prāsaṅgika and Svātantrika schools was the principal method prior to the time of Tsoṅ-kha-pa, the founder of the dGe-lugs-pa school. Furthermore, once he recognized this as the supreme method of division,[1] it became that most widely used, and the majority of later doctrinal surveys (*grub mthaḥ*) were also to adopt it.[2]

The Tibetan equivalent of "Prāsaṅgika" is "Thal-ḥgyur-pa," and it would appear that it was in fact this Tibetan term that has been reconstructed to give us the Sanskrit "Prāsaṅgika," for this term does not appear as the name of a school in any of the old Sanskrit Buddhist texts. But even if this method of division should prove to have originated in Tibet, this does not mean that we should not use it in our own inquiries, and today it is regarded as the preeminent approach to any historical

1. Nagao Gajin, *Saizō Bukkyō kenkyū* (A Study of Tibetan Buddhism; Tōkyō: Iwanami Shoten, 1954), p. 109.

2. See Tachikawa Musashi, *Saizō Bukkyō shūgi kenkyū* (A Study of the *Grub Mthaḥ* of Tibetan Buddhism; Tōkyō: The Tōyō Bunko), Vol. 1 (1974), p. 12.

consideration of Mādhyamika thought.

The Tibetan traditions do not, however, agree on whether the founder of the Prāsaṅgika school was Buddhapālita or Candrakīrti. For example, Se-ra rJe-btsun-pa and Sum-pa-mkhan-po hold that Buddhapālita was the founder,[3] while Thuḥu-bkwan says that it was "either Buddhapālita or Candrakīrti."[4] But then it is not a matter of such vital importance which of these two was the founder. The name of this school derives, needless to say, fromBuddhapālita's use of "consequential inference" (*prasaṅga-anumāna*) in commenting on the arguments of the *Middle Stanzas* in his *Mūlamadhyamakavṛtti*, but Buddhapālita's position in the history of Prāsaṅgika thought is minor in comparison with that of Candrakīrti, and Candrakīrti himself is by no means a renowned thinker in Indian Buddhism as a whole and even less so outside of Buddhism. Nevertheless, it was Candrakīrti who exerted influence on people such as Śāntideva, Prajñākaramati, Buddhaguhya and Vimalamitra, scholars who were in later times to be looked upon by the Tibetans as belonging to the Prāsaṅgika school, and it was also he who provided Tibetan Buddhism with its theoretical basis, especially that of the dGe-lugs-pa school.[5] In this sense Candrakīrti was indeed the founder of the Prāsaṅgika school.

The Prāsaṅgika school is a school that presents its arguments in terms of "*prasaṅga*" or "consequences," namely, by means of *reductio ad absurdum*. This *reductio ad absurdum* was used in order to argue that things which the ordinary person believes to really exist and to which he is attached do not exist even on the conventional level.[6] *Reductio ad absurdum* is a method of argument whereby in order to demonstrate the

---

3. *Rje btsun ḥjam dpal dbyaṅs chos kyi rgyal mtshan gyis mdzad paḥi grub mthaḥi rnam gshag* (Tibetan extracanonical works of the Tōyō Bunko, No. 167), f. 12b, l.2; Sum-pa-mkhan-po, *dPag bsam ljon bzaṅ* (C. Das [ed.], *Pag Sam Jon Zang*, Part I, *History of the Rise, Progress and Downfall of Buddhism in India*; Calcutta: Presidency Jail Press, 1908), p. 94.

4. Thuḥu-bkwan, *Grub mthaḥ śel gyi me loṅ*, ed. by Chhos Je Lama, Sarnath, Varanasi, 1963, p. 16, l.11.

5. See Tachikawa Musashi, "Chibetto shiryō ni mirareru Chūgan Purāsangika-ha no keifu" (The Lineage of the Mādhyamikan Prāsaṅgika School as Seen in Tibetan Materials), *Ajia Bunka*, Vol. 10, No. 1 (1978), pp. 66-74.

6. Tibetan extracanonical works of the Tōyō Bunko, No. 167 (see n. 3), f. 12b, ll.1-2.

truth of a proposition S, one first posits its contradictory non-S from which one then deduces a false conclusion. Since a false conclusion has been drawn from non-S, non-S may be said to be false, and therefore since non-S is false, the initial proposition S may be regarded as having been true.[7] In other words, the truth of a proposition S is held to be demonstrated by the illogical conclusion that results when the proposition S is negated and the proposition non-S advanced in its place.

This *reductio ad absurdum* initially appears rather frequently in Nāgārjuna's *Middle Stanzas*, although in a more primitive form than that employed by Buddhapālita, and *reductio ad absurdum* was in fact the most important method of argument used by Nāgārjuna. Let us now consider an example of *reductio ad absurdum* on the basis of one of the arguments developed in the *Middle Stanzas*.

As has already been explained in Chapter 5, the *Middle Stanzas*, II. 8-11, deal with the relationship between the act of traversing and the agent of this act, and it is argued that no one whosoever performs the act of traversing. Nāgārjuna's train of thought runs as follows:

a. If there is to be an act of traversing, either (a1) a traverser (*gantṛ*) traverses or (a2) a non-traverser (*agantṛ*) traverses.

b1. It is not a1. If a1 were true, it would result in the absurdity of a single traverser performing two acts of traversing. The first act of traversing is that necessary to establish a traverser, while the second act of traversing is that which occurs in relation to the traverser in his capacity as an agent established as a result of the first act of traversing. (It is considered, in other words, that the proposition "a traverser traverses" is possible only when the traverser has independent existence and functions as the locus for an act of traversing that exists apart from this locus.) Therefore, since a1 ("a traverser traverses") is false, a traverser does not traverse.

(It is evident that Nāgārjuna is here employing a type of *reductio ad absurdum*. Although Nāgārjuna's argument in the *Middle Stanzas* is not developed in exactly the same manner as described

7. Kajiyama Yūichi, *Kū no ronri* (The Logic of Emptiness), *Bukkyō no shisō* (Buddhist Thought), Vol. 3 (Tōkyō: Kadokawa Shoten, 1969), p. 149.

here, by positing a proposition contradictory to the proposition that he wishes to demonstrate, he draws a patently illogical conclusion.)

b2. It is not a2 either. This is because it is impossible for a non-traverser, namely, someone who does not traverse, to traverse. (In regard to b2, Nāgārjuna says in verse 8 simply that "a non-traverser does not traverse either," and he does not deal with it in detail as in the case of b1. But later commentaries give the above reason for this statement.)

Nāgārjuna often mentions in a single proposition two intrinsically interrelated factors or entities such as a traverser and the act of traversing, cause and effect, the seen and the act of seeing, etc. Then, positing all conceivable cases, he subdivides either of the two factors or the relationship between them. It is important to note that this division may be regarded in the final analysis as a division into *A* and non-*A*.

Let us now reconsider the above example. Traversing and the agent of traversing are the two factors dealt with here that already stand in an intrinsic relationship to one another—that of movement and its locus. If there should be a locus for the act of traversing, it will be expressed as either "traverser" (X) or "non-traverser" ($\tilde{X}$).

Here the expressions "traverser" and "non-traverser" might give the impression that Nāgārjuna has distributed the entire universe into that which is a traverser and that which is not a traverser. In this case Nāgārjuna has, however, distributed men into traversers and non-traversers. In other words, the entire universe of discourse in the present case is the set of all men in the world, not the entire universe. Hence, if we put "D" for the universe of discourse in the present case and "X" for "traverser," then a non-traverser will be symbolized as "$\tilde{X}/D$," which means the complementary set of X with reference to D.

If "traversing" is then expressed as "Y," our two earlier propositions may be expressed as follows:

a1. A traverser traverses.

gantur gamanam. (Literally, "the traversing of a traverser.")

(Xgen Ynom)

Xgen = *gantur* (of a traverser).

Ynom = *gamanam* (traversing).

a2. A non-traverser traverses.

agantur gamanam. (Literally, "the traversing of a non-traverser.")

($\tilde{X}$/*D*gen *Y*nom)

However, these two propositions result in a clearly undesirable conclusion. Nāgārjuna maintains that this is because it was a mistake to posit a1 and a2, and that in actual fact the negative form of each of these two propositions is true. Namely,

negation of a1: ~ (*X*gen *Y*nom)

negation of a2: ~ ($\tilde{X}$/*D*gen *Y*nom)

The conjunction of these two propositions implies that no one whosoever traverses. Nāgārjuna was of course aware of the fact that this runs counter to generally accepted ideas in our everyday world. It was rather because of his very awareness of this that he sought to refute the commonsense view. This contrariety between the numerous theses put forward by Nāgārjuna in the *Middle Stanzas* and commonly accepted views came to mould the basic character of Mādhyamika thought.

There was of course a close connection between Nāgārjuna's assertion of views running counter to common sense and his use of *reductio ad absurdum* as his main method of argument, and his successors attempted to demonstrate each from his own standpoint the counter-commonsense theses of their master. Buddhapālita and Candrakīrti set about presenting in a more systematic manner the arguments based on *reductio ad absurdum* that Nāgārjuna had employed in a still primitive form, while Bhāvaviveka sought to demonstrate Nāgārjuna's theses contradictory to generally accepted ideas by applying the methods of logic that had been only just established at that time.

2

According to Tibetan sources, Buddhapālita lived in southern India[8] at about the same time as or a little prior to Dignāga.[9] Today, he is thought to have lived from about 470 to 540.[10]

---

8. *Pag Sam Jon Zang*, p. 94.
9. A. Schiefner (ed.), *Tāranātha chos ḥbyuṅ* (Petropoli, 1868), p. 99.
10. Kajiyama Yūichi, *op. cit.*, p. 143.

When compared with the *Akutobhayā* and Piṅgala's commentary (preserved in Kumārajīva's Chinese translation), Buddhapālita's commentary on the *Middle Stanzas* (*Mūlamadhyamakavṛtti*) is extremely detailed, but it has no comments on Yogācāra thought, the representative school of Buddhist thought at the time, nor are there any traces of the influence of Dignāga's logic or epistemology.[11] Furthermore, although the sequence and method of explication frequently coincide with that of Candrakīrti's *Prasannapadā*, Buddhapālita's commentary contains arguments that are rather different in nature from those of the commentaries by Bhāvaviveka and Sthiramati.

As is well-known, Bhāvaviveka (died 570), who was active a little after Buddhapālita, criticized the latter's *Mūlamadhyamakavṛtti*, only to be later severely criticized in turn by Candrakīrti, who defended Buddhapālita's position. One of the most important passages in which Candrakīrti defends Buddhapālita against the criticism of Bhāvaviveka is his long commentary on the *Middle Stanzas*, I. 1. This section of the *Middle Stanzas* deals with things or existents (*bhāva*) and arising, and it posits four modes of arising, namely, from self, from another, from both, and without cause. The original Sanskrit of the main part of the first verse is as follows:

> *na svato nāpi parato na dvābhyāṃ nāpy ahetutaḥ /*
> *utpannā jātu vidyante bhāvāḥ*..... // (I.1)[12]
>
> (Things are born neither from self, nor from another, nor from both [self and another], nor without cause.)

The content of this verse may be rewritten as a conjunction of the following four propositions (cf. p. 135 ff.):

c1. Things are not born from self.
na svato bhāvāḥ utpannā vidyante.
(*na svato X*nom *Y*nom *V*)
*X*nom = *bhāvāḥ* (things).
*Y*nom = *utpannā*[*h*] (born; although it means literally "arisen," it has for convenience' sake here been translated as "born").

---

11. Yamaguchi Susumu, *Hannya shisōshi* (The History of *Prajñā* Thought; Kyōto: Hōzōkan, 1966), p. 145.

12. *Prasannapadā*, p. 12, ll. 13-14. The part omitted here reads "nowhere whatsoever and nothing whatsoever" (*kva cana ke cana*).

V= *vidyante* (are).

c2. Things are not born from another.

na parato bhāvāḥ utpannā vidyante.

(*na parato X*nom *Y*nom *V*)

c3. Things are not born from both [self and another].

na dvābhyāṃ bhāvāḥ utpannā vidyante.

(*na dvābhyām X*nom *Y*nom *V*)

c4. Things are not born without cause.

na ahetuto bhāvāḥ utpannā vidyante.

(*na ahetuto X*nom *Y*nom *V*)

In what follows, c1 and c2 are of special importance. The only difference between these two propositions is that whereas c1 has "from self" (*svato*), c2 has "from another" (*parato*). In this case, "self" and "other" are contradictories, for the intersection of self and other is equivalent to the null set while their sum constitutes the entire universe of discourse in the present context. Hence, if we express "self" as "*S*" and other as "$\tilde{S}$," c1 and c2 may be rewritten as follows:

c1'. (*na S*ab *X*nom *Y*nom *V*)

c2'. (*na* $\tilde{S}$ab *X*nom *Y*nom *V*)

(The "ab" of "*S*ab" indicates that "*S*" is in the ablative case.)

Buddhapālita's comment on c1 and c2 reads as follows:

> Things are not born of self, for a [second] arising is unnecessary and it would result in the error of continuing to be born *ad infinitum*....
>
> [Things] are not born from another, for it would result in the error of everything being born from everything.[13]

He also adduces similar arguments for c3 and c4.[14]

Buddhapālita's demonstration is a typical example of *reductio ad absurdum*, and it may be formulaically rewritten as follows:

> If things are born from self (*p*), then their [second] arising is unnecessary (*q*).

13. *Mūlamadhyamakavṛtti*, p. 11, ll. 5-13.
14. *Ibid*., p. 12.

Supposing that things are born from self (p),

This results in [the absurdity involved in] the fact that their [second] arising is unnecessary (q).

This may be symbolically expressed as follows:

$(p \supset q)\, p. \supset q$ (If p then q, and if p then q.)[15]

The statement "it would result in the error of continuing to be born *ad infinitum*," as well as Buddhapālita's demonstration of c2-c4, may also be understood in a similar manner.

By thus applying an argument based on *reductio ad absurdum* to each of the two, three or four disjuncts of which Nāgārjuna's syllogisms generally consisted, Buddhapālita sought to provide a single consistent method of explication for the arguments of the *Middle Stanzas*. The use of *reductio ad absurdum*, even though in a somewhat undeveloped form, was already in evidence in Nāgārjuna's *Middle Stanzas*, but Buddhapālita attempted to express Nāgārjuna's *reductio ad absurdum* in a more systematic fashion. Bhāvaviveka, on the other hand, who was active in the mid-sixth century and came under the influence of the system of formal logic that had evolved by then, set about interpreting Nāgārjuna's arguments by means of formal logic. He perceived that $(p \supset q)\, p. \supset q$, constituting one of the distinctive features of *reductio ad absurdum*, also implies $(p \supset q)\, \tilde{q}. \supset \tilde{p}$ [if $(p \supset q)$ and non-q, then non-p], and he utilized this in his criticism of Buddhapālita. In other words, according to Bhāvaviveka, Buddhapālita had asserted non-p ($\tilde{p}$), namely, "things are born not from self." In at least Candrakīrti's view,[16] Bhāvaviveka considered that if the proposition "things are born not from self" ($\tilde{p}$) be true, then things must be born from either another, both self and another,

15. Kajiyama Yūichi, *op. cit.*, pp. 154-155.

16. After having stated that the proposition "Things are not born from self" must be read as an absolute negative (Tibetan Tripiṭaka [Peking Edition], Vol. 95, p. 155, f. 3, l. 4), Bhāvaviveka writes, "If it is understood as an implicative negative, since priority is given to the establishment [of a certain thing], by establishing the fact that 'things are unborn' (*chos rnams ma skyes so*) the non-birth [of things] is indicated. This will consequently deviate from the thesis [that 'nothing whatsoever is born']." (*ibid.*, p. 155, f. 3, ll. 5-6) It is not clear whether "things are unborn" here means that they are "unborn from self" or whether it refers to something positive that is unborn. Cf. Y. Kajiyama, "Bhāvaviveka's Prajñāpradīpaḥ (I. Kapitel)," *WZKSOA*, Band VII (1963), p. 48.

or without cause. But there was a trick involved in Bhāvaviveka's interpretation. Let us reconsider c1' and c2'.

It is the negative particle "*na*" in (*na* *S*ab *X*nom *Y*nom *V*) that is at issue. Does it negate the whole proposition or does it negate the term "*S*" (self)? In the case of its negating the proposition as a whole, it may be understood either as modifying the verb or in the sense of "... *iti na*" (it is not that ....) placed at the end of the sentence. These two possibilities may be expressed as follows:

(*na* *S*ab *X*nom *Y*nom *V*) or

(*S*ab *X*nom *Y*nom *V*) *iti na*.

(The arrow indicates the relationship between modifier and modificand.)

These two formulae may, of course, be both expressed as:

~(*S*ab *X*nom*Y*nom *V*)

If, on the other hand, the negative particle is held to modify the term "*S*," it implies that "non-self," that is to say, one or more of the possibilities indicated by other, both or without cause is true. This is the same as "non-adult" signifying "child." In other words,

(*na* *S*ab *X*nom *Y*nom *V*)

implies at least one of the following: [17]

(*S̃*ab *X*nom *Y*nom *V*)

(*dvābhyām* *X*nom *Y*nom *V*)

(*ahetuto* *X*nom *Y*nom *V*)

As was pointed out in Chapter 8, the negation of a proposition is termed "*prasajyapratiṣedha*" or absolute negation, while the negation of a term is called "*paryudāsa*" or implicative negation. In his criticism of Buddhapālita's *reductio ad absurdum*, Bhāvaviveka took note of the danger that inevitably accompanies any *reductio ad absurdum* when it seeks to disprove the contradictory of its own postulate and conclusion, and he maintained that Buddhapālita's commentary ended up demonstrating something that contradicted Nāgārjuna's original intent. But

17. On the logical meaning of "self, other, both, and without cause," see Chapter 8.

regardless of whether he was aware of it or not, Bhāvaviveka was using a trick, for he repeatedly stated that his own negative propositions were to be understood as examples of absolute negation. As has already been pointed out, when c1' is interpreted as an absolute negation, the negative particle *na* negates the entire proposition "things are born from self," in which case there is no question of whether or not things are born from another, from both self and another, or without cause.

If that be the case, why then did Bhāvaviveka not interpret Buddhapālita's commentary too according to the dictates of absolute negation? It was an already acknowledged fact at the time that *reductio ad absurdum* disproved a proposition contradictory to its own postulate and conclusion. But it did not require that the negation of the postulate in Buddhapālita's commentary—i.e., "things are not born from self" —be interpreted as an implicative negation, namely, "things are born not from self." If Bhāvaviveka himself used the proposition "things are not born from self" in the sense of an absolute negation, it should have been possible for Buddhapālita, and in fact anyone else, to do the same. It was Candrakīrti who criticized Bhāvaviveka along these lines, but a more detailed consideration of Candrakīrti's criticism will be left until later.

One reason that the interpretation of the negative particle should have given rise to such a problem in c1-c4 was that the four terms "from self," etc., do not constitute the elements of compounds. When Nāgārjuna subjects one of two factors under discussion–for example, traversing and traverser—to a complementary distribution in order to expose the dilemma involved in his opponent's view that, for example, "a traverser traverses," he generally employs a compound with the negative prefix "*a*-," as for instance in the case of "traverser" (*gantṛ*) and "non-traverser" (*agantṛ*). Let us reconsider the negation in a1 and a2.

Negation of a1: ~ (*X*gen *Y*nom)

Negation of a2: ~ ($\tilde{X}$/*D*gen *Y*nom)

In the case of II. 8 it is obvious that the negative particle *na* modifies the entire proposition, and there is hardly any possibility of the question arising of whether or not *na* modifies a particular term—for example, "traverser"—as is the case in c1-c4. Thus it was probably the fact that the terms "from self," etc., in c1-c4 were not the elements of compounds that gave rise to two possible interpretations of the function of the negative particle *na* in I. 1. But the fact that elsewhere "from self," etc., are almost invariably expressed as elements of compounds would appear to suggest that c1-c4 should also be read as absolute negations.

Buddhapālita considered that by combining the *reductio ad absurdum* of each of the propositions c1-c4 it would be possible to demonstrate what Nāgārjuna was trying to say. Things are born neither from self, nor from another, nor from both self and another, nor without cause; they are, in a word, born from nowhere—this was what Nāgārjuna had been asserting. But in actual fact things do exist before our very eyes and form the basis of our existence. Even followers of the Mādhyamika school could not avert their eyes from this fact of reality. It was faced with such a vexed question that Candrakīrti made his appearance and further developed the methodology of Buddhapālita.

3

Once Dignāga had established his system of logic, Buddhists could not ignore it, and within the Mādhyamika school it was Bhāvaviveka who attempted to explain the idea of emptiness by employing Dignāga's system of logic. He too naturally directed his attacks first and foremost against the realists who considered that "an object exists because it is linked to language." In his commentary on the *Middle Stanzas* he presents the following syllogism of the realists:

a. Traversing exists.

b. Because a word linked to it (traversing) exists on account of it.

c. Generally speaking, when there is nothing in a certain place, one does not give verbal expression to what is linked to it (i.e., words) on account of it, as for example one does not say "a hare with a horn."

d. Words linked to it (traversing) exist on account of traversing, as in the sentence "Devadatta traverses."

e. Therefore traversing exists.[18]

Bhāvaviveka points out five errors in this syllogism.

1. The error of demonstrating anew something that is already evident and therefore does not need to be demonstrated. This

18. Tibetan Tripiṭaka (Peking Edition), Vol. 95, p. 163, f. 5, l. 4; Vol. 96, p. 266, f. 1, l. 6.

error occurs when, for example, one seeks to establish on the level of conventional truth the existence of traversing, the existence of which is already recognized by people at large.[19]

2. The error resulting from the fact that the reason (*hetu*) cannot serve as a reason because the existence of the locus or property-possessor (*dharmin*; *p*) is not recognized. If one should wish to demonstrate that coming and going to see by means of the eye of wisdom exist in the case of an enlightened person, the reason, namely , "a word linked to it exists on account of it," could not serve as a reason because the very locus—traversing—itself does not exist in the case of an enlightened person.[20]

3. The error resulting from the fact that whereas the existence of the reason in the locus *p* must be recognized by both parties, demonstration of the probandum (*sādhya*) is impossible if the existence of the reason in the locus *p* is not recognized by one of the two parties. In the present instance, the Mādhyamikans maintain that, properly speaking, traversing does not exist, while their opponents assert that traversing does exist.[21]

4. The error involved in the absence of positive concomitance (*anvaya*) such as "whenever there is *h* there is *s*." This presupposes the following counterargument: "You Mādhyamikans recognize the existence of arising, coming and going on the level of conventional truth, and we recognize the existence of arising, coming and going on the level of ultimate truth. Although there is the difference between conventional truth and ultimate truth, both parties recognize the reason, namely, the designation of the object by means of language. Therefore, there is positive concomitance." [22] In reply to this, Bhāvaviveka argues that since on the level of ultimate truth there is no utterance of words referring to any object, and since conventional truth is not an issue in the

19. Although these five errors are here not directly correlated with the aforementioned syllogism, it is obvious that they can be applied to it. *Ibid.*, Vol. 95, p. 162, f. 3, l. 6; Vol. 96, p. 258, f. 5, l. 8.

20. *Ibid.*, Vol. 95, p. 162, f. 3, l. 7; Vol. 96, p. 259, f. 1, l. 7.

21. *Ibid.*, Vol. 95, p. 162, f. 3, l. 8; Vol. 96, p. 259, f. 2, l. 4.

22. *Ibid.*, Vol. 96, p. 259, f. 2, l. 6.

present context, there is no positive concomitance.[23]

5. The error involved in the fact that the reason does not fulfill the second and third conditions of a valid reason, i.e., it exists only in the dissimilar class (*vipakṣa*). In the above example, the dissimilar class corresponds to that which does not exist. For the Mādhyamikans, on the other hand, nothing exists. Therefore, the reason exists only in the dissimilar class.[24]

Thus Bhāvaviveka's method was one in which the plane of conventional truth and that of ultimate truth were scrupulously differentiated, and although he himself recognized the validity of reasoning based on formal logic in regard to the former, when his opponent attacked him with this validity as a weapon, he immediately resorted to the "Mādhyamikan principle" that nothing exists on the level of ultimate truth. Thus the syllogisms that he presents are always accompanied by the qualification "on the level of ultimate truth." He says, for example,

a. On the level of ultimate truth a traverser does not traverse.

b. Because a traverser is associated with movement.

c. Like a person who is standing still.[25]

In this syllogism the locus or property-possessor *p* is "traverser," the probandum *s* is "traversing," the reason *h* is "association with movement," the similar class (*sapakṣa*) is "those who do not traverse," and the dissimilar class is "those who traverse." It is the understanding of the world at large and also of realists that "a traverser traverses," but Bhāvaviveka seeks to demonstrate the very opposite of this by availing himself of the premise that on the level of ultimate truth nothing exists. In this syllogism, the reason fulfills the first condition insofar that it applies to a traverser. It is worth noting that in this respect Bhāvaviveka is speaking on the level of conventional truth. In addition, the second condition is also fulfilled in that the reason applies to a person who is standing still, who constitutes one part of the similar class consisting of those who do not traverse. Finally, the dissimilar class of those who

---

23. *Ibid.*, Vol. 95, p. 162, f. 3, l. 8.

24. *Ibid.*, Vol. 95, p. 162, f. 4, l. 1; Vol. 96, p. 259, f. 3, l. 3.

25. *Ibid.*, Vol. 95, p. 164, f. 2, l. 1; Vol. 96, p. 268, f. 4, l. 2.

traverse does not exist from the Mādhyamikan standpoint. In Dignāga's system, when there is no dissimilar class, the third condition of a valid reason is considered to have been fulfilled. In this manner Bhāvaviveka seeks to demonstrate the truth of this syllogism.

This reasoning of Bhāvaviveka's represented an attempt to reformulate by means of Dignāga's formal logic Nāgārjuna's view that although ultimate truth transcends language, truth cannot be comprehended without language. It was the act of a philosopher who, although fully aware of the impossibility of grasping the absolute, still ventured to confront it. Bhāvaviveka emphasized the difference between the plane of conventional truth and that of ultimate truth, but yet it was also this same Bhāvaviveka who within the reasoning process of a single syllogism argued at one point from the level of conventional truth and at another from the level of ultimate truth.

This method of Bhāvaviveka's met with criticism even within the Mādhyamika school, and as has already been noted, in the mid-seventh century Candrakīrti took over the method employed by Buddhapālita in his commentary on the *Middle Stanzas* and established the Prāsaṅgika school in opposition to Bhāvaviveka's Svātantrika school. Although Candrakīrti was acquainted with Dignāga's system of logic, when faced with the contradictions that Bhāvaviveka had been unable to avoid, he abandoned the hope of proving emptiness by means of logic. His method was one in which, rather than formulate his own views, he applied himself primarily to pointing out by means of *reductio ad absurdum* the contradictions inherent in his opponents' views. For example, if the opponent should maintain that "a traverser traverses" (*gantā gacchati*), Candrakīrti first assumes that there can be only one act of traversing. When the act of traversing (*gamana*) is linked to the word "traverser" (*gantā*), there is nothing to which the word "traverses" (*gacchati*) may link itself, and hence this interpretation is untenable. If, on the other hand, traversing is linked to the word "traverses," "traverser" then becomes nothing but an empty word. And if one were to suppose that traversing be linked to both "traverser" and "traverses," two acts of traversing would become necessary. Therefore, according to Candrakīrti, the statement "a traverser traverses" cannot be true. This method is basically the same as that employed by Nāgārjuna, but an advance has been made on Nāgārjuna in that Candrakīrti clearly differentiates between words and their referents. Candrakīrti was extremely sceptical of logical consistency even on the level of conventional truth, and he does not assume the attitude of Bhāvaviveka, who recognized conventional truth as it is. For Candrakīrti, "a traverser does not traverse" even on the level of conventional truth, let alone on the level of ultimate truth. Whereas Bhāvaviveka's Svātantrika school was not to exert any great influence within Mahāyāna Buddhism as a whole, Candrakīrti's Prāsaṅgika school was to serve as the philosophical basis of later Mahāyāna Buddhism, especially Tantric thought. Unlike Bhāvaviveka, Candrakīrti did not attempt to demonstrate the thesis of emptiness by means of logic. In however consistent a manner logic or language might be systematized, for Candrakīrti they still represented an obstacle that had to be negated at least once in order to attain to *nirvāṇa*. For him the presentation by means of logic of the structure of a single integrated world was meaningless insofar as the attainment of liberation was concerned. Like Nāgārjuna and Buddhapālita, he too sought to point out the errors inherent in the views of his opponents by applying first and foremost the methods of *reductio ad absurdum* to their assertions.

This attitude of Candrakīrti's towards logic and language was rooted in his own understanding of the phenomenal world (or the profane) and ultimate truth (or the sacred). He considered that the absolute existed on a level totally transcending the phenomenal world, this latter being comprehended through the medium of language. If the absolute does at all manifest itself to man, it does so only to a Buddha who has attained enlightenment, and through the attainment of a mode of wisdom differing from that of everyday linguistic activity the Buddha experiences the absolute. And in order to become a Buddha, Candrakīrti maintains that one must undertake religious praxis such as meditation in a regular fashion. His main work, entitled *Madhyamakāvatāra*, describes the manner in which a practitioner passes through various stages in approaching the state of a Buddha, and he emphasizes the importance of religious praxis.

This supralogical standpoint of Candrakīrti's contrasts with that of Bhāvaviveka, for the latter considered absolute truth to indwell in the phenomenal world. It was for the very reason that the two poles of absolute truth and the phenomenal world, or the sacred and the profane, ha 'e language as their common point of contact that Bhāvaviveka believed it possible to demonstrate emptiness or ultimate truth by means of logic or language and accordingly formulated his syllogisms based on "autonomous inference" (*svatantra-anumāna*).

4

In the *Middle Stanzas* Nāgārjuna established the concept of the "two truths." This concept had already been mentioned in the Early Canon and other works such as the *Abhidharma-mahāvibhāṣā-śāstra*, but it was probably Nāgārjuna who first raised it to the level of a central doctrinal concept.[26] According to Nāgārjuna, it was by means of the two truths of "worldly conventional truth" (*loka-saṃvṛti-satya*) and "ultimate truth"(*paramārtha-satya*) that the Buddha expounded the teachings. In this context conventional truth, assuming the form of language, represents the words uttered by an enlightened Buddha in order to guide sentient beings, and it is not truth as conceived of by sentient beings from their own standpoint. This interpretation of the two truths as propounded by Nāgārjuna has traditionally been referred to as the "theory of the two truths as related to the teachings."

Candrakīrti's understanding of the two truths, however, differed considerably from that of Nāgārjuna. According to Candrakīrti, the two truths did not so much relate to the manner in which the Buddha expounded the teachings, but described the two kinds of intrinsic nature of things existing in this world. This way of thinking has been called the "theory of the two truths as related to objects," "objects" meaning objects of cognition. Of course, as will be seen below, Candrakīrti also held that the teachings of the Buddha took the form of conventional truth, but this was not its primary significance. In the *Madhyamakāvatāra* Candrakīrti deals with the two truths particularly at VI. 23-29 and VI. 79-82, and in his commentary on verse 23 they are explained as follows:

> The Buddha, the Blessed One, unerringly cognizant of the nature of the two truths, declared that all internal and external things such as mental inertia and sprouts, etc., have two kinds of nature. They are, namely, the conventional and ultimate truth. Of these, ultimate truth manifests itself as the special object of the wisdom of those with correct insight, and it does not exist of its own. This is the one type

---

26. Nagao Gajin, "Chūgan tetsugaku no konponteki tachiba" (The Fundamental Standpoint of Mādhyamika Philosophy), *Tetsugaku Kenkyū*, No. 366 (1947), p. 19.

of nature. The other is that which manifests itself by means of the erroneous cognitive powers of ordinary people whose eye of intelligence has been completely obscured by eye disease, and it does not exist of its own in the manner in which it becomes the object of the cognitive powers of ignorant people. Consequently, all things have these two natures. Of these two natures, the object of correct cognitive powers is real, which means that it is ultimate truth.[27]

Candrakīrti also considers that there are two varieties of erroneous cognitive powers, namely, those rooted in sound sense organs and those rooted in unsound sense organs (v. 24). The conventional is accordingly divided into two kinds on the basis of these two varieties of cognitive powers.

> That which is grasped by the six unimpaired sense organs is understood by the world; it is truth from the standpoint of the world. The other [objects of sense organs impaired through illness, etc.] are considered to be erroneous from the standpoint of the world. (v. 25)

The former represents the world as cognized by ordinary people possessing normal sense organs, and since they believe it to be real, Candrakīrti refers to it as "conventional truth" (*saṃvṛti-satya*). "Truth" in this case is truth only as understood by ordinary people, and not truth as seen from the standpoint of a Buddha. But the lives of ordinary people are grounded in this conventional truth, which is thus also called "worldly conventional truth" (*loka-saṃvṛti-satya*).

As for the latter case of objects as cognized by impaired sense organs, Candrakīrti maintains that they do not exist even on the level of the conventional. In fact he does not even look upon people with impaired sense organs as ordinary people belonging to the world at large (*loka*), but calls them the "non-world" (*aloka*) and declares that "their conventional is the non-worldly conventional (*aloka-saṃvṛti*)."[28] According to him, the doctrines of non-Buddhist schools, such as the three constituent elements of the world and the god Īśvara posited by the Sāṃkhya school,

---

27. Louis de la Vallée Poussin (ed.), ***Madhyamakāvatāra, Bibliotheca Buddhica*** IX (St. Petersburg, 1907), p. 102, l.12-p.103, l. 5. Cf. Ogawa Ichijō, ***Kūshō shisō no kenkyū*** (A Study of the Philosophy of Emptiness; Kyōto: Bun'eidō, 1976), pp. 80-81.

28. ***Prasannapadā***, p. 493, ll. 2-3.

all belong to the "erroneous conventional" (*ad* v. 26), which is equivalent to the above "non-worldly conventional." In passing, it may be noted that Bhāvaviveka recognizes for example the view that things are born from self, represented by the Sāṃkhya school, as belonging to the conventional.[29]

In the *Prasannapadā*, Candrakīrti gives three interpretations of the word "*saṃvṛti*" or "conventional." He first states that "it is *saṃvṛti* because it completely conceals the truth of all things."[30] In the same passage he also identifies *saṃvṛti* with "ignorance" (*ajñāna*) since ignorance conceals the truth of all things. Although the philological correctness of this interpretation remains open to question, it may be said to bring out the philosophical implications of the term. The second meaning of *saṃvṛti* given by Candrakīrti is "mutual interdependence."[31] Setting aside the question of whether or not it is permissible as far as Sanskrit is concerned to interpret the word "*saṃvṛti*" in this sense, Candrakīrti's intention here was probably to impress upon the reader the fact that the concept of *saṃvṛti* is close in its connotations to that of dependent co-arising. The third meaning he gives is "the conventions of life in general or linguistic activity as recognized by the world at large. This assumes the form of that which expresses and that which is expressed, the knower and the known, etc."[32] The standard translation "conventional" reflects most closely this third meaning of *saṃvṛti*.

For Candrakīrti, and in fact for all Buddhists, the important thing is not to know the structure of the conventional but to transcend the conventional and attain to ultimate truth. In this sense, the conventional corresponds to the profane that must be negated, while ultimate truth represents the sacred that is to be sought. According to Candrakīrti, it is in order to negate the conventional that knowledge of internal divisions within the conventional is necessary, and knowledge of logic is also necessary in order to bring everyday linguistic activity to cessation.

In the Mādhyamika school, language as used by ordinary people must be negated at least once. The use of language represents for the

---

29. *Ibid.*, p. 26, l. 3.

30. *Ibid.*, p. 492, l. 10.

31. *Ibid.*, p. 492, l. 11.

32. *Ibid.*, p. 492, ll. 11-12.

person concerned nothing less than the manifestation of the world or of linguistic proliferation. Candrakīrti considered that it was impossible to attain to *nirvāṇa* as long as the world remained an object of cognition. He did not attempt to explain the structure of the world by a series of affirmative propositions of his own. Instead he sought to point out the unreliability of language and logic by exposing the contradictions inherent in the views of his opponents. This stance of his was especially conspicuous in his criticism of Bhāvaviveka.

Bhāvaviveka, who was of the opinion that one should proceed in one's arguments on the basis of carefully formulated syllogisms, had criticized Buddhapālita for having employed in his arguments neither the "reason" nor "example" that were indispensable elements of the autonomous inference (*svatantra-anumāna*). In addition, as we have already seen, he also maintained that since one of the distinguishing features of *reductio ad absurdum* is the disproof of a contradictory postulate, Buddhapālita had demonstrated that "things are born not from self," that is to say, "they are born from another, etc." After having cited this criticism of Bhāvaviveka's in his *Prasannapadā*, Candrakīrti offers the following critique:

> [Bhāvaviveka counterargues that] when it is considered that "things are not born from self," this will give the undesirable result that "they are born from another." [We reply that] this is not so. This is because the negation of a proposition (*prasajyapratiṣedha*) was intended and because the arising from another has also been negated [by the second proposition "Things are not born from another"].[33]

Just as Bhāvaviveka repeatedly maintained that his own propositions ought to be read as *prasajyapratiṣedha* or absolute negations, so Candrakīrti held that the propositions "Things are not born from self," etc., should also be read in the same way. Furthermore, Candrakīrti did not in fact recognize any reason or example as used in syllogisms with which to convince others.[34]

In this manner, language as embodied in the propositions "Things are born from self, from another, etc." was successively negated. Nāgārjuna's aim in the *Middle Stanzas* had been to show how language

33. *Ibid.*, p. 13, ll. 4-6.

34. *Ibid.*, p.19, l. 4.

could be negated, and Candrakīrti may be said to have been faithful to this attitude of Nāgārjuna's. He believed that it was out of the question to aspire to the manifestation of ultimate truth if linguistic activity was not brought to cessation through the negation of all the disjuncts making up the dilemmas presented by Nāgārjuna. However, he did not totally disregard syllogisms. He employed them in accordance with the arguments of his opponents in order to point out the contradictions contained therein. Although he was fully aware that the language he was using was imperfect, he also believed it to be possible to negate still less perfect language or its content even by means of imperfect language. At the same time, it was impossible to negate language of superior content by means of inferior language.[35] In other words, Candrakīrti posited different levels of language.

In the final analysis, all language pertains to the conventional and not to ultimate truth. When language is functioning, this means that one is cognizing objects within the conventional. Candrakīrti held *nirvāṇa* to be unattainable as long as one is cognizing objects or "the known" (*jñeya*) or as long as one remains attached to these objects of cognition. Cognition of the outward form of objects and attachment to objects as being real represent the two obstacles to the attainment of *nirvāṇa*. Hence, those who wish to attain to *nirvāṇa* must overcome these two obstacles.

The process whereby an "ordinary person" (*pṛthagjana*) becomes a practitioner or "holy one" (*ārya*) and then a Buddha has in Buddhism been regarded as the most generally applicable process of spiritual development. The holy one in this context has already started to negate the profane and proceed towards the sacred, but he still abides within the profane and stands as it were between the profane and the sacred. This threesome of ordinary person, holy one and Buddha was also used by the Mādhyamikans as an index for the stages of religious praxis.

For example, in their comments on the *Middle Stanzas*, XXIV.9, both the *Akutobhayā* and Piṅgala's commentary contrast these three stages in virtually identical terms.[36] It is stated by both, namely, that the ordinary person persists in believing that the conventional in the every-

35. Cf. *Madhyamakāvatāra*, v. 27.

36. *Akutobhayā*: Tibetan Tripiṭaka (Peking Edition), Vol. 95, p. 43, f. 2, l. 3 ff;

day world really exists while the holy one knows that this world is empty; the Buddha, on the other hand, is said to employ both of these standpoints as a means for guiding sentient beings. The corresponding section in Buddhapālita's *Mūlamadhyamakavṛtti* is regrettably missing, and so we are unable to ascertain Buddhapālita's interpretation, but Candrakīrti presents an analogous comparison of the three standpoints corresponding to these three stages in his *Madhyamakāvatāra*.

> The ultimate (*don dam pa*) for ordinary people is the conventional-only (*kun rdzob tsam*) of the holy ones who cognize that which manifests itself [to their cognitive organs]. The emptiness of the own-being (*raṅ bshin*) of this [conventional-only] is the ultimate for them (i.e., the holy ones). The ultimate for the Buddhas is own-being itself, and since it is undeceptive, it is the ultimate truth (*don dam paḥi bden pa*).[37]

Ordinary people cognize various objects to which they then become attached. They are hampered, in other words, by both obstacles impeding their attainment of *nirvāṇa*, namely, the cognition of objects and attachment to objects of cognition. The holy ones, on the other hand, may cognize the outward form of objects of cognition, but unlike ordinary people they do not become attached to them as if they were real. They have, in other words, overcome one of the two obstacles to the attainment of *nirvāṇa*. That which is regarded by ordinary people as really existing and as the ultimate is, for the holy ones, something that merely assumes the form of objects but does not become an object of attachment. This conventional that does not become an object of attachment is designated by Candrakīrti as "conventional-only" (*saṃvṛti-*

Piṅgala's commentary: Taishō Tripiṭaka, Vol. 30, p. 32c ("On account of perverted views the world produces false *dharmas* which are real within the world. The worthy and holy ones know the nature of perverted views and so they know that all *dharmas* are empty and unborn. For the holy ones this is the ultimate truth and is designated as real. Relying upon these two truths, the Buddhas preach the Dharma for sentient beings."). We may note that a passage almost identical to this section in Piṅgala's commentary appears in the Chinese translation of Bhāvaviveka's *Prajñāpradīpa, ad* XXIV. 10 (Taishō Tripiṭaka, Vol. 30, p. 125b), although a corresponding passage is not to be found in the Tibetan translation of the *Prajñāpradīpa* (cf. Tibetan Tripiṭaka [Peking Edition], Vol. 95, p. 247, f. 1, l. 3 ff).

37. *Madhyamakāvatāra*, p. 108, ll. 13-18; cf. Ogawa Ichijō, *op. cit.*, p. 100. "Ultimate" is probably similar in meaning to "real" appearing in the passage quoted from Piṅgala's commentary in n. 36.

mātra). This term, not to be found in the *Akutobhayā* or the commentaries by Piṅgala and Bhāvaviveka, constitutes a distinctive feature of Candrakīrti's interpretation of the two truths. He thus divides the conventional into "conventional-only" and "conventional truth."

A Buddha neither perceives the outward form of objects nor does he become attached to them. This is because he has overcome the two obstacles to the attainment of *nirvāṇa*. Needless to say, language does not function in the realm of ultimate truth. As is indicated by the above quotation, the ultimate for holy ones is the emptiness of the own-being of conventional-only, whereas the ultimate truth for a Buddha is own-being (*raṅ bshin*) itself. When we refer to the emptiness *of* something, this implies the act of viewing a certain thing as empty, and the reason that in contrast to the emptiness of the own-being of conventional-only, representing the ultimate of the holy ones, Candrakīrti described the ultimate truth of a Buddha simply as own-being is probably that he wished to point to the very essence of truth itself such as does not imply any act of viewing a certain thing as empty. In the *Prasannapadā* Candrakīrti refers to the essence or emptiness of a *dharma* as "own-being" (*svabhāva*).[38] In the *Middle Stanzas*, apart from some ambiguous instances such as XXII. 16, the term "own-being" is used almost exclusively in the meaning of "own-being" as propounded by Nāgārjuna's opponents, that is to say, in a negative sense. Candrakīrti also uses this term in the sense of "own-being" as propounded by advocates of the existence of own-being or an intrinsic reality, but he further uses it in the sense of truth. Although for Candrakīrti ultimate truth was nothing other than emptiness, his conception of this ultimate truth may be considered to have been somewhat more positive than that of Nāgārjuna, which was expressed through the medium of negation.

The ultimate truth represents the goal of all people aspiring to the attainment of the sacred, and it is none other than Buddhas who may reach it and dwell there. Thus the explanation of the existence of the world in which ordinary people have their actual being was a task that fell also upon the Mādhyamikans.

---

38. *Prasannapadā*, p. 264, l. 12.

5

If everything were empty, then things would neither arise nor disappear, and there would also be no Four Noble Truths (*Middle Stanzas*, XXIV. 1), in which case Nāgārjuna's viewpoint would be equivalent to a form of nihilism advocating that nothing exists. Nāgārjuna replied to this criticism by introducing the distinction between conventional truth and ultimate truth. He argued, namely, that although ultimate truth does transcend language, the Buddha expounds the teaching by relying upon conventional truth in the form of everyday language, and it is impossible to expound ultimate truth without relying upon conventional truth (*ibid*., XXIV. 10). This conventional truth was recognized as the locus of existence for ordinary or unenlightened people. Nāgārjuna defined conventional truth in terms of "provisional designation" (*prajñaptir upādāya*: provisionally establishing [the existence of a certain thing] in reliance upon [another thing]). This basic conception remained the same for Candrakīrti. Unless one were to assert that everything is essentially equivalent to nothing, that the world is without any order whatsoever and that all human endeavour is totally meaningless, even a Mādhyamikan maintaining that "everything is empty" could not avoid explaining the structure of the world and the basis of human activity.

But Nāgārjuna did not, however, evince any great interest in the structure of the world and the nature of human activity. For him it was sufficient to realize that regardless of the nature of the world's structure, this structure was in the final analysis empty, and it was only in this respect that an understanding of the structure of the world was required. Candrakīrti, on the other hand, differed somewhat from Nāgārjuna in his understanding of the structure of the world, for he took a far greater interest than Nāgārjuna in the very structure of the world itself, and he emphasized the fact that the phenomenal world evolving before the very eyes of man was necessary as the basis of human existence. This difference to be seen between Nāgārjuna and Candrakīrti in their respective attitudes towards the world is also reflected in differences in their understanding of basic concepts such as the two truths and dependent co-arising.

We have already noted that in response to the criticism of nihilism the two truths were propounded and that conventional truth was posited as the actual locus of the activities of ordinary people. But how is conventional truth to be explained? According to Candrakīrti, it comes about through the principle of dependent co-arising. In the *Prasannapadā* he writes as follows:

> It is only on the basis of "dependence upon this" (*idaṃpratyayatā*; i.e., dependent co-arising) that the establishment of the conventional (*saṃvṛti*) may be recognized, and [the conventional] is not [established] by recognizing the four views [of birth from self, other, both, or without cause], for they lapse into the view [of things as] possessed of [an eternal and immutable] own-being and are unreasonable.[39]

A similar view point is also presented in the *Madhyamakāvatāra*.

> Question: If the birth [of things] from self, other, both [self and other], or without cause is denied by you [a Mādhyamikan] in both [the conventional and ultimate truth], how is it to be explained that consciousness and sprouts, etc., are born as the conventional from ignorance, formative forces (*saṃskāra*), seeds, etc.?
>
> Answer: Nothing whatsoever is born without cause or from the cause of Śiva or from self, other or both. Therefore things are born in dependence [upon others]. (v. 114)[40]

We have already seen that in the *Middle Stanzas* Nāgārjuna postulated that if things were at all to be born, there were only four possible ways in which they could be born and, furthermore, that by negating all four possibilities he attempted to demonstrate the fact that nothing whatsoever is born. And the reason that the permanent world manifests itself before our eyes as if it did exist, in spite of the fact that nothing whatsoever is born, he considered to be explained by the truth known as dependent co-arising that had been expounded by the Buddha. This latter point was emphasized still more by Candrakīrti.

But their opponents could also maintain that for them too the phenomenal world existed. Candrakīrti's reply to this was that the world appeared to exist to them because they believed in the existence of an eternal and immutable own-being which could under no circumstances be true; they were unable to argue for dependent co-arising, which represented the truth as taught by the Buddha, but he could. Candrakīrti

39. *Ibid.*, p. 54, ll. 11-12.

40. *Madhyamakāvatāra*, p. 226, ll. 1-9.

held that according to the principle of dependent co-arising, the arising of things—namely the phenomenal world—was established in a manner totally different from the four cases of birth from self, other, both, or without cause.

In the *Middle Stanzas* the term "dependent co-arising" embraced two contrasting meanings. On the one hand it signified a locus free of both arising and disappearing and in which all activity has ceased and no causal relationships obtain, while on the other hand it also meant quite literally "arising in dependence upon other." But Candrakīrti would appear to have attached greater importance to the latter sense. He refers to dependent co-arising as "pertaining to the conventional" (*saṃvṛta*) [41] and describes conventional truth in which own-being appears to exist as "fabricated and dependently co-arisen" (*rten ciṅ ḥbrel bar ḥbyuṅ ba*). [42]

The conventional established as something dependently co-arisen was, for Candrakīrti, even superior to the ultimate truth in which all elements of the conventional have been eliminated. Towards the end of Chapter IX of his commentary on the *Catuḥśataka* he states that just as when seeking to cure a disease of the eyes one should not go so far as to remove the eyes themselves, so too when eliminating the suffering of *saṃsāra* it is inadvisable to do away with the body itself, and hence it is the conventional that is of superior value. [43] In other words, he maintains that the body, which serves as the locus of action and represents the conventional, is necessary.

The conventional is established through dependent co-arising. More specifically, dependent co-arising occurs through the medium of provisional designation, which means that the Buddha gives names to various phenomena by using the verbal expressions current in the world at large and establishes them as the actual basis of human existence. But the act of applying language to the phenomenal world does not simply provide the basis of human existence but also functions as a means (*upāya*) for leading people to ultimate truth. It should not be forgotten that the philosophy of both Nāgārjuna and Candrakīrti was of a religious

41. *Prasannapadā*, p. 10, 1. 13.

42. *Madhyamakāvatāra*, p. 107, 1. 11; cf. Ogawa Ichijō, *op. cit.*, p. 91.

43. Yamaguchi Susumu, *Yamaguchi Susumu Bukkyōgaku bunshū* (Collected Papers on Buddhology by Yamaguchi Susumu; Tōkyō: Shunjūsha, 1973), p. 747.

nature, its final aim being to lead people from the conventional to ultimate truth.

The use of verbal expression as a means for attaining to *nirvāṇa*, in spite of the ineffability of *nirvāṇa*, is possible only with the compassion of an enlightened one. At the start of his *Prasannapadā* Candrakīrti writes that Nāgārjuna, who had comprehended the essence of *prajñāpāramitā* (perfection of wisdom), composed the *Middle Stanzas* out of compassion (*karuṇā*) in order to awaken others,[44] and in his commentary on the *Middle Stanzas*, XXIV.10, he further states that since the conventional is a means for obtaining *nirvāṇa*, it should be utilized before anything else just as someone desirous of water avails himself of a drinking vessel.[45] Since the conventional assumes the form of everyday linguistic activity (*vyavahāra*), conventional truth (*saṃvṛti-satya*) is also known as the "truth of everyday linguistic activity" (*vyavahāra-satya*). In the *Madhyamakāvatāra* Candrakīrti also writes:

> The truth of everyday linguistic activity is the means and ultimate truth the goal. (v.80)

It is the teachings of the Buddhas that lead ordinary people dwelling in the conventional to the goal of ultimate truth, and these teachings too assume the form of language. Insofar that they represent a form of language, the Buddhas' teachings also belong, according to Candrakīrti and except for certain special instances, to the conventional.[46]

> All these teachings of the Buddhas endowed with the knowledge of means born of great compassion are established as a means (*upāya*) for entering the nectar of truth.[47]

For Candrakīrti the Buddhas' teachings were no more than a means for attaining to ultimate truth, and he gave virtually no thought to

44. *Prasannapadā*, p. 2, l. 7-p. 3, l. 2.

45. *Ibid.*, p. 494, ll. 14-15.

46. According to Candrakīrti, the truths of suffering, the origination of suffering and the path belong to conventional truth, while the truth of cessation is equivalent to ultimate truth itself (*ad Madhyamakāvatāra*, V.1; p. 71, l. 5). Hence, among the Buddha's teachings, the truth of cessation alone is not subsumed under conventional truth.

47. *Prasannapadā*, p. 372, ll. 1-2.

their aspect as a manifestation of ultimate truth itself in the form of language. The Svātantrika Bhāvaviveka, on the other hand, recognized a "true conventional" (*tathya-saṃvṛti*) in which the ultimate truth "functions in the world of experience and has become the veridical logic of the world."[48] Candrakīrti regarded the conventional as existing totally cut off from ultimate truth.

Thus, in Candrakīrti's system, importance was attached to the conventional as the basis of human existence, and at the same time it was understood as something far removed from ultimate truth. These two characteristics are by no means unrelated, for in order to establish the conventional and simultaneously prevent the ultimate truth from being defiled by the conventional, he had to set the conventional and ultimate truth—namely, the two poles of the profane and the sacred—far apart from one another. Candrakīrti would appear to have acquired this understanding in the course of his criticism of Bhāvaviveka, who held that it was possible for the profane to demonstrate the sacred by its own resources in the form of language. But Candrakīrti had seen in the unsuccessful endeavours of Bhāvaviveka that in the case of the Mādhyamika school, which had since the time of its founder held up a slogan contradictory to the conventional usage of language, regardless of the systematization of one's syllogisms, and even because of still greater systematization, one was bound to expose one's own errors through the syllogisms that one had oneself formulated. Candrakīrti instead adopted a supralogical method in which he employed logic only for the purpose of refuting all counterarguments and thereby sought to bring all linguistic activity to cessation. At the same time, he considered the actual world constituting the foundation of our existence to be established on the basis of the principle of dependent co-arising.

In that case, how is one to bridge the gap between language and the ultimate truth that transcends language? In the *Madhyamakāvatāra* Candrakīrti seeks to solve this problem by means of religious praxis. There have been instances when the abandonment of logic and the appeal to praxis have opened the way to irrationalism and mysticism, and in point of fact Candrakīrti's successors were to have close connections with Tantrism. Many Tantric treatises were attributed to Candrakīrti himself, and in Tibet these were to be avidly studied in later times. Tantrism is not

48. Kajiyama Yūichi, "Chūgan tetsugaku no ronri—jo" (An Introduction to Logic in Mādhyamika Philosophy), *Tetsugaku Kenkyū*, No. 402 (1951), p. 25.

of course equivalent to irrationalism and mysticism, but Candrakīrti may be considered to have provided a model for a logical basis to the irrational and mystical aspects of Indian and Tibetan Buddhist Tantrism. Candrakīrti's use of the term "own-being" as a synonym of "emptiness" should also be understood in relation to later Tantric thought.

The seventh century in which Candrakīrti is thought to have lived was a period when Hinduism was rapidly extending its influence. The Hinduists did not look upon the world as something non-existent. Even though this world might indeed have made its appearance as a result of illusion (*māyā*), they still believed it to exist insofar that it had appeared. For them, the world as the locus supporting their existence was an existent, and as a result the Hinduists sought to comprehend the structure of the world by means of their cognitive faculties and establish their own world view. By the time of Candrakīrti orthodox Brahmanical schools such as the Sāṃkhya, Nyāya and Vaiśeṣika had already formulated detailed theories concerning the structure of the world. These represented a prelude to the eventual golden age of Hinduism. Of course even within Buddhism Abhidharma, the Yogācāra school and the logicians had each from their own standpoint undertaken an examination of the phenomenal world, and this represented in fact a form of Hinduization. The establishment of a system of knowledge concerning the conventional was a historical trend that enveloped both Hinduists and Buddhists, and Candrakīrti too was doubtless an observer of this movement. The Mādhyamika school had originally been indifferent towards the structure of the world and the foundations of cognition, and its philosophical methods were in themselves unsuitable for dealing with such questions. The path taken by Candrakīrti as a Mādhyamikan was such that while preserving the unique nature of ultimate truth or emptiness (i.e., the sacred) by setting it far apart from the conventional (i.e., the profane), he explained the plane of the conventional by means of the principle of dependent co-arising and recognized the significance of the conventional as the basis of human existence inasmuch as it could be recognized within the conventional. In this manner, although remaining within the confines of Mādhyamikan thought, Candrakīrti attempted to respond to the contemporary philosophical situation while preserving his own standpoint as a Buddhist.

BIBLIOGRAPHY

Chhos Je Lama (ed.), Thuḥu-bkwan. *Grub mthaḥ šel gyi me loṅ*, Sarnath, Varanasi, 1963.

de la Vallée Poussin, Louis (ed.). *Madhyamakāvatāra*, *Bibliotheca Buddhica* IX. St. Petersburg, 1907.

__________ (ed.). *Prasannapadā*, *Bibliotheca Buddhica* IV. St. Petersburg, 1913.

Eliade M. (tr. Willard R. Trask). *The Sacred and the Profane: The Nature of Religion*. New York: Harcourt Brace Jovanovich, 1959.

__________ (tr. Willard R. Trask). *The Quest: History and Meaning in Religion*. Chicago: The University of Chicago Press, 1969.

Hatani, Ryōtai. *Kokuyaku Issaikyō* (Japanese Translation of the Tripiṭaka), Chūganbu (Mādhyamika), Vol. 1, 1925.

Imai, Kunihiko. *Henkei bunpō no hanashi* (On Transformational Grammar). Tōkyō: Taishūkan, 1979.

Kajiyama Yūichi. "Chūgan tetsugaku no ronri–jo" (An Introduction to Logic in Mādhyamika Philosophy), *Tetsugaku Kenkyū*, No. 402, 1951.

__________. "Bhāvaviveka's Prajñāpradipaḥ (I. Kapitel)." *WZKSOA*, Band VII, 1963.

__________. *Kū no ronri* (The Logic of Emptiness), *Bukkyō no shisō* (Buddhist Thought), Vol. 3. Tōkyō: Kadokawa Shoten, 1969.

Kajiyama, Yūichi, and Uryuzu, Ryūshin. *Ryūju ronshū* (Treatises by

Nāgārjuna), *Daijō butten* (Mahāyāna Scriptures), Vol. 14. Tōkyō: Chūō Kōronsha, 1974.

____________. "Chūganha no jūnishi engi kaishaku" (The Interpretation of the Twelvefold Chain of Dependent Co-arising in the Mādhyamika School). *Bukkyō Shisōshi* (The History of Buddhist Thought), Vol. 3, 1980.

Levi-Strauss, C. "Introduction à l'oeuvre de Marcel Mauss." In Marcel Mauss, *Sociologie et anthropologie*, Paris: Presses Universitaires de France, 1950.

Nagao, Gajin. "Chūgan tetsugaku no konponteki tachiba" (The Fundamental Standpoint of Mādhyamika Philosophy). *Tetsugaku Kenkyū*, No. 366, 1947.

____________. *Saizō Bukkyō kenkyū* (A Study of Tibetan Buddhism). Tōkyō: Iwanami Shoten, 1954.

Nagao, Gajin. "Bukkyō no shisō to rekishi" (The Thought and History of Buddhism). *Sekai no meicho. Daijō butten* (Famous Books of the World: Mahāyāna Scriptures). Tōkyō: Chūō Kōronsha, 1967.

Ogawa, Ichijō. *Kūshō shisō no kenkyū* (A Study of the Philosophy of Emptiness).. Kyōto: Bun'eidō, 1976.

Robinson, R. *Early Mādhyamika in India and China*. Delhi: Motilal Banarsidass, 1976.

Ruben, Walter. *Die gesellschaftliche Entwicklung in alten Indien*, IV, *Die Entwicklung der Philosophie*. Berlin: Akadamie-Verlag, 1971.

Saigusa, Mitsuyoshi, and Kuga Sunao. *Daijō Bukkyō no seiritsushiteki kenkyū* (Studies in the History of the Development of Mahāyāna Buddhism). Tōkyō: Sanseidō, 1954.

Saigusa, Mitsuyoshi. "Ryūju no kū ni tsuite" (On Nāgārjuna's Emptiness). In *Daijō Bukkyō no seiritsushiteki kenkyū*. Tokyō: Sanseidō, 1954.

____________. "Engi no kōsatsu" (A Consideration of Dependent Co-arising). *Indogaku Bukkyōgaku Kenkyū*, Vol. 6, No. 2, 1958.

Schiefner, A. (ed.) *Tāranātha chos ḥbyuṅ*, Petropoli, 1868.

Stcherbatsky, Th. *The Conception of Buddhist Nirvāṇa*, Leningrad, 1927.

Sum-pa-mkhan-po, Das, C. (ed.), *dPag bsam ljon bzaṅ* (*Pag Sam Jon Zang*) Part I (*History of the Rise, Progress and Downfall of Buddhism in India*). Calcutta: Presidency Jail Press, 1908.

Tachikawa, Musashi. *Saizō Bukkyō shūgi kenkyū* (A Study of the *Grub mthaḥ* of Tibetan Buddhism), Vol. 1. Tōkyō: The Tōyō Bunko, 1974.

________________. "*Chūron* ni okeru sezoku to shōgi" (The Conventional and Ultimate Truths in the *Middle Stanzas*). *Tōyō Gakujutsu Kenkyū*, Vol. 16, No. 5, 1977.

________________. "Chibetto shiryō ni mirareru Chūgan Purāsangika-ha no keifu" (The Lineage of the Mādhyamika Prāsaṅgika School as Seen in Tibetan Materials). *Ajia Bunka*, Vol. 10, No. 1, 1978.

________________. "Gengo katsudō no shimetsu to kūshō–purapancha ni tsuite" (The Extinction of Linguistic Proliferation and Emptiness: On *prapañca*). *Bukkyōgaku*, Vol. 9-10 Special Issue, 1980.

________________. "*Chūron* ni okeru nishu no hitei–*Chūron* no ronrigakuteki kōsatsu (3)–"(The Two Types of Negation in the *Middle Stanzas*: Logical Considerations of the *Middle Stanzas* (3). In *Nasu Seiryū Hakushi beiju kinen ronbunshū* (Collected Papers in Honour of Dr. Nasu Seiryū's 88th Birthday). Narita: Naritasan Shinshōji, 1984.

Teramoto, Enga (transl. and annotated). *Ryūju-zō Chūron Muisho* (The Commentary *Akutobhayā* on the *Mādhyamakakārikā* by Nāgārjuna). Tōkyō: Kokusho Kankōkai, 1974.

Tibetan Tripiṭaka (Peking Edition). Tōkyō: Suzuki Research Foundation, 1952-59.

Ueda, Yoshifumi. *Daijō Bukkyō shisō no konpon kōzō* (The Basic Structure of Mahāyāna Buddhist Thought). Kyōto: Hyakkaen, 1957.

Ui, Hakuju. *Kokuyaku Chūron* (Japanese Translation of the *Mādhyamakakārikā*), *Kokuyaku Daizōkyō* (Japanese Translation of the Tripiṭaka), Ronbu (Treatises). Vol. 5, 1920.

Walleser, Max (ed.). *Buddhapālita. Mūlamadhyamakavṛtti, Bibliotheca Buddhica* XVI. St. Petersburg, 1913.

Yamaguchi, Susumu. *Hannya shisōshi* (The History of *Prajñā* Thought). Kyōto: Hōzōkan, 1966.

__________________. *Yamaguchi Susumu Bukkyōgaku bunshū* (Collected Papers on Buddhology by Yamaguchi Susumu). Tōkyō: Shunjūsha, 1973.

Yutsugi, Ryōei. *Kegon gokyōshō kōgi* (Lectures on the *Hua-yen wu-chiao chang*). Kyōto: Hyakkaen, 1927.

INDEX